CHRIST
IN THE
HOME

CHRIST
IN THE
HOME

ROBERT R. TAYLOR, JR.

BAKER BOOK HOUSE
Grand Rapids, Michigan

Library of Congress Catalog Card Number:
73-86807

ISBN: 0-8010-8811-9

Printed in the United States of America

In loving tribute this book is affectionately dedicated to the six people with whom I have lived in the family framework.

R. R. Taylor, who died December 18, 1971, and **Vera Bell Taylor,** my parents, who gave me being, who early set my feet toward the Master, and who have been fervent boosters in my gospel ministry.

Sue Henley, my sister, for whom I have the fondest of feelings.

Irene, my helpmeet, my constant companion, the apple of my eye, and the joy of my heart. Her worth exceeds what a legion of gifted scribes could portray. She adds luster to the beauty, worth, and wonder of womanhood.

Rebecca Irene, my teen-age daughter, our firstborn for whom we have aspirations of Christian womanhood, Christian wifehood, and Christian motherhood.

Timothy Robert, my son and namesake, our second born for whom we have the prayerful aspiration that he will one day be a proclaimer of Calvary's saving message.

ACKNOWLEDGMENTS

The following authors and publishers have graciously given permission for the use of quotations from their works.

Jimmy Allen, *The American Crisis and Other Sermons,* 1971.

B. C. Goodpasture, *Sermons and Lectures of B. C. Goodpasture,* (Nashville: Gospel Advocate Company, 1964.)

Gordon Hanna, Editor, *The Commercial Appeal,* 1963, 1971.

Ann Landers, *The Commercial Appeal,* (Chicago: Hall Syndicate, 1971.)

Guy N. Woods, *A Commentary on the New Testament Epistles, Vol. VII,* (Nashville: Gospel Advocate Company, 1954.)

Special thanks is due to Basil Overton who encouraged the writing of the book, read the material in manuscript form, offered many helpful hints and sage suggestions, and penned the Foreword.

A special thanks is due the Ripley Church of Christ in general and its excellent eldership in particular for their continued willingness to allow me to spend a portion of each day in a writing ministry. Were it not for their understanding, encouragement, and patience this book and my other writings could never have seen the light of printed day.

I owe a great debt to every preacher and teacher under whom I have sat as an auditor through the years. I am grateful to every author I have read. I am grateful for every Christian home in which I have been an honored guest. From all of these I have learned. The influences of all these educative experiences permeate this book from beginning to end.

Above all I am grateful to the Godhead for length of life, health of mind, and strength of hand to complete this literary endeavor.

FOREWORD

Someone has said that a book can be more important than a battle. America is suffering because so many of its homes have been destroyed. And, sad to say, the pace of the destruction is not slowing. Authorities say that more than half of the world's societies have an even higher rate of destruction of homes than America has.

Truly, America may be struggling for survival. The percentage of broken homes in the United States is about eight times what it was at the beginning of the Civil War.

The military might of America cannot do as much to truly protect and preserve this great nation as this book could do if all readers in this country would read it and really follow the foundation principles emphasized in it.

The principal feature of this book is that the author very skillfully points its readers to the Book of Books! Robert R. Taylor, Jr., stresses the Bible and its importance in this book. He presents much good advice regarding many home situations and the advice is always in harmony with passages and principles that are in the Bible. In most instances Scripture is quoted to support the advice.

Some say the Bible is not relevant for our times. The author shows how truly foolish this conclusion is. He focuses attention on many human interest stories in the Bible and effectively demonstrates how interesting, profitable, and dramatic these stories are in their portrayal of human nature. The great educator William Phelps is credited with having said that one can learn more about human nature by reading the Bible than he can by living in New York City. Robert Taylor, Jr., supports this interesting comment on the practical value of reading the Bible. It is truly refreshing and encouraging to read a good book that focuses attention on the Bible in this age when so many authors either ignore the Bible or make efforts to destroy it.

It is with pleasure that I commend this book. My heart's desire and prayer is that multitudes will read it.

Basil Overton

INTRODUCTION

This book is an outgrowth of many years of studying, preaching, and lecturing on the home. The concept "Christ in the home" has been developed from strongly felt conviction that enthroning Christ in the heart of every family member is the only way to solve the complex problems facing today's homes. *Christ in the home* means a Christian home. Christ separate and apart from the home means a Godless and Christless home. Where the Godhead does not reign in the home, Satan will be on that home's throne.

It has long been my prayer and dream to write this book. The spring of 1971 opened the door for the fruition of this literary goal. I gave four lectures at the Memphis School of Preaching Lectureship on "Lifting up The Bible —The Home." Several people indicated a keen interest in having these lectures in written form. I began immediately and have worked on this book almost daily for seven months. Much of the work was done early in the morning and late at night so as not to interfere with a heavy schedule of local church work, gospel meetings, speaking engagements, and writing an average of four articles per week for religious journals and newspapers.

A frequent criterion for most books lies in their heavy documentation of what others have written along the same line. Submitting this work to such a standard would no doubt result in its being considered a literary failure. It has not been our intent to concentrate on what uninspired people have written relative to the home but to picture what God's Book has said. Hence Scripture has been employed as documentary evidence and also used as illustrative material undergirding the various propositions and principles submitted for the reader's consideration. Scripture quotations are frequently given and their locations are supplied. This will enable the reader to check for accuracy and for his own personal profit. I believe in "book, chapter and verse" preaching and writing. Unless otherwise designated, Scripture quotations are taken from the King James Version.

Each chapter is divided into various sections of thought. These divisions could well serve as advantageous spots to conclude a study if less than one chapter is covered in a setting. Questions for discussion are given at the conclusion of each chapter for the benefit of those who wish to use the book in Bible classes or study groups.

This book is sent forth with the prayerful hope that it may be a leavening ingredient in helping homes of the twentieth century to practice diligently the *Christ in the home* concept and philosophy in every facet of the family framework. May our Heavenly Father bless this work toward this noble goal.

Robert R. Taylor, Jr.

Ripley, Mississippi

CONTENTS

"I will behave myself wisely in a perfect way. O when wilt thou come unto me? I will walk within my house with a perfect heart" (Ps. 101:2).

"Except the Lord build the house, they labour in vain that build it: except the Lord keep the city, the watchman waketh but in vain" (Ps. 127:1).

"And forthwith, when they were come out of the synagogue, they entered into the house of Simon and Andrew, with James and John. But Simon's wife's mother lay sick of a fever, and anon they tell him of her. And he came and took her by the hand, and lifted her up; and immediately the fever left her, and she ministered unto them" (Mark 1:29-31).

"Now it came to pass, as they went, that he entered into a certain village: and a certain woman named Martha received him into her house. And she had a sister called Mary, which also sat at Jesus' feet, and heard his word. But Martha was cumbered about much serving, and came to him, and said, Lord, dost thou not care that my sister hath left me to serve alone? bid her therefore that she help me. And Jesus answered and said unto her, "Martha, Martha, thou art careful and troubled about many things: But one thing is needful: and Mary hath chosen that good part, which shall not be taken away from her" (Luke 10:38-42).

"Zacchaeus, make haste, and come down; for to day I must abide at thy house. And he made haste, and came down, and received him joyfully . . . And Jesus said unto him, This day is salvation come to this house, forsomuch as he also is a son of Abraham" (Luke 19:5-6, 9).

1

Christ in the Home

The home of the twentieth century does not enjoy the Scripturally wholesome and supremely important position it maintained in previous ages. Crumbling home foundations constitute one of the saddest portraits of our day. Rapid deterioration of the home has been noted by religious and secular thinkers alike. The sinister forces of mounting materialism, licentious living, and sinful sensualism are undermining the stability of the home throughout the world. Pessimistic prophets appear everywhere and predict that home and family as we have known them will continue to erode and are destined to fade into complete oblivion. I beg to differ. Our eyes cannot be closed to these realistic happenings in our day but we do not believe that what began so beautifully and majestically in Eden's innocence will experience a permanent fatality at the hands of unbelieving men. The hand of Jehovah God has not yet vacated the realms of home and family.

Many of the problems facing our homes today can be traced to the irresponsible manner in which marriages are contracted and homes are begun. Immature youth and even ill-prepared adults frequently enter this sacred and binding institution with lighthearted flippancy and little regard for Jehovah's law touching marriage and its permanent obligations. Marriage thus begins on an extremely shaky foundation and amounts to little more than a trial-and-error experience. When the trials begin to mount higher and higher, both marital mates may decide an error was made in the selection of a life's companion. To them a divorce seems the shortest way to write the finale of their ill-mated marriage. The divorce evil hangs as a darkening blight over our beloved country. Nothing currently appears on the horizon to curb this growing evil in our midst save Jesus Christ and Christianity.

Annually this country witnesses approximately 500,000 divorces. For each three to four couples who march down the happy aisle toward matrimony, another couple appears in a divorce court room and seeks to obtain those fatal words from the presiding judge, "Divorce Granted." These words are spoken on an average of fifteen hundred times each day in our nation alone. Perhaps no two other words spoken in our country on any given day are fraught with more evil than are these. Every sixty to ninety seconds a home is broken in our land. Among the family of nations we are becoming the country of the broken home. These statistics tell the sordid story about the marital instability of the American people. The broken home with the bitter attitudes it produces and the innocent and precious children it harms for life is one of the most tragic occurrences in our generation. It forms a taproot from which springs so much evil in other forms. Good homes on a universal scale could soon eliminate many of the Herculean problems we face in other areas of life.

Truly our homes need to be saved. They need to be happy. They deserve to be productive of goodness and the powerful protectors of manly virtue and womanly purity. They need to be schools where the pliable minds and tender hearts of impressionable youth can be trained for the good life here and that home of immortal souls in the hereafter. Enshrining the abiding presence of Jesus Christ in the heart of each family member is the only way that our homes can be what Jehovah intended them to be. Jesus can restore the home to its first foundations which were laid in Eden's bliss. Let us catch some beautiful glimpses of Jesus as the divine guest in a few first-century homes.

A VISIT TO THE HOME OF SIMON PETER AND ANDREW

Jesus was engaged in His Galilean ministry. Following a busy and eventful day in a synagogue at Capernaum, the Master visited the humble home of Simon Peter and Andrew. Mark briefly describes this interesting visit, "And forthwith, when they were come out of the synagogue, they entered into the house of Simon and Andrew, with James and John. But Simon's wife's mother lay sick of a fever, and anon they tell him of her. And he came and took her by the hand, and lifted her up; and immediately the fever left her, and she ministered unto them" (Mark 1:29-31). We shall talk about this visit later.

A VISIT IN JAIRUS' HOME

Somewhat later the evangelist Mark pictures the coming of the deeply distressed Jairus to Jesus with a fervent request couched in words of moving gravity. "And, behold, there cometh one of the rulers of the synagogue, Jairus by name; and when he saw him, he fell at his feet, And besought him greatly, saying, My little daughter lieth at the point of death: I pray thee, come and lay thy hands on her, that she may be healed; and she shall live. And Jesus went with him; and much people followed him, and thronged him" (Mark 5: 22-24). The compassionate ear of the great physician was always opened to such a call. With steady steps the Son of God traveled with the concerned father. Mark 5:25-34 relates the story of the woman who touched the hem of Christ's garment and received an instant cure from her serious blood disease. This must have delayed somewhat the arrival of Jesus to the home of Jairus, and every minute counted as far as Jairus was concerned. But if there is any disapproval of Jesus' actions on the part of the troubled Jairus, Scripture does not reveal it. This should impress us that Jesus knows best and we should allow Him to be Master in every sense of the term. It is never the prerogative of the servant or the seeker to dictate the actions of the Master. That amounts to fallibility seeking to direct the course of affairs for the sovereign of the universe.

Shortly before Jesus' arrival at Jairus' home, a delegation brings the sad message that the seriously ill child has now died. Their words are, "Thy daughter is dead: why troublest thou the Master any further?" (Mark 5:35). The compassionate healer has a precious word of comfort for the distraught father. Mark describes the dispatch with which Jesus offered treasured assurance. "As soon as Jesus heard the word that was spoken, he saith unto the ruler of the synagogue, Be not afraid, only believe" (Mark 5:36). The Master is not detoured in the least. The direction of travel is still toward the home of Jairus. Moments before it had been the home of sickness; now it becomes the chamber of death. Before the services of the great physician were needed; now the task demands the presence of the resurrection and the life.

The Lord is met at the house by the weeping and wailing throng of mourners. Quickly He informs them that the damsel is not permanently dead but temporarily asleep. The scorn of unbelieving laughter filled the air and must have pained deeply the great heart of Him who was about ready to perform one of His greatest miracles. How inexcusable was their infidelity for nearby Nain had witnessed a similar miracle shortly before and it is highly unlikely that this miracle had escaped their attention. All persons are now put forth except the bereft parents and the "inner three" — Peter, James, and John. Jesus and these people enter the room where the "king of terrors" had invaded but moments before. The merciful Master tenderly takes the lifeless hand into that of His own and His lips give utterance to that authoritative expression, "Talitha cumi; which is, being interpreted, Damsel, I say unto thee, arise" (Mark 5:41). The child's departed spirit reenters the little tabernacle of clay stilled moments before by death's chilling hand. Life is her precious possession again. Death could not hold captive the child that the author of life willed to live again.

BETHANY — A SECOND HOME TO THE LORD

The beloved physician Luke records Jesus accepting an invitation to visit the lovely and hospitable home of Mary and Martha. Perhaps no home in first-century Palestine, other than His own with Joseph and Mary while growing up, ever afforded Jesus a more wonderful welcome or a more permanent type of hospitality than did this one in the quiet setting of Bethany. Luke records this interesting account, "Now it came to pass, as they went, that he entered into a certain village: and a certain woman named Martha received him into her house. And she had a sister called Mary, which also sat at Jesus' feet, and heard his word. But Martha was cumbered about much serving, and came to him, and said, Lord, dost thou not care that my sister hath left me to serve alone? bid her therefore that she help me. And Jesus answered and said unto her, Martha, Martha, thou art careful and troubled about many things: But one thing is needful: and Mary hath chosen that good part, which shall not be taken away from her" (Luke 10:38-42). I have seen the rather large outdoor plaque in Bethany inscribed with the words from Luke 10:42.

This is a lovely picture of what a visit from the divine guest meant. Martha in her domestic-centered world is taught a needed lesson. Mary learns that her decision was the wiser of the two and that eternal dividends would accrue therefrom. Jesus would forcefully fix the attention of all to the wisdom of Mary's decision.

AT HOME WITH ZACCHAEUS

Near the end of the Saviour's ministry He is passing through Jericho on His way to Jerusalem. Zacchaeus, chief of the publicans but short in stature, determines to obtain a glimpse of the famed Galilean prophet. Nature may have bypassed him in supplying average height but it had not left him lacking in practical planning. He determines to turn his liability into an asset. Running well ahead of the great throngs traveling with the Lord he finds himself a position in a sycamore tree. Jesus was to pass that way and a bird's eye view of the Lord would amply repay Zacchaeus' efforts. Luke says, "And when Jesus came to the place, he looked up, and saw him, and said unto him, Zacchaeus, make haste, and come down; for today I must abide at thy house" (Luke 19:5). The Bible says that "he made haste, and came down, and received him joyfully" (Luke 19: 6). Jesus was eager to bless his host and Zacchaeus was eager to know the Lord more fully. But, as is frequently the case, the performance of a good work provides fuel to generate the tongues of murmurers and increase the carping of hostile critics: He has "gone to be guest with a man that is a sinner" (Luke 19:7). It is doubtful if these critics would have lifted a little finger to alleviate the spiritual bankruptcy of the many Zacchaeuses of that day. As a rule the publicans were a hated lot. "Guilty of treason" and "taxing traitors" were the common designations by which they were known among the Jews of that era. In the second place, it is doubtful that these critics would have extended a warm welcome and a royal reception to the itinerant teacher from Nazareth had they been in the place of Zacchaeus. Carping critics usually are quite inefficient in any service save wrecking what talented builders have erected. A heart of selfishness, a soured disposition, a quick tongue, and a regular refusal to do good works are the guaranteed prerequisites for success in destructive criticism. The cutting snipes of the supercharged critics did not keep Jesus from going home with Zacchaeus nor did they bar the chief publican from extending God's Son the warmest welcome at his personal command. Deep admiration is raised in our hearts as we look at Jesus and Zacchaeus. Nothing but utter abhorrence describes the attitude we feel for the faultfinders.

Zacchaeus says to Jesus, "Behold, Lord, the half of my goods I give to the poor; and if I have taken anything from any man by false accusation, I restore him fourfold" (Luke 19:8). Some think Zacchaeus was telling the Lord what had been his past practice. However, it seems safer to assert that the chief publican is stating a present conviction of what he purposed to do in the future. The very fact that Jesus announces in the succeeding verse the arrival of salvation for this home seems to warrant our conclusion that Zacchacus' past left many things to be desired. It seems that from this moment onward he was determined to be a different person.

Before His departure the Lord was able to say, "This day is salvation come to this house, forsomuch as he also is a son of Abraham. For the Son of man is come to seek and to save that which was lost" (Luke 19:9-10). The narrative ends with a saved family and a pointed reminder of Christ's supreme mission in coming to this earth — the salvation of the lost.

SOME COMMON THREADS

These four accounts, two from Mark and two from Luke, contain several common threads of thought interestingly interwoven. Jesus visited four first-century-Palestine homes. Two of these homes were located in Galilee, the northern province of the Holy Land. The other homes were located in Judaea, the southern province. Jesus was welcome in each home. Simon and Andrew were delighted to have their beloved Master visit their humble home near the shores of the northwestern edge of the Galilean sea. Jairus begged Jesus to come home with him and heal his dying daughter. Jesus always experienced a warm welcome in the Bethany household of Martha and Mary. Jesus became the self-invited guest in the home of the chief publican; nevertheless we conclude that He received a royal reception from Zacchaeus. Jesus was no intruder in these homes. There was no hypocritical outward show of hospitality accompanied by an inward aversion to His being there. Both attitudes and actions conveyed their happiness to have God's Son as the divine guest in their humble homes. Jesus has never stayed long where He was unwanted and unwelcome. His departures from Nazareth in Luke 4 and from the materialistic Gadarenes in Mark 5 testify to this point. Revelation 3:14-22 sets forth the thought that He will not dwell in one of His own congregations when lukewarmness and listlessness drive Him out. It is a foregone conclusion therefore that Jesus does not live in our homes today unless we have made Him welcome.

There was a real need in each of these homes. The home of Simon and Andrew had a serious sickness. Mark says Peter's mother-in-law had a fever (Mark 1:30). Luke writes as a physician and he calls it "a great fever" (Luke 4:38). J. W. McGarvey, in commenting on this passage, referred to Galen, the father of medicine, as one who divided fevers into little and great. Simon's mother-in-law had the more serious type of the two. Luke informs us that the concerned members of this home besought Christ for her (Luke 4: 38). Such concern reveals the deep bond of love, kindness, and consideration which permeated this family relationship. It is just what we would expect. A home that welcomes Jesus usually has many worthwhile qualities. Another of these homes had a critical illness that resulted in death. Truly there was a need in the home of Jairus. Evidently there was a need for the wonderful words of life to be spoken in the Bethany household. This is what Jesus did and He never did anything but what wise propriety demanded. In the words of His admiring contemporaries, "He hath done all things well . . ." (Mark 7:37). Though this was specifically stated concerning His miraculous manifestations it becomes a standing commentary on all His practices. The home of Zacchaeus needed salvation far more than it needed additional success from his thriving tax collection business. Four homes and each had a specific need.

Jesus came as a bearer of blessings into each of these homes. The divine guest did not come empty-handed. The rich storehouse of universal bounties was at His disposal. Not only did Jesus come as a blessing to each home but He also brought the blessing most needed. He came as the great physician to Simon's home. His arrival found a beloved member of the family sick and the remainder of the household compassionately concerned. Before He left the sick had been made well and was left in perfect health. We can almost see the cured mother-in-law walking with the great physician to the door. A beaming countenance radiates her joy for returned health. Jesus came as the resurrection and the life into the home of Jairus. His services had been requested as the great physician at first but the arrival of the pale horse and his rider death changed the need from that of a healer of sickness to that of a restorer of life. How fortunate indeed was Jairus when he received the death message about his only daughter. He had Jesus right by his side. You and I frequently do not know what to say when in similar circumstances but the Maker of men knew exactly what was needed by way of a comforting expression. He uttered four words according to the Greek text in Mark 5:36. They were, as would literally appear in English, "Not fear; only believe." They have been translated into five and four words respectively in our King James and American Standard Versions. Volumes of human words could be written on how to deal with death and they would not say nearly as much as Jesus packed into a quartet of consoling words. Jesus went into that room of death and made a lifeless corpse into a radiant, living, loving child again. Jesus brought the wonderful words of life to Mary's home. She knew their worth. Solomon said, "A word fitly spoken is like apples of gold in pictures of silver" (Prov. 25:11). If anyone ever spoke fitly, it would have been God's Son. Mary indeed would have appraised His words as being "like apples of gold in pictures of silver." Jesus supplied the needs of Mary's longing heart by the words He uttered.

Jesus came as Saviour to the Jericho home of Zacchaeus. This was the blessing this household needed and Jesus supplied it. He is the only one who can bring salvation to our homes today just as He was the only one who could come as Saviour in the first century.

Jesus left these homes in much better condition than He found them. In the home of Simon and Andrew He left restored health where there had been serious illness. In the home of Jairus He left a live and well daughter where there had been a sick and dead child. In the Bethany household He left a gratified Mary and a wiser Martha. In Zacchaeus' home He turned the words *lost* into *life* and *sin* into *salvation*. Four homes, four visits, four blessings conferred, and four homes lifted to a higher plateau of spiritual eminence.

If we will receive Jesus into our homes and lift up the Bible in every heart of the household, Jesus and the Bible will lift up our families. *Christ in the home* is God's formula for successful marriages, happy homes, and well-adjusted children who are being reared in the nurture and admonition of the Lord. Has the divine guest ever visited your home?

QUESTIONS FOR DISCUSSION

1. In your judgment, what are some of the factors contributing to the collapse of so many homes today?
2. Is there any cause for possessing optimism toward the future stability of the home? If so, what is it? Discuss in detail.
3. List some things men and women should bring with them to the marriage altar.
4. Describe the shaky foundations upon which many marriages begin.
5. Discuss the divorce problem as it currently exists. Has it affected the church? In what ways?
6. List reasons why our homes need to be saved.
7. Describe in detail the visit of our Lord to Simon Peter's home.
8. Why did the home of Jairus need Jesus? Tell of the details of this visit.
9. How was Bethany almost a second home to the Lord during His personal ministry? Tell of His visit there in Luke 10:38-42.
10. Describe the Lord's visit in the home of Zacchaeus.
11. Are God's glory and man's betterment ever promoted by the work of carping critics and malicious murmurers? Tell why you answer as you do.
12. Do you believe Luke 19:8 refers to Zacchaeus' past actions or a

pledge for a future course to pursue in his human relationships? Give reasons for your answer.

13. What was the mission of Jesus to earth? How did it tie in with His visit to the home of Zacchaeus?

14. List and discuss as many common threads interwoven among these four sacred narratives as you can.

15 What will happen when we lift up Christ and the Bible in our homes?

16. Do you believe most members of the church whom you know are seeking to enthrone Christ in their homes? Why, or why not?

17. What does "Christ in the home" mean to you?

18. What would happen if every congregation were composed of homes where Christ is truly the head, ruler, and guide?

2

Christ in Today's Home

The same divine guest who visited various Palestinian homes of the first century seeks admittance into the homes of today. Homes of the first century desperately needed His inspiring and consoling presence. Every home needs Him today. Homes which are happy in the true sense of the term already have His abiding presence. In order to remain happy they must retain Him and His way of life. Homes which are unhappy need Him to show them the way to live happily and harmoniously within the framework of the family. (Those who cannot get along in the family seldom have any assurance that they can fare successfully outside the home in other personal relationships.) Homes which are tottering on the brink of disaster need the help of Jesus Christ. He brings the cementing ties of salvation into our homes and purifies and elevates every relationship. The great physician frequently mended lame limbs, gave sight to the blind, hearing to the deaf, speech to the dumb, cleansing to the leper, and gave real meaning to those whose lives had been totally purposeless. He can be the great physician in healing the problems of every home today. He knows what these problems are. He has the solution to them. After all His Father instituted the home in Eden. The Son knows how to restore the home to its original moorings. He can mend and make well the ills that presently plague the home. He can open blind eyes to the real beauties of a Christian home. He can open deaf ears to the pleas of precious little children who want and deserve a father and mother who will live together, love each other,

22

and rear their offspring "in the nurture and admonition of the Lord" (Eph. 6:4). He can restore the lines of communication that for all practical purposes have become as useless as dumb tongues. He, and He alone, can cleanse the leprosy of sin which is behind every unhappy home and the prompting cause of every broken home. He supplies purpose to life and enriches the home with the formulation of worthwhile goals. "Christ in the home" was the answer for every family in the first century. "Christ in today's home" is the answer for twentieth-century families. Lift up Christ and His Holy Book in your home and your household will be lifted up. This will follow as surely as night follows day.

The divine guest visited many homes while He tabernacled in human flesh. These homes extended Him a warm welcome and a ready reception. He came as the heavenly blessing to each of these homes. He conferred the blessing most needed. Without exception He left all these homes better than He found them. No home was ever more corrupt because Jesus had been there. No home ever became irreligious due to our Lord's visit. He raised homes. He purified family relationships. Jesus recompensed the happy hospitality He received in these homes with blessings that none other could bestow. He can still bless our homes today. The blessings most needed will be conferred when families meet the conditions He demands. As long as He lives in today's homes they will become better, glow more brightly, and perform family functions more efficiently. Let us now take a look at some of the current needs in our homes and suggest how Jesus is the solution.

ILLNESS IN THE HOME

Is there illness in our homes as Simon Peter's family experienced in Mark 1:29-31? Jesus desires to be present. We are long past the age of miraculous cures such as the great physician performed upon Peter's mother-in-law, yet the consoling presence of Christ can be felt in our sick rooms. During my twenty-two year ministry I have visited hundreds of homes where illnesses were present. Some of these sicknesses were critical; others were less serious and only temporary in duration. Some of these people did not recover; others fully regained their health. Some of these homes were Christian and the members were very devout in their service to the Lord. Other homes were totally irreligious. With but few exceptions it has been my experience that Christian homes were much better equipped to accept, endure, and profit from sicknesses than were homes void of the Lord's help. Christians had learned that bodily afflictions could bring one closer to God. The afflicted psalmist wrote, "Before I was afflicted I went astray: but now have I kept thy word . . . It is good for me that I have been afflicted; that I might learn thy statutes" (Ps. 119:67, 71). The sick saint knows the importance of patience. James writes, "My brethren, count it all joy when ye fall into divers temptations; Knowing this, that the trying of your faith worketh patience. But let patience have her perfect work, that ye may be perfect and entire, wanting nothing" (James 1:2-4). The saint knows that "tribulation [even bodily ailments] worketh patience; And patience, experience; and experience, hope: And hope maketh not ashamed; because the love of God is shed abroad in our hearts by the Holy Ghost [Spirit] which is given unto us" (Rom. 5:3-5). Paul's thorn in the flesh experience aptly illustrates this point (II Cor. 12:1-10). When ill the afflicted saint is counseled to approach the Father's throne of grace and help. "Is any among you afflicted? let him pray" (James 5:13). As a righteous man his prayer "availeth much" (James 5:16). Members of his righteous family can pray in his behalf and their prayer likewise will avail much in the heart of Him who is their Heavenly Father. Being of a righteous family will insure the sufferer that Christian sympathy will be his lot through this sickness. He can face this illness with Christian courage, and even brave victoriously the icy hand of death if such is to be. If a restoration of health be his, then he can come through the sickness and be a better man. Illness has proved to be a blessing in disguise to many a saint.

Sin loses its magnetic power to attract when a man is seriously ill. The gay old time of the world loses its glitter of attraction. The beauty of spiritual needs and realities glows more brightly than ever when a saint is sick. Sickness enables him to see more clearly that his choice of Christianity was indeed wise. Sin has no power to bolster the sick; Christianity does. Sin is totally impotent in extending help in the hour of pain; Christ is again all-powerful in this realm.

Sickness in irreligious homes is a double reason for pity. There is first of all the pain, discomfort, and inconvenience which attend all forms of illness. The second pitiable condition is that these people do not have the Lord upon whom to lean. They have registered total unbelief toward His cause in their healthy years. They have never enlisted His sympathetic help as burden bearer. They are not in covenant relationship with Him. They neither tread praying grounds nor enjoy pleading terms with Him who occupies the throne of grace. Paul portrays vividly their spiritual poverty. They are "without Christ, being aliens from the commonwealth of Israel, and strangers from the covenants of promise, having no hope, and without God in the world . . ." (Eph. 2:12). People who are physically well but are spiritually lost are in a pitiable position. People who are physically sick and lost in sin are even more to be pitied. Misery is their daily lot. It is true that the sickness may wake them into a sobering realization of their helpless, hapless, and hopeless condition. On the other hand, it may harden them in their sin and confirm their lifelong contempt for all realities of religion. There is always the possibility that the illness could result in death. This is the tragedy of all tragedies — death outside of Christ. Homes of illness where Jesus has never been present are lamentable indeed. I know. I have visited many of them.

A home where all are vigorously healthy certainly also needs Jesus Christ. Each member needs Him as the friend that will remain with us in health and will never forsake us in illness and need. Christ is the type of friend that sticketh closer than a brother (cf. Prov. 18:24). Solomon says, "A friend loveth at all times, and a brother is born for adversity" (Prov. 17:17). The love of this heavenly friend knows neither limitation nor duration. He loves us in prosperity and adversity. Tender affection is given us in health and undying interest is the conferred blessing in illness. In life and in death we have a real friend in Jesus. "What A Friend We Have in Jesus" has been sung by millions through the years. It is truly one of the greatest of all Christian hymns. John tells us that Jesus loved His disciples to the end (John 13:1). It does not take much at times to dampen our love and chill our affection for each other. But it is not that way with Jesus. His friendship knows neither bounds nor ends. All the family members need Jesus as Saviour. Each needs Him as guide and comforter. But when there is sickness we have an additional need for the compassionate presence of the divine guest.

DEATH IN THE HOME

Has death recently visited your home? Is there an empty chair at the family table that was once filled by a radiant and loving member of the home who has now ceased the walks of men and no longer frequents the settings of family togetherness? We know that the pale horse and its ominous rider death are never far removed from the threshold of any home. Without warning and instant as a flash of unexpected lightning the "king of terrors" can strike. Death does not always follow a strict chronological arrangement. Death may bypass the senior member of the household and strike down first a younger member.

During the years of my gospel ministry I have stood by the side of hundreds of families left bereft by death. Sometimes death was sudden and without prior warning. Sometimes it was expected and time had been supplied to brace for the sure shock of its certain coming. Some of these people have been Christian families. Other families have had absolutely no Christian connection. There is all the difference in the world between offering comfort to a Christian family who possesses the precious hope of seeing their departed one on that eternal shore of fadeless day and in standing by the side of those who are without God and Christ in this present world. Preachers of truth cannot do as preachers of error frequently do. The latter can get most anyone ready to meet death in the closing moments of the deceased's life. Such preachers frequently furnish words of hope and assurance to the surviving family regardless of how wicked and profane the life of the deceased might have been. If there has been no profession of faith prior to death, such preachers will often manufacture one by the time of the funeral. I have conducted numerous funerals where I could offer no word of comfort to the family without departing from Biblical truth. This I will not do for either the dead or those who remain. Respect for God's feelings must always take precedence over family feelings even in the day of death. I will not unnecessarily offend but neither will I deceive the family by words of false hope.

The desolateness of one dying outside the Lord is never more keenly realized than in moments when standing by families who have no truthful basis of hope in the wake of death. Some years back an elder, a deacon, and I went to see a grieving mother who was to bury her fifty-year-old son the following day. He had died in a tragic manner but a far greater tragedy weighed upon that Christian mother's heart. She told us that her son just "leaned" toward the Lord's church. He never became a Christian. But leaning is not equal to being born of water and the Spirit which places one into the kingdom of God (John 3:5). Leaning is not equal to belief and baptism which are the Lord's stated stipulations for salvation (Mark 16:16). Leaning is not the equivalent of repentance and baptism which result in the remitting of one's sins (Acts 2:38). Leaning is not the same as obeying that form of doctrine which frees one from sin (Rom. 6:17-18). Leaning is not the way to be delivered from the power of darkness and experience the joys of a triumphant translation into the heavenly kingdom. Leaning is not equal to a faithful life lived in the Lord Jesus with an attendant death in the faith (Heb. 11:13). This Christian mother would soon follow the mortal remains of her son to the silent city of the sleeping dead and every truth she had ever learned from God's Book told her he would not be buried in hope. There was little we could say. Any reader who is currently "leaning" toward Jesus and the gospel should take this story to heart. The next time it is told *your* mother may be the grief-torn parent near *your* lifeless tabernacle of clay inside the open casket.

The same comforting Christ who was with Jairus when the death message was delivered desires to be with us both in life and at the hour of death. No resurrection of the dead will immediately restore our loved one as in Jairus' case but the promise of a future resurrection of life will undergird our faith and give us courage and solace. Jairus needed Jesus when death claimed his loved one. We need Him today in similar situations. We must have Him in life if He is to be by our side in the day of death.

THE HOME AND JESUS' WORDS

Have you ever reflected on how important words are to the functioning of a home? Someone has suggested that the average person speaks 4,800 words a day. Many of these words are spoken in the home. Think of the words exchanged between husbands and wives, parents and children, brothers and sisters, and even those between the family and guests. Words can be angry or kind, inspirational or destructive, pure or sensual, religious or profane, dignified or unworthy. Words can build homes or destroy families. Words can mend or fester wounds. Words can add radiant chapters of happiness to a marriage. Words can produce the type of unhappiness that ultimately leads to broken homes. The Bible teaches the importance of words. "A word fitly spoken is like apples of gold in pictures of silver" (Prov. 25:11). "Let no corrupt communication proceed out of your mouth, but that which is good to the use of edifying, that it may minister grace unto the hearers" (Eph. 4:29). "Let your speech be alway with grace, seasoned with salt, that ye may know how ye ought to answer every man" (Col. 4:6). "But I say unto you, That every idle word that men shall speak, they shall give account thereof in the day of judgment. For by thy words thou shalt be justified, and by thy words thou shalt be condemned" (Matt. 12:36-37). James writes of the great power that lies in the tongue in James 3:1-12.

Of all potential words which should permeate the family framework the words of Jesus stand rank first in priority. Any other words are so far behind that they are scarcely discernable. Our homes today need the wonderful words of life just as Mary's hom did in the first century. Jesus did not visit the Bethany household without His message of eternal life. Neither will He enter our homes separate and apart from His word. No home can say yes to Jesus and no to His book, the Bible. To think that we can have Him separate and apart from His word is vain thinking indeed. The slogan frequently heard from young people today, especially those of the Jesus movement, is senseless. They tell us that they are saying yes to Jesus but no to the church. If by the word *church* they have in mind a man-made religious institution, then we stand ready to voice a louder no than do they. We have been saying a loud no to the need of denominationalism far longer than have they. But if they have the Lord's church in mind, then they are as wrong as they can be. They cannot have Jesus and reject what He promised to build in Matthew 16:18. They cannot have Jesus and turn up their noses at what He accomplished on Pentecost in Acts 2. They cannot have Jesus and reject that over which He reigns as head and king (Col. 1:18; Eph. 1:22-23). A *no* to the church of the Lord means a decisive *no* to Jesus Christ. The same is true about Him and His word. How would one go about separating Jesus and the Bible? What would the Bible be without Jesus as its central personality? It is impossible to think of Jesus without thinking of that only volume which reveals Him to us. Were it not for the Bible we could not have Jesus as the divine guest in our homes and the bearer of these wonderful words. If the Bible is not welcome in your home, then Jesus is not welcome. If the Bible is not revered, then Jesus is not revered. If the Bible is archaic, outdated, and outmoded to you, then Jesus is archaic, outdated, and outmoded to you also. Those who imagine they can say yes to Jesus and no to His church and covenant do not know the very first principles about the Jesus revealed in the Bible. Jesus and the Book of God come together. You cannot have one without the other.

Jesus comes as the bearer of good tidings of heavenly peace for the suffering and dying sons and daughters of wrecked and ruined humanity. His wonderful words of life tell us about the Father and the Spirit. These two, along with Him who became flesh, compose deity or the Godhead. Many misconceptions currently exist because people have not listened to what Jesus said relative to the Father and the Holy Spirit. The wonderful words of Jesus impart the attitude that we should possess toward the holy scriptures. Those who do as Mary did in Luke 10:39 will learn how we ought to view the Mosaic Covenant and the writings of the Old Testament. The wonderful words of life will reveal how lonely and lost man is without God. The words of Jesus will direct a man toward the relevant realms of life and will detour him from the trivial toys that fatally fascinate most of mankind. The words of Jesus will lead him to salvation and a life of loyalty in serving the Saviour. They will be his chart and compass as he sails the ocean of opportunities in this life. These words are true and tested. They are steadfast and sure. They will lead him into the right church, the right worship, the right mission in life, the right manner of daily demeanor, and ultimately to the right destination.

The words of Jesus are powerful. As agent of creation He brought all things into existence (John 1:1-3; Col. 1:15-17; Rev. 3:14). The Hebrew penman affirms that all things are upheld and undergirded "by the word of his power" (Heb. 1:3). His word "is quick, and powerful, and sharper than any twoedged sword, piercing even to the dividing asunder of soul and spirit, and of the joints and marrow, and is a discerner of the thoughts and intents of the heart" (Heb. 4:12). God's Son paid truthful tribute to the power of His word when He said, "It is the Spirit that quickeneth; the flesh profiteth nothing: the words that I speak unto you, they are spirit, and they are life" (John 6:63). Christ solemnly warns what rejection of His word means. "He that rejecteth me, and receiveth not my words, hath one that judgeth him: the word that I have spoken, the same shall judge him in the last day" (John 12:48). Jesus calmed a stormy sea and made peaceful the great winds by a dynamic directive of preeminent power. The power flowed through the channel of three words, "Peace, be still" (Mark 4:39). Jesus healed lame limbs, extended sight to the blind, cleansed lepers, made deaf ears hear, dumb tongues speak, and even called back to life those who were dead — all by the power of His word.

Is it any wonder that Mary cherished those words? Is it any wonder that each of His words was a pearl of great price to her? It is really a wonder that all did not practice this same brand of dynamic discipleship. Sitting at the feet of Jesus and hearing His wonderful words constitutes the very foundation of discipleship. Then the educated disciple is ready for spiritual action. It is strange that the masses of today prefer their own words to those spoken by the Master. They prefer the words of sensualism, secularism, and sensationalism to the words of that wonderful counselor from heaven. Do not the many broken homes and ruined lives of today bear irrefutable evidence and undeniable testimony to the fact that too few homes have made Jesus and His gospel welcome? Does Jesus reign in your home? Are His precious words of redemption inscribed upon the hearts of every accountable soul in your home? If not, why not?

SALVATION IN THE HOME

Jesus came as Saviour to the home of Jericho's chief publican. Though we do not know all the needs of this man and his household, we feel safe in asserting that his need for salvation was paramount. There is no conceivable need of a physical nature which compares with the need of spiritual salvation. This was true in Zacchaeus' case. The same is true in regard to all our homes today.

Every accountable husband and father needs Christianity. Every responsible wife and mother needs to know Christ as Lord and Saviour. Every child old enough to realize he is responsible before God needs Jesus as Saviour. The same Jesus who brought salvation to the Jericho household of Zacchaeus still comes to confer the same gift today.

Jesus does not come into our homes separate and apart from Christianity. We cannot make Him welcome and then demonstrate contempt for the gospel of salvation. Has it occurred to you that Jesus is the only guest who can bring salvation to your home? He was the only one who could confer this gift upon the household of Zacchaeus. Even if the high priest of the Jewish nation had come down from Jerusalem to Jericho to visit Zacchaeus, he could not have brought salvation. It was not within his prerogative of powers to confer such a gift. Even if Pilate, a Roman governor, or Herod Antipas, a ruling king, had visited the household of Zacchaeus, they would have been totally impotent in conferring salvation upon this lost family. The power to remit sins was not within political Roman dominion then or within papal prerogative from the Vatican now. Even one of the apostles could not have come to Jericho as the saviour of Zacchaeus. Only Jesus could bring salvation then; only He can bring it now. A visit from the governor of our state, a senator, or even the nation's chief executive would be a great honor for any loyal lover of America. However, these men could not bring salvation. Only Jesus can do that.

It may be that some sincere searcher for salvation will read these words long after the author has left earthly scenes. This person may not know how to become a Christian. Therefore, we now choose to relate how Jesus proposes to make Christians. A Christian is a member of God's kingdom. The entrance requirements are set forth by means of a birth. To the inquiring Nicodemus, Jesus said, "Verily, verily, I say unto thee, Except a man be born again, he cannot see the kingdom of God . . . Verily, verily, I say unto thee, Except a man be born of water and of the Spirit, he cannot enter the kingdom of God" (John 3:3, 5). In every birth there is a begetting and a bringing forth. These prerequisites are met when one obeys the gospel. To be a Christian one must be added to the church. Luke says of those early converts in Acts 2, "Praising God, and having favour with all the people. And the Lord added to the church daily such as should be saved" (v. 47). To be a Christian one must be delivered from the power of darkness and be translated into the kingdom of God's dear Son (Col. 1:13). To become a Christian one must cease being a servant of sin and become a servant of righteousness. Paul explains how this is done, "But God be thanked, that ye were the servants of sin, but ye have obeyed from the heart that form of doctrine which was delivered you. Being then made free from sin, ye became the servants of righteousness" (Rom. 6:17-18).

Jehovah has not enshrouded behind an impenetrable wall of mystery how one is born from above, anew, or again He has not left us in the dark as to how we obey the gospel. One must *hear* the Lord's word. Paul wrote, "So then faith cometh by hearing, and hearing by the word of God" (Rom. 10:17). *Belief* is imperative. Jesus said, "I said therefore unto you, that ye shall die in your sins: for if ye believe not that I am he, ye shall die in your sins" (John 8: 24). It is to the believer that the Lord dispenses power to become a son of God (John 1.12) Hence, salvation is not achieved at the point of faith. Sonship in the heavenly kingdom will never be attained by those who espouse the "faith only" dogma. James says justification is not by faith only (James 2:24). When the Bible says something is not so, then it is not so; even if millions say it is so. God determines truth - - not fallible men. Error would be error even if believed by all men. Truth is truth whether anyone accepts it or all reject it. Possibly there has never been a religious error that has done more harm than the dogma that salvation is achieved at the point of faith only. One religious group says that this is a most wholesome doctrine and affirms that it is very full of comfort. We ardently attack both stated aspects of this grave religious error. This dogma is not wholesome because it is unscriptural and antiscriptural. It is void of *any* comfort because it has no truth to undergird it. Man also must *repent*. Jesus presents the two great alternatives for humanity in Luke 13:3, 5: "I tell you, Nay: but, except ye repent, ye shall all likewise perish." Paul taught the Athenian philosophers on Mars Hill concerning the imperative nature of this divine directive, "And the times of this ignorance God winked at; but now commandeth all men every where to repent" (Acts 17:30). Paul immediately supplies a motive for repentance as he says, "Because he hath appointed a day, in the which he will judge the world in righteousness by that man whom he hath ordained; whereof he hath given as-

surance unto all men, in that he hath raised him from the dead"
(Acts 17:31). In Romans 2:4 Paul set forth God's goodness toward
humanity as another heavenly derived inducement leading to repentance. *Confession* of Christ is a part of becoming a Christian.
Such is a prerequisite for His confession of us to the Father (Matt.
10:32). Paul penned these words to his Roman readers, "That if thou
shalt confess with thy mouth the Lord Jesus, and shalt believe in thine
heart that God hath raised him from the dead, thou shalt be saved.
For with the heart man believeth unto righteousness; and with the
mouth confession is made unto salvation" (Rom. 10:9-10). People
who have complied with the foregoing commandments are now
ready to become candidates for Bible baptism. Jesus said, "He that
believeth and is baptized shall be saved; but he that believeth not
shall be damned" (Mark 16:16). Matthew quotes Jesus as saying,
"Go ye therefore, and teach all nations, baptizing them in the name of
the Father, and of the Son, and of the Holy Ghost [Spirit] . . ." (Matt.
28:19). Persons pricked in their hearts on Pentecost were told, "Repent, and be baptized every one of you in the name of Jesus Christ
for the remission of sins, and ye shall receive the gift of the Holy
Ghost [Spirit]" (Acts 2:38). When people hear the gospel message and desire to obey God's will, they will also desire baptism
(Acts 8:35-39). Sound preachers of truth will eagerly assist. Baptism puts one into Christ (Gal. 3:27). One comes into the body
(church) of Christ by baptism (I Cor. 12:13). The cleansing bene-
fits of Christ's blood are reached at the point of baptism and not one
moment earlier (Rom. 6:3-4). Baptism is connected with the washing away of one's sins (Acts 22:16). It is rather significant that the
Bible's final mention of baptism occurs in I Peter 3:21 where he says,
"The like figure whereunto even *baptism doth also now save us*
[not the putting away of the filth of the flesh, but the answer of a
good conscience toward God,] by the resurrection of Jesus Christ"
(italics added). That is how Christ will confer salvation upon each
member of the home. There is no other way for our homes to become Christian except by gospel obedience. Is your home a complete Christian household? If not, why not?

Has your home heard these words of Christ: "This day is salvation
come to this house" (Luke 19:9)? Christ in today's home is the
most pressing need of the twentieth-century family. When the family
lifts up the Christ and His book of divine love, that home will be
lifted to a higher spiritual eminence than it has ever enjoyed previously.

QUESTIONS FOR DISCUSSION

1. List some reasons why modern homes need the presence of Jesus today.
2. List some problems modern homes face and then list how Jesus can provide the solution.
3. What did Jesus do for the homes He visited in New Testament times?
4. Contrast Jesus as the guest who always blessed homes and many guests today who come to confer curses, stir up sorrow, and create confusion.
5. Will Jesus miraculously heal the sick in our homes as He did in Simon's home in Mark 1:29-31? Why, or why not?
6. Tell about some people of your experience, both Christians and non-Christians, who have faced sickness and how they reacted to the illness.
7. Who is better able to face and profit from sickness, the Christian or the non-Christian? Why do you answer as you do?
8. What blessings accrue to sick believers?
9. What blessings are withheld from unbelievers while in illness?
10. Do you believe each illness will draw us closer to God or push Him further away?
11. Are there blessings in illness? What did the psalmist say? Memorize Psalm 119:67, 71.
12. Does a home of healthy people need Jesus? Why?
13. What undergirds a Christian family when death comes into its midst?
14. Why is death so terrible for an irreligious family?
15. Why is there no real comfort to Christians left behind when the deceased only "favored" or "leaned" toward the Lord's church?
16. Who was with Jairus when the death message came concerning his daughter?
17. Why is it so important that we have Jesus by our side when we face the death of a loved one?
18. Discuss the importance of words.
19. Why are the words of Jesus so important to our homes?
20. Will Jesus come into our homes separate from His word? Why, or why not?
21. Discuss the modern attitudes of "Jesus, yes; the church, NO" and "Jesus, yes; His gospel, NO."
22. Discuss the power of Jesus' words.

23. Why is salvation the number-one need of every home today?
24. Can we have Jesus separate and apart from Christianity? If so, how?
25. Discuss in detail how Jesus makes Christians. Have you ever obeyed these instructions? If not, why not?

3

Needs of Today's Homes

The previous chapters have depicted Christ as the divine guest visiting a number of homes during the first century. In each He was the welcome guest. All these homes possessed needs and God's Son satisfied those needs. Some of the same needs which faced them face us today. The same Jesus who is able to bless our homes in the hour of illness, the day of death, and the time when salvation is needed can bless our homes with solutions to any other needs they might have.

Jesus did not fail with these homes in the first century. Instead He enjoyed phenomenal success. Save for the miracles which belonged to that age exclusively due to the need to confirm the Word, Jesus still does for our homes today what He did then. His power to protect our homes from the sinister forces of destruction is no less today than it was nearly twenty centuries ago. He blessed homes then. He still does today as multiplied thousands of devout Christian families can attest.

Counteracting the prevalent influences of secular society, finding solutions to marital and parental problems, and aiding families, society's most basic unit, to achieve a deep degree of success and happiness are among the home's most pressing needs in these critical days. An honest appraisal of every home would surely reveal that all homes have many needs. Some needs are more pressing in one home than perhaps in another home. This may be true because some homes have already made Jesus and His claims the hub around which the whole family framework revolves. Other homes have left the Master completely out of all family planning and purposes. He was not welcome at the beginning of marriage. He was not welcome during the birth of the first child. Such homes have been Christless all their existence and the greatest of all needs has been unfulfilled. The supreme blessings have been persistently withheld. The fountain of real happiness has never sent forth its copious stream of genuine joy and wholesome delight into these homes.

It is my solid conviction that Jesus Christ has a solution to every problem we face in today's home. Remember, His Father instituted marriage in Eden's beautiful garden. The Son surely knows of the essentials for a happy home.

THE NEED FOR LOVE AND COMPANIONSHIP

Do not our homes need more love and companionship between husband and wife? What peaceful atmospheres could descend on our homes if there could be a deepening of the bond of love and companionship which binds husband and wife in marriage. In today's extremely loose and lax times should not every marital mate work diligently to strengthen that cementing tie of fidelity that binds him or her to the lifetime companion? Should not all Christian couples determine that their marriage will be just as close to heaven's marital standards as frail humanity is capable of making it? A dedicated attachment to Jesus Christ and His manner of life is the surest way to achieve blissful success in your home. You cannot claim heaven's guarantee for a happy home unless you have heaven's Son as the captain of your household. Does He now occupy that position in your home?

Jesus brings real love and satisfying companionship into our marriages. From the sacred beginning of marriage Jehovah God intended this intimate bond to be fully expressive of the deepest love one human can extend another human. The wisdom of Almighty God created this institution to provide man and woman the most intimate human association known. The creative Father surveyed His garden of earthly paradise. He observed that it was not good that the man Adam remain alone. Jehovah determined to provide a companion for Adam. Moses wrote, "And the Lord God said, It is not good that the man should be alone; I will make him an help meet for him" (Gen. 2:18).

Succeeding verses inform us that the beasts of the field and the birds of the air were brought "unto Adam to see what he would call them: and whatsoever Adam called every living creature, that was the name thereof. And Adam gave names to all cattle, and to the fowl of the air, and to every beast of the field; but for Adam there was not found an help meet for him" (Gen. 2:19-20). These verses expertly refute the theory of man's organic evolution commonly accepted by the unthinking masses today. Adam was neither part nor parcel of these lower forms of animal life to whom he ascribed acceptable names. They had not produced him. They were not a part of his family tree. He was made one day later than water life and fowls of the air. He was made the same day as were the land animals. Lower forms of life could not supply him with the help meet that he needed. Female animals were perfectly adapted to their male counterparts but for Adam there was yet no human counterpart. God did not choose theistic evolution to solve that need. What the Almighty proposed to make was not something that would correspond to one of the animals Adam had just named. The creature to be formed was to be of human kind, not animal kind. There was a male and female of each animal kind; there must be a male and female of human kind. God had made man in His own image and after His own likeness (Gen. 1:26). No male animal of the field, fowl of the air, or creature of the sea enjoyed this unique distinction. Woman would have to be made — as man, that is, in the image and likeness of her maker. Moses said in Genesis 1:27, "So God created man in his own image, in the image of God created he him; male and female created he them." Human beings that stand at the marriage altar today and feel that they are highly evolved animals on the ladder of organic evolution are off to a poor start. God was not planning for this anticipated help meet to be an evolved offspring from lower forms of life. That was never Adam's appraisal of the glorious creature God gave him to complete his incompleteness and satisfy his loneliness. What people believe about their origin has a direct bearing on their self-decided plans for a destiny. What people believe about their origin cannot help but strongly affect their marriage and the erection of their future home.

The anticipated creation of his help meet was to fill the vacuum in Adam's life. The one to be made would answer fully his needs and be for him a spiritual and physical complement. Moses had described the making of man in language that was majestic and marvelous (Gen. 2:7). The language is just as lovely as he describes the wonders of woman's creation. "And the Lord God caused a deep sleep to fall upon Adam, and he slept: and he took one of his ribs, and closed up the flesh instead thereof; And the rib, which the Lord God had taken from man, made he a woman, and brought her unto the man. And Adam said, This is now bone of my bones, and flesh of my flesh: she shall be called Woman, because she was taken out of Man. Therefore shall a man leave his father and his mother, and shall cleave unto his wife: and they shall be one flesh" (Gen. 2:21-24).

Jehovah God fully intended that this sacred bond be nourished in the bosom of affection, love, and gentleness. But alas, its glorious origin was not destined to continue. Sin would soon make its tragic entrance into the perfect holiness of the first home. Its adverse effects would touch every human relationship, including that of matrimony. What had been love would in the future become hatred. What had been affectionate companionship would deteriorate into angry communications. What had been pure would become perverse.

The perverse hardness of man's heart toward his wife in Moses' day prompted the famed lawgiver to depart from Eden's original intentions. Jehovah had Moses write, "When a man hath taken a wife, and married her, and it come to pass that she find no favour in his eyes, because he hath found some uncleanness in her: then let him write her a bill of divorcement, and give it in her hand, and send her out of his house. And when she is departed out of his house, she may go and be another man's wife. And if the latter husband hate her, and write her a bill of divorcement, and giveth it in her hand, and sendeth her out of his house; or if the latter husband die, which took her to be his wife; Her former husband, which sent her away, may not take her again to be his wife, after that she is defiled; for that is abomination before the Lord: and thou shalt not cause the land to sin, which the Lord thy God giveth thee for an inheritance" (Deut. 24:1-4). It is quite obvious that later Jewish generations misunderstood this passage. Jews in Jesus' day affirmed that Moses had *commanded* the putting away of their wives. "They say unto him, Why did Moses then *command* to give a writing of divorcement, and to put her away?" (Matt. 19:7, emphasis added). Jesus, in answer, suggested that they had not correctly read their own lawgiver. "He saith unto them, Moses because of the hardness of your hearts *suffered* you to put away your wives: but from the beginning it was not so" (Matt. 19:8 emphasis added). Had there always been real love and companionship between Jewish mates, the laws given in Deuteronomy 24:1-4 would not have been used. In our day there would never have to be a resorting to Matthew 19:9 if all mates really and truly loved each other and shared in the marital companionship the way God intended.

From Moses to Malachi there stretches a full millennium of Israelite history. If anything, marriage deteriorates during this time. There are a few bright spots of real marital love but the deterioration in matrimonial love was becoming more evident with each passing generation. In the critical closing days of the Old Testament some men were dealing treacherously against the wives of their youth. Jehovah's stern and courageous prophet thundered out in no uncertain sounds concerning God's hatred of divorce (Mal. 2: 14-16).

Four centuries later conditions were even worse. Jewish rabbis were advocating divorce for such trivial excuses as a wife burning her husband's bread. The celebrated rabbi Hillel had taught such and a school of rabbis who sided with him were vociferously active in Jesus' day. Some came to the Master, as recorded in Matthew 19:3, with a query partly based on this exceedingly lax approach to the whole scope of binding marital ties. Temptation lay behind this query, no doubt. They surely hoped to trap Jesus and place Him in a tight dilemma from which He could not honorably extricate Himself without contradicting Moses or His own earlier teachings on the subject. They asked, "Is it lawful for a man to put away his wife for every cause?" (Matt. 19:3). They expected Him possibly to go back to Moses' law. Instead, He went back even further. He tersely queried them in return and embarrassed them with their woeful ignorance of Genesis 2. "Have ye not read, that he which made [not evolved] them at the beginning made them male and female, And said, For this cause shall a man leave father and mother, and shall cleave to his wife: and they twain shall be one flesh? Wherefore they are no more twain, but one flesh. What therefore God hath joined together, let not man put asunder" (Matt. 19:4-6). In His answer Jesus sought to restore marriage to its original status. True monogamy will result when the principles of Christ are faithfully followed. The husband will love the wife and be a real companion to her. He will love his wife even as Christ loves the church (Eph. 5:25). As he loves his own body and cherishes it, so will he deal with the treasured wife of his bosom (Eph. 5:28). He will dwell with her according to knowledge (I Peter 3:7). Humanly speaking, she will be the one person upon whom he showers his deepest love and most ardent affection. He will seek to be a real companion to her. His approach toward life will be the "our" attitude and not the "my" philosophy. She will never be far from his thoughts. Love and loyalty will protect her interests in his heart even when great distances separate them. She in turn will love, honor, cherish, respect, and be a true "help meet" toward him in every conceivable way. Humanly speaking, he will be number one in her life. Total fidelity will be her attitude toward him all the days of their married life.

The triangle of real marital bliss has Christ on one side, the husband on the second side, and the wife on the third side. Perhaps an even better way to express it would be to have Jesus at the top angle and the two marital mates occupying the two base angles. From the first date, through courtship, the engagement period, and on through marriage it should be a threesome arrangement, never a twosome agreement. The title of Tom Warren's excellent book on marriage says it perfectly, *Marriage Is for Those Who Love God and One Another*. The correct emphasis has been properly placed in this unique title: God first, each other next. Humanly speaking, husband and wife should be first in each other's hearts. But when duties toward divinity are included God has to be first. When He is really placed first, both husband and wife will more nearly fulfill their respective responsibilities toward each other in the royal realm of marvelous matrimony.

Is your wife still living? Be grateful. Show her the love, honor, and respect she truly deserves. The words "I love you" should often be upon your lips and just as frequently demonstrated in deeds. Do not wait until you view her lifeless form inside the cold casket to express words of love, affection, and gratitude. Then her ear will be deaf to your affectionate expressions. Then her eyes cannot sparkle with wifely pleasure for they will then be closed in the sleep of death. Then her heart cannot be lifted and made happy because it has lost its ability to feel. Then her spirit will not be stirred because it has already vacated the tabernacle in which it was housed. Do not wait until you bury your loved one before you express in motive, attitude, words, and deeds just how much she means to you. Do not wait until that empty chair at the table bears mute testimony of her absence or the other side of the marital bed is sadly empty before expressing your real appreciation for the leaves of love and the chapters of companionship with which she has filled the book of your marriage. I have conducted many funerals for wives whose husbands would give anything to have them back.

Is your husband still alive? Does he still shed the protective powers of his manly strength over you? Be grateful. Show him today how much he means to you. The words "I love you" should be a daily expression. By actions let him know that he is the most important human being in your life. Making him happy will add immeasurably to your own happiness. It will produce a stronger bond of marriage between you. Do not wait until you view his silent, spiritless form inside the cold casket before you realize how much you loved and appreciated him. Utterances expressed then will be too late to enter his closed ears and brighten his stilled heart. Post-mortem kindness cannot raise a sparkle of appreciation. Do not wait until he no longer brings home the paycheck to recognize his great worth as your breadwinner. Do not wait until his voice is no longer heard around the house or his arms of affection no longer embrace you as loving wife before you let him know what his love has meant to you. I have helped many women bury their devoted husbands. They would give anything to see the head chair occupied with his presence again. They would give anything to see his familiar frame cross the threshold again. They would give all they have of earthly goods to hear his manly voice echo through the house or feel the gentle embrace of his powerful arms again. But those days are passed forever. They can never recall them. But the days are not gone for you if your husband yet lives. Form a resolution as you finish this paragraph that your husband will have a more appreciative wife during the remainder of your marriage. You are the only one in the world who can confer such a generous gift upon him. Is this not what Jesus and His Father would have you do?

What about the love and companionship between parents and children? Parents need children as worthy objects of deep love. Children need parents as objects of their deep and responsive love. Do your children yet live? Show them Christian love. Enjoy the companionship of their company. Do things for them and with them. Aid them in forming sound guidelines for later adulthood. Because you do love them you will be head and guide of the home and never abdicate your positions. You will not allow your children to become little dictators of household policies. Because you do love them you will discipline them within the full framework of the child rearing guidelines established by Scripture. Are your children yet with you? Show them real parental love and regard now. Do not wait until premature death may snatch them from your presence to realize their worth to you. I know parents who have buried little ones. They would give a million worlds like this one to see that sunny smile again, to hear that radiant "Hi, Daddy" or "You know what, Mommy?" ring through the house again and to hear the patter of little feet racing through the house. A bereft mother would not complain at all if there were little fingerprints all over the back storm door which she finished cleaning less than one hour ago. A bereft father would utter no complaint at all if that little fellow were only here needing a new pair of shoes or a baseball glove. If we still have our children let us show them real love and appreciation now. Does not Jesus Christ expect us to do this?

Many who read these lines are fortunate enough to have their parents yet living. If you are married and living away from home, how long has it been since you last wrote your parents, called them, or made a special visit home just to see them? If you live nearby, how long has it been since you had them over for a meal or spent an evening with them? Opportunities for entertaining business associates and friends your own age will be present long after your parents have gone "the way of all the earth" (Josh. 23:14). Too many children wait until the parental hand is lifelessly still and the parent's eyes are closed in the sleep of death before they really appreciate the worth of parental love and concern. Would not Jesus desire you to manifest love, regard, and filial feeling of companionship to your parents now? Tomorrow may be too late. Now it can brighten and bless a lonely heart of some parent in his or her sunset years. Let each of us do it without delay.

Jesus does not come into our homes separate from love and companionship. He brings these needed blessings in the true sense of the term. The gift the enthroned Christ brings will result in a rich supply of real love and lasting companionship.

THE NEED FOR GREATER PURITY AND FIDELITY

Our age is lax in its morals and loose in its practices, and this is apparent also in relations between members of the opposite sex who are not married to each other. The dating game in today's permissive atmosphere often includes the practice of premarital sex, apparently without feelings of regret and with no evidence of scruples. Recent statistics crossing my desk indicated that possibly one-third of the babies conceived annually in our nation are conceived out of wedlock. Many couples do later marry but in about 300,000 cases no marriage occurs and these mothers give birth to babies who have no legal father.

But this does not tell the full story of rampant fornication in our sex-charged generation. Many unmarried couples engage freely in sex play and protect themselves from a possible pregnancy by employing the various birth control devices so easily available. Premarital sex is a paramount sin of flagrant proportions in our day.

Each occurrence means a sin has been committed. Its occurrence means a departure from the standards of the Saviour. Of all the couples guilty of fornication whom I have counseled, I have yet to have a couple tell me: "Our night of sin and shame was prompted because each of us sought to practice the moral standards of Jesus." Before fornication develops between a young man and woman there is first a departure from Jesus.

Before a boy and girl engage in premarital sex they have to trample underfoot all the following passages of Scripture: "Blessed are the pure in heart: for they shall see God" (Matt. 5:8). "Ye have heard that it was said by them of old time, Thou shalt not commit adultery: But I say unto you, That whosoever looketh on a woman to lust after her hath committed adultery with her already in his heart" (Matt. 5:27-28). Jesus would cut off adultery at its beginning place — the lustful heart. Those who commit fornication or adultery have ignored the counsel of Christ here unfolded. "And he said, That which cometh out of the man, that defileth the man. For from within, out of the heart of men, proceed evil thoughts, adulteries, fornications, murders, Thefts, covetousness, wickedness, deceit, lasciviousness, an evil eye, blasphemy, pride, foolishness: All these evil things come from within, and defile the man" (Mark 7:20-23). "Flee fornication. Every sin that a man doeth is without the body; but he that committeth fornication sinneth against his own body. What? know ye not that your body is the temple of the Holy Ghost which is in you, which ye have of God, and ye are not your own? For ye are bought with a price: therefore glorify God in your body, and in your spirit, which are God's" (I Cor. 6: 18-20). "Now the works of the flesh are manifest, which are these; adultery, fornication, uncleanness, lasciviousness, idolatry, witchcraft, hatred, variance, emulations, wrath, strife, seditions, heresies, envyings, murders, drunkenness, revellings, and such like: of the which I tell you before, as I have also told you in time past, that they which do such things shall not inherit the kingdom of God" (Gal. 5:19-21). "Abstain from all appearance of evil" (I Thess. 5: 22). "For this is the will of God, even your sanctification, that ye should abstain from fornication: That every one of you should know how to possess his vessel in sanctification and honour; Not in the lust of concupiscence, even as the Gentiles which know not God: That no man go beyond and defraud his brother in any matter: because that the Lord is the avenger of all such, as we also have forewarned you and testified. For God hath not called us unto uncleanness, but unto holiness" (I Thess. 4:3-7). "Let no man despise thy youth; but be thou an example of the believers, in word,

in conversation, in charity, in spirit, in faith, in purity" (I Tim. 4:
12). Paul informed Timothy that in his relationship with younger
women he was to treat them "as sisters, with all purity" (I Tim.
5:2). "Keep thyself pure" is the great imperative of I Timothy
5:22. Timothy was to "Flee also youthful lusts . . ." (II Tim.
2:22).

God has not placed the sex relationship in any part of the dating
game. Sex belongs to marriage and marriage alone. Experienced in
any other relationship it is spelled in great big letters S-I-N. Jesus
can bring a needed degree of fidelity between unmarried couples
in their courtship. Following Him will keep the dating game on the
high level of moral integrity. Each will be a protector of the other's
virtue if both are following in the steps of Jesus. We do not believe
there is any power in the universe that can restore the dating game
to the lovely levels of purity and uprightness save Christ and Christianity. Christian youth should remember that they represent the
Lord's cause and their home in any given situation. This includes
behavior on dates. The happiness of many a home has been
wrecked because of immoral behavior by one of its young people
while on a date. Young people who have Christian homes and
Christ-like parents need to be constantly aware of the fact that
there is no surer way to break a parent's heart than in this area.
I know a man who had once experienced this heartbreaking event
not with one child but with two. He summed up the feelings of his
broken heart: "I have buried my first wife, followed to the silent
city of the dead the remains of some of my own children, and have
also buried my parents. But what my daughters have done in these
cases of flagrant fornication has hurt more than any happening
of my long life." Situations like this are repeated hundreds of
thousands of times each year. Some parents could care less about
the amoral practices of their children. In fact, their children are but
emulating their own amoral lives! But other parents really do care.
And their hearts can be broken. The harvest from this sown crop
of wild oats is anything but pleasant. Young people who follow Jesus
will keep themselves from committing this heinous sin, thus preserv-
ing their own purity and keeping happy the homes from which they
come. Contrary to what the world thinks love does not make lust
proper. Love is still not spelled with lust. Real love says a firm and
decisive *no* to illicit lusts and actions.

Not only is there much moral laxity and ethical looseness among
the unmarried in their relations with those of the opposite sex but
extramarital affairs are also rampant. Reports from various studies
suggest that a high number of husbands and wives in our country

frequently travel the forbidden path of adulterous affairs. A leading women's magazine in our nation some years back reported that mutual adultery or "wife swapping" is practiced by millions of couples today. Many other mates stray into sinful relationships without knowledge or approval from the innocent partner who may be doing his or her best to have a successful marriage as far as the physical relationship is concerned. The infamous crime of infidelity thus rears its ugly head and wrecks many marriages. The Lord Jesus identified this sin as the only factor which would break the marriage bond and allow another marriage for the innocent partner while both yet lived. Jesus commented on this awful sin in Matthew 5:31-32: "It hath been said, Whosoever shall put away his wife, let him give her a writing of divorcement: But I say unto you, That whosoever shall put away his wife, saving for the cause of fornication, causeth her to commit adultery: and whosoever shall marry her that is divorced committeth adultery." Near the end of His personal ministry Jesus repeated, "And I say unto you, Whosoever shall put away his wife, except it be for fornication, and shall marry another, committeth adultery: and whoso marrieth her which is put away doth commit adultery" (Matt. 19:9). Following Jesus will not lead to a divorce on the ground of adultery or any other ground. A divorce always means that one or both parties have failed to follow the Master in His directions about marriage and the home.

When Jesus Christ and His principles of purity are inscribed in the hearts of both husband and wife, mutual and lasting fidelity is the beautiful fruit. No husband ever strayed from the plainly marked pathway of marital fidelity without first making a sharp deviation from the pure principles taught by Jesus Christ. No wife ever had an illicit affair with another man without first departing from the teachings of Jesus. Following Jesus Christ cements a husband and wife to each other. Obeying Jesus never prompted a husband to be unfaithful to his wife or a wife to be unfaithful to her husband. Faithfulness to Christ and infidelity in the marriage realm are mutually exclusive. One cannot be loyal to the Lord and unfaithful to a marital mate.

I have worked with many couples having marriage difficulties. Some of these homes were saved; others hit the disastrous rocks of divorce with all its attendant evils. I may have encountered unusual circumstances but I firmly believe that marital difficulties and trouble among brethren in the church are the gravest problems we face in the ministry today. Of each husband and wife whom I have counseled, I never have had a couple even remotely indicate that their marriage was coming apart at the seams and divorce was pending because each was following the Lord so closely. Those who have a right to live together as husband and wife do not encounter a break-up of their home by following closely Christ's commands. Divorces develop because someone has not been following the Master. Broken homes become tragic realities because Jesus never really lived in that home or has not been allowed to guide and govern that home in the months preceding the destructive finale.

Some years ago I received a letter from a lovely couple who were about to celebrate their forty-eighth wedding anniversary. (Since then they have celebrated their fifty-first anniversary.) Both affirmed that the precious vows of marital fidelity had been kept. In their long, useful years of fruitful activity for the Lord they had found contentment and supreme satisfaction in the earnest embrace of a pure and uplifting love. They had never stooped to something low, ugly, and degrading. They had not accepted Satan's advertisement encouraging extramarital affairs with the enticing words, "Stolen waters are sweet, and bread eaten in secret is pleasant" (Prov. 9:17). They knew that the aftertaste of such relations is always bitter. In a world of broken vows, broken homes, broken lives, and broken hearts they have succeeded beautifully in keeping intact their promises to the Lord and to each other. How beautiful and praiseworthy is this type of marital fidelity. How ugly and shameful the picture becomes when infidelity breaks the bond that cements a husband and wife together. Christ is the author of marital fidelity; Satan is the author of marital infidelity. Unfaithfulness will not occur until Christ has been ousted and His law disobeyed.

THE NEED FOR TOTAL ABSTINENCE

The mountain of misery erected by strong drink includes the break-up of homes. Often King Alcohol comes in by way of the twin doors of social drinking in the homes of others and of returning that hospitality with cocktails in one's own home. Liquor is easier to bring in than it is to send out. It has a way of going right to the throne room of a person's heart. When perched successfully thereon it will rule without mercy or compassion. Alcohol is a merciless master and a cruel conqueror.

The entrance of King Alcohol always means the exit of real happiness. Contentment is one of the first blessings to depart. Then woes will begin to descend with lightning speed. An avalanche of adversity begins to rumble. Endless contentions and constant bickerings replace what once were pure and elevated conversations.

The statements of "I love you" and "I am so happy being married
to you" will be said less frequently. The wounds will be many.
Red eyes will replace what once were sparkling windows of the soul
radiating joy and happiness. The blighting effects of strong drink
will soon permeate every facet of home and personal relationships. Solomon described how liquor works and with what end
results three thousand years ago. Note the terse questions, the
logical answer, and the certain recompense of it all. "Who hath
woe? who hath sorrow? who hath contentions? who hath babbling?
who hath wounds without cause? who hath redness of eyes? They
that tarry long at the wine; they that go to seek mixed wine. Look
not thou upon the wine when it is red, when it giveth his colour
in the cup, when it moveth itself aright. At the last it biteth like a
serpent, and stingeth like an adder" (Prov. 23:29-32). The context of this pointed appraisal of what strong drink will do also
connects the vicious habit with a strange woman and her sinful
allurements. The two preceding verses say, "For a whore is a deep
ditch; and a strange woman is a narrow pit. She also lieth in
wait as for a prey, and increaseth the transgressors among men"
(Prov. 23:27-28). The succeeding verse says, "Thine eyes shall
behold strange women, and thine heart shall utter perverse things
(Prov. 23:33). The utter foolishness of such a life is vividly portrayed in Proverbs 23:34, "Yea, thou shalt be as he that lieth
down in the midst of the sea, or as he that lieth upon the top of a
mast." Strong drink and adultery form an unholy union. Solomon
says those who embrace this unholy union are as foolish as a person
who lies down in the middle of the sea or seeks to lie upon the top
of a ship's mast. Neither was made for a man's bed. Strong drink
and flagrant forms of fornication with which it is so frequently
connected will destroy a home quickly.

No one ever became a social drinker by following the principles
of Jesus Christ. No man or woman was ever led to become a problem
drinker or an alcoholic by following Jesus. The fifteen hundred
people in our nation each day who become alcoholics do so because
they have failed to follow Jesus. The journey to alcoholism began
with the first drink. That first drink would have never been taken
if the person had been totally following Solomon's wise counsel. A
young man once sought to defend liquor. He said to me, "The Bible
does not say it is wrong to drink. It just says it is wrong to get
drunk." With immediate dispatch I countered by saying, "The Bible
not only condemns drinking but also says not to look upon it when
it is in its intoxicative stage" (Prov. 23:31-32). The conversation
ended as abruptly as it had begun.

Following the steps of Christ never leads to strong drink but rather always in the opposite direction. Let no one counter with the feeble quibble that Jesus turned water into wine in John 2. There lives not a man on earth who can prove that contention to be accurate. Prove that Jesus turned that water into an alcoholic beverage in Cana of Galilee and one has Him an open violator of Proverbs 23:31-32. Oh, the depths to which some people resort in order to defend liquor! They will even make Jesus a transgressor of God's law in order to prove their point. God's law said not to look upon intoxicative wine. They would not only make Jesus a manufacturer of the devilish liquid but also cast Him in the role of commanding the servants to bear some out and take to the governor of the feast (John 2:8). Habakkuk pronounced a woe upon every person who gave his neighbor to drink. "Woe unto him that giveth his neighbour drink, that puttest thy bottle to him, and makest him drunken also, that thou mayest look on their nakedness!" (Hab. 2:15). If Jesus did in John 2 what the liquor lovers say He did, He would be under Habakkuk's woe. In this miracle Jesus simply turned water into grape juice. The Greek word for wine here is *oinos* and according to *Young's Analytical Concordance* can mean grape juice. Christ and the Father had been turning water into grape juice by the working of natural law from the beginning of time. In this miracle Jesus did instantly what it took nature, moisture, and a grapevine several months to accomplish. It does not come in its intoxicative state when first taken from the vine. Neither was this intoxicative when it came from the Master's hand of miraculous power. Desperate indeed is a cause that would seek to turn our Saviour into a first-century bartender. Yet some of our preachers will do that to the Lord they profess to love, revere, and follow. They feel that the sensitivities of the drinkers are of top priority and must not be offended. The Lord's feelings take a back seat in the thinking of such preachers and religious leaders.

Jesus brings abstinence to our homes. This is the only sane and sensible course for the Christian to pursue and insures the well being of the home. I stand ready to contend for total abstinence against any and all opposition, some of our liquor-supporting preachers and whiskey-loving members nothwithstanding. Liquor has slain its millions and broken innumerable homes and yet some contend that social drinking (the breeding ground for problem drinkers and alcoholics) is innocuous. I say it is sin — S I N. No home is big enough for two kings. King Jesus and King Alcohol do not reside in the same home. Solomon wisely observes, "Wine is a mocker, strong drink is raging: and whosoever is deceived thereby is not wise" (Prov. 20:1). Paul commands that there be an abstaining "from all appearance of evil" (I Thess. 5:22). There is no way to look at alcoholic beverages with even an unprejudiced eye without seeing evil written all over the fiery liquid. Jesus brings total abstinence to our homes; the devil brings the disposition, desire, and opportunity to drink.

THE NEED FOR FORGIVENESS, KINDNESS, COURTESY, AND CONSIDERATION

Forgiveness is a must whether we speak of home relationships or church relationships. Jesus said our own forgiveness from God rests upon our willingness to forgive those who trespass against us. "For if ye forgive men their trespasses, your heavenly Father will also forgive you: But if ye forgive not men their trespasses, neither will your Father forgive your trespasses" (Matt 6:14-15). An incentive to be forbearing and forgiving is clearly outlined in Colossians 3: 13. Among many prescriptions for the renewed soul, Paul gave this one, "Forbearing one another, and forgiving one another, if any man have a quarrel against any: even as Christ forgave you, so also do ye." Though this counsel is not restricted to home relationships, it certainly includes them. The Epistle is directed to "the saints and faithful brethren in Christ which are at Colosse . . ." (Col. 1:2). Colossian Christians lived in home environments and knew of family relationships. Note what Paul wrote to wives, husbands, and parents in Colossians 3:18-21. A refusal to forgive has broken the bond of marital happiness between many mates. Marriage does not make perfect men and women. If every husband and wife were perfect, then no sins would ever mar their relationship. With the commission of no sins there would be no cause for forgiveness. Forgiveness implies a wrong has been done and mercy is ready to cover the sin when penitence is shown. One of the popular movies currently shown across our nation has an utterly false concept. The advertising quotation which has appeared in our newspaper to help sell the movie says, "Love means never having to say you're sorry." Real love always demands a confession of regrets and is to be followed immediately by full forgiveness. When God forgives He treats the forgiven party as though He had never sinned. When we forgive we are to treat the forgiven person as though the sin had never existed. You may be thinking, "This is asking too much!" But it is not asking too much when we are on the receiving end of forgiveness, whether from God or a fellow human. The difficulty in practicing forgiveness comes when we are the ones to grant the forgiveness. Then an ugly spirit of reluctance raises itself and stubbornly refuses to extend what we expect to receive when the situation is reversed. Many marriages would still be together had a greater measure of the forgiving spirit been present in the hearts of both husband and wife. Forgiveness can shed its beautiful mantle over any and all sins for which the transgressor is truly penitent. Some today do not wish to extend forgiveness more than a very few times. But forgiveness should not be a one-, three-, or seven-time arrangement. Certain rabbis in Jesus' day evidently extended the number of times one must forgive to three. This was two more times than some wished to give. Peter raised forgiveness to seven, thinking this was really a sufficient number of times. Jesus took Peter's seven and raised it to an indefinite number of times. He said, "I say not unto thee, Until seven times: but, Until seventy times seven" (Matt. 18:22). To take the attitude that the 491st transgression calls for a refusal to forgive is to miss the whole point of the Lord's teaching. Forgive an indefinite number of times is the basic thrust of this injunction. Forgiveness is to occur time and time again even upon a given day. Jesus said, "Take heed to yourselves: If thy brother trespass against thee, rebuke him; and if he repent, forgive him. And if he trespass against thee seven times in a day, and seven times in a day turn again to thee, saying, I repent; thou shalt forgive him" (Luke 17:3-4). Following Jesus will produce hearts that are tender and forgiving. He truly brings the blessings of real forgiveness into our homes. "To err is human; to forgive is divine."

Does any home practice as much kindness as it could and should? This is another most pressing need for modern homes. Kindness usually permeates the period of courtship. Voices are seldom raised toward each other in this happy period of coming to know, love, and appreciate each other. Why should the beautiful raiment of kindness be put aside when marriage is entered? That husband who may speak kindly to all his business associates during the day may come home and have nothing but words of hardness and harshness for his wife. Every word may be spoken in a framework of anger and resentment. How exceedingly strange that he should so treat the very one who ought to mean more to him than any other human being. She wears his ring. She changed her name in order to be known by his name. She keeps his home by day and caresses him by night with her love. She deserves much more than unkind and harsh treatment. Other cases may see the very opposite in marital behavior. The man will be kind and compassionate. He will deal gently with his wife. Yet there will fall from her lips ten words of anger to every word of kindness. He deserves better than this. Why will she talk kindly to friends and neighbors during the day but allow hostility to corrupt communication with the man who has made her his? He honored her at marriage by saying in essence, "Of every girl in the world, you are my voluntary choice to be queen of them all." Such an honor should not be taken lightly. She is obligated to treat her husband with gentleness, deep respect, and lasting affection. Kindness is not an optional matter if one wishes to have a happy home. It is also commanded by Scripture. Paul says, "And be ye kind one to another, tender-hearted, forgiving one another, even as God for Christ's sake hath forgiven you" (Eph. 4:32). "Therefore all things whatsoever ye would that men should do to you, do ye even so to them: for this is the law and the prophets" (Matt. 7:12). These rules could work wonders in the home. Whatever each member of the family would have all other members think of him, let him be kind and think likewise of them. Whatever each would have the rest speak of him, let him be kind and speak likewise of them. Whatever one would like other members do to him, let him be kind and do likewise to them. Jesus is a kind Lord. Jehovah is a gentle God. Christianity is beautifully built upon the firm foundation of kingly kindness. Truly Christ brings kindness to our homes.

Common courtesy and consideration are also absolute musts for a happy home. Courtesy is not a robe we wear during the daily pursuits of business and shed at the doorway upon our return home. If one member can come home and be discourteous and inconsiderate, then all members have the same right. If one member is obligated to practice courtesy and consideration, then all members of the home are equally obligated. Our homes could become havens of harmony with a generous mixture of courtesy and consideration. Jesus also brings the twin blessings of courtesy and consideration into our homes.

QUESTIONS FOR DISCUSSION

1. List some of the most pressing needs of today's homes.
2. Take each need you have named and explain how Jesus offers the real solution.
3. Why do our homes need a greater degree of love and companionship?
4. Did man, woman, and marriage have an evolutionary origin? Discuss the divine origin of each.
5. How are atheistic and theistic evolution refuted by a study of Genesis 2:18-24?

6. What concepts will evolutionists not take to the marriage altar?
7. What concepts will they take to the marriage altar?
8. Which view of life's origin, evolution or creation, will be more conducive to a happy, lasting, and successful marriage? Tell why.
9. Tell of woman's creation in Genesis 2:21-24.
10. Describe the downgrading of marriage from Eden to Moses' time? Do the same from Moses' time to Malachi's era. Trace the downward course from Malachi's time to the Saviour's earthly sojourn.
11. Discuss thoroughly Matthew 19:3-9.
12. Is there need for more teaching on this and similar passages today? Why, or why not?
13. Describe what will happen when husbands and wives really follow Jesus in their marriage.
14. What is the triangle of marital success?
15. Where should love for God be placed in marriage and the home?
16. List reasons why gratitude should be shown to other members of the family now.
17. Where has God placed the sex relationship? Is it ever right elsewhere?
18. Why are premarital and extramarital relationships wrong?
19. According to Bible teaching, are moral standards relative or absolute? Who has the real right to establish moral standards?
20. Before fornication or adultery can occur what must one first do with respect to his relation to Christ?
21. Discuss the beauty of a long and fruitful marriage where both partners have kept the marriage vows.
22. List some of the accompanying evils of alcoholic beverages. How do they affect the home?
23. What is wrong with social drinking?
24. List several Scriptural injunctions that would be violated if liquor were brought into the home and consumed.
25. Discuss how Christ entering into our homes brings forgiveness, kindness, courtesy, and consideration.

4

Marriage in the Home

Jehovah's great wisdom is beautifully portrayed in many realms of divine activity. Wisdom guided the voice that spoke the universe into existence. "The Lord by wisdom hath founded the earth; by understanding hath he established the heavens" (Prov. 3:19). Wisdom is vividly portrayed in His providential care and the preservation of what He made. Wisdom is superbly shown in the unfolding of the unique scheme of human redemption. God intends for the church to be an eloquent exhibition of the many-sided facets of His prudent planning and wonderful wisdom (Eph. 3:10). The making of man and woman in His own image and after His own likeness is a marvelous manifestation of His tremendous wisdom (Gen. 1:26-27). Those who can see how wonderfully made man is and yet deny God's hand in the process, are of all men most miserable and possess eyes totally blind to one of the most obvious of all truths.

From the very beginning God wisely provided marriage and the home for humanity's good. It was not good for the innocent and sinless Adam in Eden to be void of woman's companionship. Certainly it is not good today for fallen humanity to avoid the marriage relationship. Paul makes it clear that those who can live pure lives as single people have the right to do so but he recognized that many could not do as he did (I Cor. 7:1-9). Marriage is a mark of God's beautiful wisdom. Marriage can be beautiful as young people make their plans to enter its blessed and hallowed relationship. Marriage can be beautiful in its beginning, its continuation, and at its close when death honorably ends the sacred tie that binds human hearts together. However, this beauty cannot be achieved by a twosome arrangement. It can only be accomplished by a threesome arrangement. Let it be emphatically recalled that "Marriage is for those who love God and one another" as the title of Tom Warren's excellent book states. The love of Christ and two human hearts that deeply love each other are the imperative ingredients which every marriage should possess in abundant measure. Dating within a Christless framework grows into marriage at a Christless altar, blossoms into a Christless honeymoon, and continues in a Christless home. That life-style is a basic cause for unhappy marriages, unsuccessful homes, untrained children, and ultimately broken homes. In this chapter we propose to look at the basic beauty of this intensely interesting institution.

MARRIAGE IS REAL IN ITS NATURE

For many years when performing marriage ceremonies I have begun with this observation to the couple following the father's answer to "Who giveth this woman in marriage?" "The institution that the two of you are now entering is not an imaginary one but is real in its nature." It is not one that is entered today and treated as though it never existed on some tomorrow. Marriage is just as real as Jehovah God who first instituted it in the beauties of blissful Eden. Marriage is just as real as the Christ who once blessed a marriage feast in Cana of Galilee with His divine presence. The couple whose marriage was then occurring in the small Galilean village has been left nameless by Scripture. However, they were fortunate that their marriage began with Jesus present. Any marriage has a marvelous beginning if the Lord is there to bless it. So many couples today enter marriage and they care nothing at all for the Lord and His blessed presence. This couple at Cana was greatly blessed because Jesus was there. Marriage is just as real as the Holy Spirit who in Scripture has given wise words and prudent practices for successful marriages. Marriage is just as real as the Bible which maps the direction the anticipated home must travel if success is to be achieved. Marriage is just as real as the two who form it, the state which gives it legal sanction, the witnesses who observe it, and the civil or religious person who performs the ceremony. Marriage is not just a game that fertile imaginations create for a passing fancy. Let there be no doubt of its reality. It is just as real as any institution can be.

MARRIAGE IS DIVINE IN ITS ORIGIN

Unbelieving sociologists may vociferously vindicate the idea that we can never know for sure just how marriage came to be. This is understandable from their viewpoint because they reject the only book which sheds light on the beginning of marriage. Let a man reject the Bible and he is at a total loss to determine how marriage came to be. He will be in the same boat as are his unbelieving colleagues in science who supposedly seek for man's origin in the evolutionary hypothesis. They reject the premise of creation and thus have to build on a series of highly unlikely assumptions which have no factual basis whatsoever. The same is true with infidels in the field of sociology. They reject the very information that could lead them to a proper understanding of how marriage came to be a part of human relationships. Those who have placed their feet upon the Rock of Ages can say with firm assurance, "By faith, we know the origin of marriage." Marriage did not first exist in the minds of men. It was not by an experiment conducted by two consenting adults that the marital institution first came into being. Man's Maker first conceived of marriage and made it possible. He had made the man a little earlier. Then he made the woman. He made them adaptable to the needs of each other. He made them so they could enjoy the beauties of the physical union and thus supply one of the basic urges of the human heart. He made them so they could enjoy spiritual communion. Man and his hunting dog may enjoy many hours of pleasure seeking game. But when it comes time to pray the dog is no part of the experience. Man cannot enjoy spiritual fellowship with lower forms of God's creation. But man and woman can pray together, read God's Word together, and be "heirs together of the grace of life" (I Peter 3: 7). This separates humanity from the lower forms of life and is one of the strongest of all reasons for refuting the damnable doctrine that man's family tree has mammals, reptiles, amphibians, and simpler forms of life on its lowest branches. God supplied the spirits and made the minds of man and woman so they could enter and enjoy the physical and spiritual blessings of the marriage union.

Moses describes the thrilling beginning of marriage: "And the Lord God said, It is not good that the man should be alone; I will make him an help meet for him. And out of the ground the Lord God formed every beast of the field, and every fowl of the air; and brought them unto Adam to see what he would call them: and whatsoever Adam called every living creature, that was the name thereof. And Adam gave names to all cattle, and to the fowl of the air, and to every beast of the field; but for Adam there was not found an help meet for him. And the Lord God caused a deep sleep to fall upon Adam, and he slept: and he took one of his ribs, and closed up the flesh instead thereof; And the rib, which the Lord God had taken from man, made he a woman, and brought her unto the man. And Adam said, This is now bone of my bones, and flesh of my flesh: she shall be called Woman, because she was taken out of Man. Therefore shall a man leave his father and his mother, and shall cleave unto his wife: and they shall be one flesh. And they were both naked, the man and his wife, and were not ashamed" (Gen. 2:18-25). Jesus had His eye upon this passage of Scripture when He answered the query placed before Him in Matthew 19:3-9. To confess that man cannot know the origin of marriage, as some have done, is to blind one's eyes to Moses' message, close one's eyes to what the Christ disclosed, and reject what the Spirit prompted the Sinaitic Sage and the disciple Matthew to write.

Let the couple who stand upon the threshold of marriage disclose their real feelings toward how marriage originated and we can quite accurately analyze their feelings toward the whole realm of matrimony. Young men and women who reject the Genesis account of how marriage began are not likely to respect what Paul said about marriage, or the Lord's word about the duration of the marital bond. Genesis 2 therefore becomes the pivot upon which marriage revolves. Those who reject God as the author of marriage will not accept His Son as guide and director of the home.

MARRIAGE IS INTIMATE IN ITS RELATIONSHIP

In the Genesis 2:18-25 account, the following facts have been eloquently enunciated in multitudes of marriage ceremonies. When Jehovah came to choose a bone from man's body for the making of woman He did not choose a bone from man's head as though He intended the woman to be man's ruler and head. He did not choose a bone from man's foot as though He intended the man to trample upon her rights, despise her worth, and ignore her privileges. He chose a bone from man's side. Perhaps this signified that the woman was to be worthy of walking by man's side down the rocky pathway of life. Where the Bible has not gone, woman has been treated as cheap chattel and simply the object of man's passion and pleasure. In the Oriental world of the past many women never knew what it meant to walk by the side of their husbands. They accepted the teaching that they were deeply inferior to men and kept several paces behind. Where the blessed effects of Christianity have made an impact, woman has been lifted to her rightful position as the esteemed companion and partner of man. Jehovah God chose a bone from underneath man's arm. The arm has always been a symbol of power. Perhaps this emphasized the great need for man to protect her person and defend her interests through any of the perils of their mutual pilgrimages in life. Being the stronger of the two as far as physical strength is concerned, the chivalrous male has always treasured his right to protect his beloved all his life. The husband who would balk at such protection does not deserve the designation of *man*. The name does not fit such cowardly refusal of a universally recognized duty and privilege. The bone God chose was near man's physical heart — that most important body organ. This indicates the importance that every husband should attach to the wife of his bosom. She provides, as it were, the very heartbeat of their marriage. God took man's own bone and flesh and made for man his intimate companion. God could have put to sleep one of those animals whom Adam had just named and taken one of its bones and part of its flesh for the making of woman. But He chose not to do so. He took a part of man to make the woman. Each time Adam looked upon Eve he would see a part of himself in her make-up. She was not a highly evolved animal but a product from God's hand and made out of Adam's flesh and bones. It is a completely carnal and totally depraved mind that can reject the beauty of Genesis 1 and 2 and accept Godless, Christless, and Spiritless evolution.

The Hebrew terms for *man* and *woman* reveal something of the deep intimacy which God intended to exist between the first human couple. *Ish* is one of the Hebrew terms for man; *ishshah* is a Hebrew term for woman. The Hebrew people could not speak this word for woman without being reminded of her closeness to man. The speaker of English cannot pronounce the word *woman* without mentioning that which constitutes most of the term, *man*. Use of the words *husband* and *wife* shows the intimacy of this sacred union. A man talks of himself as husband. That immediately implies the half part of a unit, the marital unit. People who hear him speak as a husband automatically assume that he has a wife. A woman who speaks of herself as wife always implies the other half of the unit, the husband. When people think of husband and wife they think of two people who live intimately with each other. No other terms describing human relationship are so universally connected with physical intimacy.

Jehovah God placed the sexual urge in the human personality.

Throughout human history it has been recognized as one of the strongest drives known to man. God made provision for it to be enjoyed in one relationship and one only. That relationship is marriage. Paul states the matter very clearly in I Corinthians 7:2, "Nevertheless, to avoid fornication, let every man have his own wife, and let every woman have her own husband." The writer of Hebrews says, "Marriage is honourable in all, and the bed undefiled: but whoremongers and adulterers God will judge" (Heb. 13:4). The physical intimacy between a man and his wife is a lawful and God-approved relationship. Within marriage it is sacred and beautiful. There is no shame attached. There is no reason for regret after the act is concluded. It acts as a cementing tie. It is one of the deepest expressions of love. It truly is the extra language of the marital union. Though physical in its nature, it also has a spiritual dimension provided from two hearts deeply in love and two lives closely entwined. The Bible speaks of husband and wife becoming one flesh. Paul said, "For this cause shall a man leave his father and mother, and shall be joined unto his wife, and they two shall be one flesh" (Eph. 5:31). Jesus taught the same truth in Matthew 19:5-6, "For this cause shall a man leave father and mother, and shall cleave to his wife: and they twain shall be one flesh? Wherefore they are no more twain, but one flesh. What therefore God hath joined together, let not man put asunder." The Bible praises the one union that is experienced in the marriage bond. Without exception, when the union of a man and woman not married to each other is comtemplated, the act is always considered to be sin. God Almighty does not recognize any circumstances where fornication or adultery would be right and praiseworthy. The new morality and situation ethics which permissively permit such are unscriptural.

It is interesting to observe another Biblical term describing the intimacy of this union. That word is *know* or one of its derivatives. "And Adam knew Eve his wife; and she conceived, and bare Cain, and said, I have gotten a man from the Lord" (Gen. 4:1). "And Cain knew his wife; and she conceived, and bare Enoch: and he builded a city, and called the name of the city, after the name of his son, Enoch" (Gen. 4:17). "And Adam knew his wife again; and she bare a son, and called his name Seth: For God, said she, hath appointed me another seed instead of Abel, whom Cain slew" (Gen. 4:25). This description is given of Rebekah, "And the damsel was very fair to look upon, a virgin, neither had any man known her: and she went down to the well, and filled her pitcher, and came up" (Gen. 24:16). A virgin in Old

Testament times was one who has never known a man. The same expression is used in New Testament times. When the angelic announcement of Jesus' birth was made to Mary of Nazareth she said, "How shall this be, seeing I know not a man?" (Luke 1:34). Of Joseph and Mary it is stated, "And knew her not till she had brought forth her firstborn son: and he called his name Jesus" (Matt. 1:25). The use of this word throughout the Bible for the sexual relationship strongly implies that there is a unique way in which God intends a man to know about a woman. This knowledge should never be obtained save in the one relationship of marriage. In this sense boys and girls on dates should never "know" each other. In this sense men and women unmarried to each other should never "know" each other. This "knowing" experience is for the marriage bed only (Heb. 13:4). In all other cases it is a crimson crime, a terrible transgression, a serious sin, and a pernicious practice. No right thinking and right-acting man will ever know a woman in this sense save his own wife. To know one not his wife means he has given in to wrong thinking and wrong acting. No right-thinking and right-acting woman will ever seek to be known by a man in this sense save by her own husband. Her body is sacred and any man seriously trespasses who lays a hand on that which may be enjoyed only by her husband. When a woman agrees to be known by a man other than her husband she is acting under wrong thoughts and is committing a sinful action. Following Jesus will prompt men and women to know each other in the marriage relationship and there alone.

The intimacy of marriage is beautifully illustrated by the procreation of children. Jehovah has always had but one approved way of continuing the race. This is by marriage and the family, and in that precise order. He has always intended that a child be conceived within marriage and be born a part of the family framework. This makes for approved pleasure in the moments of conception and happiness at the hour of birth. The conception and ultimate birth of a child to a husband and wife are two of the most rewarding moments of their marriage. The physical union of their bodies results, by God's help, in the formation of another human personality. The fruit of their union is far more important than the fruit accruing from the mating of animals. The offspring of animals have no soul. The offspring of humans have souls. As that little baby grows into a little boy or girl the proud parents are bound that much closer. A child adds much cement to the marital tie. Those parents can look upon that little bundle of heavenly sunshine sent down by the Father's love and feel at all times that a part of each parent helps to constitute that child. A part of the father went into his making; a part of the mother also went into the infant. They can share the blessed memory of the love that produced him and the happiness with which they received him. As the child grows he will ever be a vivid reminder of the tie that binds their hearts, souls, and bodies to each other. The intimacy of the marriage institution is also beautifully portrayed in the rearing of children. It took both parents with God's help to get the child here. Both should keenly feel that the child's best interests absolutely demand that both parents, with God's grace and guidance, see him to maturity. This is one of the signal failures of the broken home where children are concerned. The broken home means that only one or perhaps neither parent will be rearing the child. Many tragedies abound in our time but this one just has to be near the top.

The intimacy of marriage is seen in the fact that God approves of the sexual relationship only in this sphere and this sphere alone. It is difficult to think of any act more intimate than is this one. This intimacy is sweet, beautiful, and fully expressive of real love when used as God's wisdom intended.

The intimacy of this bond is seen in the fact that it transcends in importance all other human relationships. The person getting married is to "leave his father and his mother, and shall cleave unto his wife: and they shall be one flesh" (Gen. 2:24). Jesus reiterated the same abiding obligation in Matthew 19:5. Therefore this relationship transcends the relationship to parents. The relationship in marriage even transcends that which we owe our children. There will come a time when they will leave the family to form marriages and establish homes of their own. But the marriage continues. God intended it to last as long as the two of them shall live. The love a husband feels for his wife should be greater than that he knew for his parents or that he has for his own children. The love a wife feels for her husband should be greater than that she feels for either her parents or her own children. When this affirmation is offered some stand aghast. In astonishment they ask, "What! Love him more than my father, mother, son, daughter or sister?" Yes! "What! Love her more than I do the parents that begat me or the children whom I have begotten?" Yes! Some will respond by saying such is impossible. No, it is not. It may seem incredible to them because they have never caught a vision of real marital love.

Let us consider carefully the following thoughts. God expects us to love Him best. Our love for Jesus transcends all other loves. He said, "He that loveth father or mother more than me is not worthy of me: and he that loveth son or daughter more than me is not worthy of me" (Matt. 10:37). The parallel account in Luke is slightly different. "If any man come to me, and hate not his father, and mother, and wife, and children, and brethren, and sisters, yea, and his own life also, he cannot be my disciple" (Luke 14:26). Here the term *hate* must mean that all earthly relationships must be loved less than the relationship that spiritually links the Christian to the Christ. This use of *hate* for *love less* is observed with Jacob, Leah, and Rachel. "And he went in also unto Rachel, and he loved also Rachel more than Leah, and served with him yet seven other years. And when the Lord saw that Leah was hated, he opened her womb: but Rachel was barren" (Gen. 29:30-31). When some learn that love for Christ must transcend other relationships of affection, they balk. They say such is impossible. But it is not, for many have done it. Some feel that such love for Christ would cause one to be unmindful of his family. Not so! The person who loves Christ preeminently will be far kinder to parents, brethren, wife, and children than the person who thinks he loves family first and puts love for God in a secondary category. A husband will be a better husband if he puts Christ first. A wife will be a better wife if Christ is really primary in her heart. A son or daughter will be a far more loving, obedient, and respectful child if he puts the Lord and His kingdom into position Number One. Father and mother will be far better parents if God is first in their lives. The same principle is true with reference to the primary obligation of marital love. A man can be a far better son to his parents by fulfilling God's will toward his wife. If he fails to love his wife, he will bring heartache to the parents who prayerfully desire his home to be happy and permanent. A man can be a far better parent to his children if marital allegiance to their mother is what it should and must be to meet heaven's standards. The wife can best honor her own Christian parents and most successfully promote the best interests of her own children by placing the husband in the primary position of earthly affections. The only love which should transcend marital love is our love for God. Remember that proper love for God will make marital love what it should be.

The intimacy of marriage is further emphasized in the sharing of happiness and the facing of adversity. Any right-thinking husband or wife goes first to the companion when good news is in the making. The affectionate reciprocation of a smile, a prayer of gratitude, or the warm grasp of holding hands tells the sweet story of sharing joys and happiness. When adversity sweeps into the life of one of the companions, there is no other person whose hand of help and word of optimism bring so much needed solace and encouragement as the trust, faith, reliance, and total commitment of the marriage mate. I have known the bliss of a happy marriage for nearly twenty years. Moments of happiness and times of sorrow shared with the wife of my youth have made this truth a constant reality.

Marriage is deeply intimate in its relationship. A firm grasp on Christ and Christianity gives proper direction for this intimacy throughout married life.

MARRIAGE IS MATURE IN ITS RESPONSIBILITIES

Marriage is not for children. They are not prepared in years, training, or experience to cope with the mature decisions that have to be made daily in the marital realm. In reading the story of Adam and Eve as they were made on the sixth day and entered marriage we never have received the impression that Adam was a little boy and Eve a little girl. We naturally think of them at the beginning as grown people. The Bible speaks of a *man* taking a *woman* but not of a little boy taking a little girl for marriage. Isaac possessed maturity before Rebekah became his bride. Jacob was mature enough to make his own provisions for a living when he agreed to work seven years for Rachel's hand in marriage in the land of Padan-Aram (Gen. 29:15-20). Jacob's love for Rachel was not the passing type of transient affection a little boy may feel for his girl-friend today and yet change the object of his infatuation a dozen times before mature love finally captures his heart and beckons him toward the matrimonial altar. Jacob served vigorously for seven years for Rachel's hand at the marital altar. Such was his feeling for her that the seven years "seemed unto him but a few days for the love he had to her" (Gen. 29:20). These cases could be multiplied in the Bible. N. B. Hardeman used to tell his students in Bible class at Freed-Hardeman College that when he married "Miss" Joe that he did not have to borrow buttermilk from his father-in-law the next morning. Sometimes boys and girls who are not old enough even to be dating think they are so madly in love that marriage just has to occur immediately. Both have yet so much of the child in them that they have not thought about where they will live, who will make the living, or any other important pre-requisites for marriage. They are like children who request an expensive toy. The price tag does not bother them at all. After all, that is a matter for parental concern. Many who stand upon the brink of early teen-age marriages do the same. They have not made one concrete plan for living after the honeymoon. Many feel their parents ought to work out all the details concerning living expenses. Such youngsters are not ready for marriage. If they unwisely wed, they may never celebrate their first anniversary together. The author of the phrase "Marry in haste; repent in leisure" may have had something like this in mind when he first coined that wise observation. Marriage-bound boys and girls who are so immature, have nothing with which to begin, and little prospect of anything for the next few years might do well to keep the following in mind:

> "If he ain't got nothing,
> And she ain't got nothing.
> Don't wed.
> Cause nothing plus nothing makes nothing,
> And that don't chew like bread."

It is my firm conviction that many parents are to blame for the conditions I have just described. They cannot or will not let their children be children. Constantly they push them toward adulthood. Mothers do not want their daughters left spinsters. We doubt that a mother of a ten- or eleven-year-old daughter must worry now about spinsterhood! At an age when little girls should still be living in a little girl's world, some mothers push them toward the sophisticated world of adult behavior. When boys should be interested in fishing and the latest score of their favorite team, a foolish father or unwise mother may be making plans to introduce little Johnny to the exciting world of boy-girl relationships. If parents would be wise and patient, nature would solve that problem and at an age when such relationships should begin to bud. But many parents do not trust the safe workings of nature along this line. It is so cute for fourth, fifth, and sixth graders to have little dates with each other, so they think. By the time some of these children get into junior high school dating is already an old game with them. Now they are ready for a steady. By the time some of them are ready to enter the freshman or sophmore classes in high school the game of steadies has gone stale and they think about marriage. For four or five years now they have been in constant company with those of the opposite sex. They may begin to take liberties with each other's body. Fornication may be the end result. An unwanted pregnancy may be the next chapter in this heart-breaking book of young people pushed too much and entirely too early into the world of boy-girl relationships. Whether they marry in their early teen-age years because of an unplanned pregnancy or decide against marriage, two people have been emotionally scarred for life. They will never be the same. The teen-age years which could have been so rewarding may end up as a horrible nightmare. The parents who paved the way for it to happen may not even realize the tragic contribution they made in this sad chapter in the life of their youthful son or daughter.

Some years ago I knew a lady with two daughters. She desperately wanted her girls to be popular. By the time the girls were ten or twelve years of age, boys filled the yard each afternoon after school. The lady worked and often there was no adult home. Her daughters and their boy friends had free use of the home for an hour or so each day before she arrived home. Friends tried to warn her about what was happening but she didn't listen. Her girls were popular and that is what she wanted for them. They had more boy friends as they stepped into their teen-age years than almost any other girls that age in the community. Do we need to relate the rest of the story? By the time one of the girls was fourteen or fifteen she was pregnant. The girl was not ready for marriage and the boy was not either. They married even with these three strikes against them: ill-prepared bride, ill-prepared groom, and a baby on the way. Marriages similar to this sometimes do succeed. Frequently they do not. Let your children be children. They will reach the adult world too soon anyway. It is not fair to make them into adults before by years, training, and experience they are equipped to be adults.

Marriage means earning a living. It means taking care of children when they come. It means being head and guide of the home for the husband and the wife respectively. It means making responsible decisions about a place to live. It means bringing home a paycheck, for those bills are going to come with clock-like regularity. It means keeping a house and being a homemaker. It means assuming one's duties toward the church, nation, the state, and the community in a way never before realized. Married people, regardless of age, are assumed to be mature enough to take on and discharge the obligations owed by every responsible citizen.

We are not trying to establish a definite age for marriage. Some mature earlier than others and some never become mature. But it should be emphasized that marriage is not for children. It is not for the immature. People need some degree of maturity before entering this institution. Maturity makes for better and more lasting marriage; static immaturity prompts marital mismanagement and ultimately a broken home. I have counseled couples who could have made a go of their marriages if both had been willing to grow up, to face their problems as mature men and women, and had stopped acting like spoiled children determined to have their own way with absolutely no give or take.

MARRIAGE IS MONOGAMOUS IN ITS CHARACTER

From the very beginning God intended that marriage would be a monogamy. When Jehovah planned the making of woman He did not say, "I will make him some help meets for him." There was to be only one Eve for Adam. There was to be only one Adam for Eve. Had polygamy been the wiser part of the marriage planning processes, God would have made a multiplicity of companions for the man. Had polyandry been the wiser part of God's wisdom, He would have given Eve a number of husbands. Marriage began with one man and one woman. "Therefore shall a man leave his father and his mother, and shall cleave unto his wife: and they shall be on flesh" (Gen. 2:24). Jesus taught this same truth in Matthew 19:4-6, and so did Paul in Romans 7:1-4 and I Corinthians 7:39.

Marriage began with monogamy in Genesis 2. Polygamy first became known in Genesis 4. There we read, "And Lamech took unto him two wives: the name of the one was Adah, and the name of the other Zillah" (Gen. 4:19). Abraham is remembered for taking Hagar as a secondary wife in order to have children. "Now Sarai Abram's wife bare him no children: and she had an handmaid, an Egyptian, whose name was Hagar. And Sarai said unto Abram, Behold now, the Lord hath restrained me from bearing: I pray thee, go in unto my maid; it may be that I may obtain children by her. And Abram hearkened to the voice of Sarai. And Sarai Abram's wife took Hagar her maid the Egyptian, after Abram had dwelt ten years in the land of Canaan, and gave her to her husband Abram to be his wife" (Gen. 16:1-3). The Egyptian maid soon was with child. This caused trouble between Sarah and Hagar even before the child was born. There was much trouble afterwards, even to the point of the handmaid and her child being cast out. As descendants of the founder of the Israelite nation, the subsequent generations that came from Abraham's loins should have learned a lesson for all time. They should have learned that when a man has two wives, there will be trouble: trouble between the man and his first wife, trouble between the man and his second wife, trouble between the two women, and trouble between the children of the two wives. But Abraham's descendents did not learn these obvious lessons. Jacob became husband to Leah and Rachel, though his original intentions included only Rachel. He added

Bilhah and Zilpah for secondary wives. These four wives bore him
twelve sons and one daughter. History relates the jealousy that
existed between Rachel and Leah and among the sons of Jacob.
This jealousy erupted when the sons of Leah, Bilhah, and Zilpah
conspired to sell Joseph, their despised brother, into captivity.
More than one wife in the household and children of more than one
mother living together caused trouble even in the patriarchal homes
of great and godly men like Abraham and Jacob. Certainly households with less substantial leadership will fare even worse.

The opening verses of I Samuel introduce us to an Ephrathite
named Elkanah. This Hebrew of old "had two wives; the name of
the one was Hannah, and the name of the other Peninnah: and
Peninnah had children, but Hannah had no children" (I Sam. 1:2).
The fruitful womb and the barren womb became a bone of contention in this polygamous household. Hannah's adversary (we
presume this to be Peninnah) "provoked [*angered her* — marginal
rendering] her sore, for to make her fret, because the Lord had shut
up her womb" (I Sam. 1:6). Righteous Hannah should not have
had to put up with the provocations of the prideful Peninnah.
It seems that Elkanah was very good to Hannah. When time arrived for the household head to dispense goods and gifts he gave
portions to Peninnah and her children (I Sam. 1:4). "But unto
Hannah he gave a worthy portion; for he loved Hannah: but the
Lord had shut up her womb" (I Sam. 1:5). The worthy portion, according to the marginal reference, was a double portion. Elkanah
questioned Hannah: "Hannah, why weepest thou? and why eatest
thou not? and why is thy heart grieved? am not I better to thee
than ten sons?" (I Sam. 1:8). Elkanah's deep generosity toward
Hannah could not compensate for her barren womb. No home is
big enough for polygamy or polyandry. Jehovah never intended it
from the beginning and these Old Testament examples vividly tell
the sad consequences of the various violations of Eden's original
standards.

David had many wives. During his brief reign in Hebron, sons
were born to him of six wives: Ahinoam, Abigail, Maacah, Hag-
gith, Abital, and Eglah (II Sam. 3:2-5). In earlier life he also
had married Michal, the daughter of Saul (I Sam. 18:27). This
makes at least seven wives for David by the time he was thirty-
seven years of age. The capture of Jerusalem and his subsequent
reign there witnessed an addition of more wives to the king's harem.
"And David took him more concubines and wives out of Jerusalem,
after he was come from Hebron: and there were yet sons and
daughters born to David" (II Sam. 5:13). In later life he also

took Bathsheba as wife. Every student of David's life is aware of the tremendous troubles that plagued his home. There was a very obvious lack of love between the half-brothers that lived there. A modern computer could have been kept busy in calculating the number of marriages contracted by Solomon. As he added wives to his harem, he also multiplied his own personal transgressions against the God who generously and lovingly had given him a powerful throne along with wisdom that exceeded any possessed by his ancestors or contemporaries. Centuries later Nehemiah reflected on this and declared, "Did not Solomon king of Israel sin by these things? yet among many nations was there no king like him, who was beloved of his God, and God made him king over all Israel: nevertheless even him did outlandish women cause to sin" (Neh. 13:26). Those who followed David and Solomon still continued the practice of a plurality of wives. In the words of Romans 15:4, "For whatsoever things were written aforetime were written for our learning, that we through patience and comfort of the scriptures might have hope." However, the most obvious lessons of history are frequently overlooked by succeeding generations of mankind.

Today's picture is little different from the foregoing accounts of the Old Testament. Where the laws of a land permit, men still have plurality of wives. This problem has been met frequently by missionaries. The Mormons practiced polygamy in our land until our laws finally took effect in their lives. Quite foolishly they used Old Testament examples for vindicating their sinful practice. The possession of more than one mate takes another route today. A man or woman may have many mates during the course of adulthood by having one at a time. Marriage is entered. The fascination wears off in a few weeks, months, or years. Divorce is sought and obtained. A new marriage is contracted. This cycle is repeated throughout life. By the time a man or woman reaches the end of life, two, three, four, or more companions may have been had and all may still survive. Laws of the land may allow this deviation from God's marriage law but God's law still stands: one man and one woman form a marriage unit and continue therein until death. There will not be any separation, divorce, or entrance into adulterous second or third marriages as long as both parties follow Jesus. Following Christ means monogamy in marriage. Eden first witnessed this wise constitutional arrangement and the Messiah still demands it (Matt. 19:6). Homes by the millions now pay the wages for violating God's marriage laws.

MARRIAGE IS PERMANENT IN ITS DURATION

From the moment that a man and woman enter into the holy estate of matrimony Jehovah God fully intends that this union will be indissoluble save by death. God's Word furnishes the glue and cement which will keep the union firmly connected. There will have to be a serious departure from the "Christ in the home" concept before a marriage of Christians will break asunder. Jesus wisely said, "For this cause shall a man leave father and mother, and shall cleave to his wife: and they twain shall be one flesh? Wherefore they are no more twain, but one flesh. What therefore God hath joined together, let not man put asunder" (Matt. 19: 5, 6). Does not Jesus here forbid the husband to put asunder the wife? Does He not forbid the wife to put asunder the husband? Does not God's Son forbid any and all attempts to put this institution asunder by a third party, whether an in-law or an outsider seeking to steal the affections of a heart that is committed for life? Many a marriage would still be together were it not for an interfering in-law. Stealing the affections of another's mate may be thrilling to the thief but the theft is grievous in the sight of God. Yet complacent society looks on this type of robbery with but little alarm. If neither husband nor wife puts asunder the marital tie but together they forge such an indissoluble unit that no third party can wreck their marriage, then that marriage will indeed be permanent. Only death can end it.

While speaking of a third party in marital interference, I would like to offer the following observations. While a young preacher I heard one of our most experienced and able preachers remark that in marriage counseling he had seen marriages that he could have kept together had it not been for an interfering in-law. That statement impressed me at the time. After many years of marriage counseling I can reiterate that statement. It never fails to deeply disturb me that Christian (???) in-laws will actually help to break up a marriage on a most trivial ground. They will encourage the son or daughter to come back home at the first sign of trouble instead of insisting firmly that the problem be maturely met and the marriage saved. What makes them think that their daughter, whom they have encouraged to leave a husband on some trivial ground, will return home, and never seek another marriage? Such thought, if possessed, is quite unrealistic. That divorced daughter with maybe two or three little children may not be home two months after the home has been broken before her lonely eyes settle on some available man. The man may not be available when she first spots him but she encourages him to divorce his own wife, break up his own home, turn his back upon his own children, and marry her. This woman may then enter a marriage which is condemned on his part as well as hers. It is adulterous from the first day onward. Yet parents will actually help pave the way for its occurrence by encouraging or condoning the destruction of the only legal marriage their child will ever know. When parents encourage a divorce they are casting their votes in favor of son's or daughter's second marriage. If that divorce is for any cause except the lone ground given in Matthew 19:9, then a second marriage is adultery. There is absolutely no way to avoid this inescapable conclusion. When your children have their first spat, encourage them to go right back home and solve their problem. Going home to Papa and Mama at that first cross word or sharp disagreement of decision-making is not the answer. Breaking up a home and entering an adulterous second marriage, whether done solely by the mates themselves or at the instigation of a third party, constitute two of the most serious sins of our time. They are high crimes that will bear devastating dividends in generations yet to come. Who but God Himself can fathom the total disaster resulting from the destruction of a home and the formation of an adulterous union? These are deadly blows aimed at the very annihilation of our society.

Paul taught the permanence of marriage. "For the woman which hath an husband is bound by the law to her husband so long as he liveth; but if the husband be dead, she is loosed from the law of her husband. So then if, while her husband liveth, she be married to another man, she shall be called an adulteress: but if her husband be dead, she is free from that law; so that she is no adulteress, though she be married to another man" (Rom. 7:2-3). Almost the same time Paul wrote the Corinthians emphasizing the same basic truth. He closes his great chapter on marriage, I Corinthians 7, with this pronouncement: "The wife is bound by the law as long as her husband liveth; but if her husband be dead, she is at liberty to be married to whom she will; only in the Lord" (I Cor. 7:39).

The marriage vows emphasize the lifetime bond of this union. "Until death do ye part," or its equivalent, has been used millions of times by those officiating. This is a vow made to God. It is a vow made to each other. It is a vow made in the presence of interested witnesses. It is a vow that ultimately will affect every child born to that home. It is a vow affecting society as a whole for society is composed of people from homes. This vow affects the church. The church cannot be composed of light-bearing Christians if they become negligent in the keeping of marital vows.

Let us begin to do a better job of teaching our boys and girls that marriage is permanent in its duration. The latest *World Almanac* suggests that in excess of 600,000 divorces were granted in this country during 1969. We, as a people, have not been doing an efficient job of conveying the importance of the marriage vows, or else our people are not abiding by what they have learned. We cannot help but conclude that there is an almost hopeless wave of ignorance in our nation concerning what the Bible has to say about marriage.

MARRIAGE IS UPLIFTING IN ITS DESIGN

Men and women need worthwhile goals to furnish purpose for life and to provide direction for their God-given energies. Those who have no purpose and direction in life are misfits in human society. They make the world a worse place to live. In marriage and the home are found noble purposes and goals. Jehovah said at the very beginning that it was not good for the man to be alone (Gen. 2:18). Solomon suggested, "Whoso findeth a wife findeth a good thing, and obtaineth favour of the Lord" (Prov. 18:22). The discovery of a good mate for life is far more valuable than possessing all the gold stored in Fort Knox or owning all the diamonds that South Africa has ever produced.

Marriage keeps men and women from living like animals of the field. Were there no bond of marriage, there could be no approved union of man and woman in the physical relationship. It is only the marital bed that reflects honor to its two occupants and God above. Unions outside of marriage are dishonoring to the sinful participants and bring down the vengeance of an offended heaven. Most men and women are so constituted that they cannot be pure in living single lives. Some like Paul can do it (I Cor. 7:7-9). Paul counsels that it is far better to marry than to burn with passion which cannot be gratified legally save in the marital union. Earlier in this great chapter on marriage Paul said "to avoid fornication, let every man have his own wife, and let every woman have her own husband" (I Cor. 7:2).

The establishment of a home and ultimately the rearing of a family offer some of the greatest incentives for right living, industrious work habits, and dedication to decency. Paul knew that younger women needed to "marry, bear children, guide the house, [and] give none occasion to the adversary to speak reproachfully" (I Tim. 5:14, brackets added). Such excellent incentives would keep them from the dangers set forth previously, "And withal they learn to be idle, wandering about from house to house; and not only idle, but tattlers also and busybodies, speaking things which they ought not" (I Tim. 5:13). Husbands and wives have something else for which to live rather than pleasing self. Fathers and mothers have something else for which to live rather than the selfish gratification of their own desires. The responsibility of bringing little children into the world, setting the proper example before them, rearing them in the nurture and admonition of the Lord, and seeing them to the place where they can successfully function on their own in this complex world are noble concepts which can lift people to higher plateaus of successful and happy living. Marriage and family responsibilities should bring out the best in people. Many a man has ceased participating in a sinful habit because of that little fellow that bears his image. The fact that he looks so trustingly to Dad for a standard of human behavior is a powerful incentive to live a better life. Many a woman has quit a long habit of sinful indulgence because a little girl is watching and will be emulating her as she grows to maturity.

A family that studies God's Word together, prays together, works together, eats together, plays together, and attends church together will provide a great inspiration for wholesome living. "Christ in the home" leads to such togetherness.

MARRIAGE IS MUTUAL IN ITS RESPONSIBILITIES

Too many marriages are entered with a selfish intent. The man thinks in terms of what the woman can mean and do for him. The woman thinks in terms of what the man can mean and do for her. The concept of what this marriage can do for me has self at the center. How much better for the man's love to be of such high character that he will think, "Now what can I do to make her happy that she has chosen to become my wife? What can I bring to this marriage that will make it a success?" How much better if the wife comes to the matrimonial altar with the concept, "Now what can I do to make my husband happy? What can I bring to this marriage that will make him be grateful daily that he chose me above all others to be his life's companion?" The concept of each individual should be, "Think not what this marriage can do for me but what can I do for this marriage?" The discharge of responsibilities is frequently lost sight of in the selfish thought of what will I receive from this planned union of two people. One of these is the attitude of giving; the other is the attitude of receiving. It is more blessed to give in marriage than to receive (cf. Acts 20:35). As a rule the person who gives most to marriage will receive most in return. There are responsibilities in marriage that pertain to husband, wife, father, and mother. Subsequent chapters will deal with these sacred obligations.

MARRIAGE IS DESIGNED FOR MAN AND WOMAN

The Commercial Appeal of Memphis, Tennessee, in its September 8, 1971, edition, carried the following (UPI) release, "Marriage of 2 Male Students First in U.S." It came from Minneapolis, Minnesota, and concerned two 28-year-old men who were students of the University of Minnesota. One of the men was president of the University of Minnesota Student Association. According to the news release they were married (???) in "a small private ceremony" on September 3. A mutual friend of both men said, " 'Jack and Michael were married at 8 p.m. Friday by Roger Lynn, a Methodist minister . . . in America's first legally recognized same-sex marriage.' " According to what this spokesman told newsmen, the two "have asked 'that they not be bothered during a one-week honeymoon.' " The spokesman also said, " 'As the two men love each other, Jack and Michael want to live together openly and with respect. Marriage is a serious personal affair for them.' "

The remainder of the release says, "Baker and McConnell were denied a marriage license last year in Hennepin County (Minneapolis). That attempt wound up in the Minneapolis Supreme Court, which is scheduled to rule on the case Sept. 21.

"Last week Baker was legally adopted by McConnell, and shortly afterward the pair obtained a bona fide marriage license in Blue Earth County, Preston said.

" 'There is no question in our minds that last week's ceremony constituted a legal ceremony. It was performed by a licensed minister of the Methodist church,' Preston said."

We stand amazed and aghast at this shocking disclosure. We do not know whether to be alarmed most over the two men who entered this so-called marriage union, the Methodist minister who said the ceremony and thus gave this beastly act his blessing, or the county which issued them a marriage license. All three conspired to perform an act of depravity. Such an act goes against every principle of marriage that is taught in God's Book. To form such a union with the words *love* and *respect* is to show total naiveness toward both of these majestic terms. That a so-called "man of the cloth" could stoop to such depravity shows how far some religious leaders are from Biblical teaching. That such a license, endorsing the very thing that prompted the destruction of the sinful cities of the Jordan plain in Abraham's day, could be obtained in any county in this nation must come as a shock to every decent-minded citizen in our land. The shades of Sodom have moved a big step closer to America. Lot made a tragic mistake as he "pitched his tent toward Sodom" (Gen. 13:12). It becomes even more of a tragedy when Sodom's standards become the accepted guidelines for a so-called marriage union between those of the same sex. For years now religious leaders and others have suggested that we ought to extend social approval to these highly unclean relationships. The revelation of this grievous and shocking act in Minnesota shows some of the fruit of this movement. The full harvest of such sinful teaching has not yet been reaped.

Everything that God's Book teaches relative to marriage makes it absolutely impossible for two members of the same sex to marry. God Almighty designed marriage with man and woman in mind. Marriage is not for two men. Marriage is not for two women. These two men in Minnesota, the Methodist minister, the spokesman that condoned the act, and the county that issued them the license should read carefully the last half of Romans 1. "Christ in the home" is not possible in that situation. This "marriage" is another point for Satan in his efforts to annihilate the home as God would have it. Is it not high time that America awakes to the perils that lie before us?

The home travels a fast course toward destruction when Satan is in control. When Christ and the Bible are lifted up in the home, the home will be lifted up. "Christ in the home" will make for a good beginning, a successful continuing, and a crowning conclusion.

QUESTIONS FOR DISCUSSION

1. List some of the ways God has manifested His great wisdom.
2. Describe the beauty of real marriage.
3. What are the ingredients of every marriage?
4. List some things which come from Christless dates, Christless marriages, and Christless homes.
5. Just how real is marriage?
6. Why was the couple being married in Cana in John 2 so signally blessed?
7. Can the origin of marriage be known if one rejects Biblical testimony? Tell why or why not.
8. How can we really know the origin of marriage?
9. Tell the thrilling story of how marriage first began.
10. What did Jesus say about marriage?

11. Can those who disrespect Genesis 2:18-24 really respect other Biblical teachings about marriage? Why, or why not?

12. What bone was chosen from Adam's body for the making of Eve? May there be some points of significance here? If so, what would they be?

13. Discuss the Hebrew words for man and woman. What is their significance in English?

14. Where did God place the physical relationship between man and woman?

15. How does the Bible describe this act between man and his wife?

16. Discuss other ways in which the intimacy of marriage is manifested.

17. Humanly speaking, what love is to be deepest in the human heart? Does this detract from other types of human love? Tell why it does or does not.

18. Discuss the mature responsibilities of marriage.

19. Why is marriage not recommended for immature boys and girls?

20. How do parents frequently contribute to early teen-age marriages?

21. Discuss the wisdom of keeping marriage monogamous in its character.

22. How does modern man with his laws about divorce deviate from the monogamous aspects of marriage?

23. Relate some of the consequences of polygamy in Bible times.

24. Discuss in detail the permanence of marriage.

25. Explain the various ways in which marriage is uplifting in its various designs.

26. Discuss the right concept that one should have on entering marriage. How does selfishness usually rule the situation?

27. Discuss God's design in marriage as including man and woman as opposed to those of the same sex attempting to enter this union.

28. What would Satan like to do to the home as God would have it to be?

5

The Husband in the Home

A handsome man follows the preacher out of the waiting room into the auditorium just before the "Wedding March" begins. The groom, his best man, and the preacher await the coming of the other members of the wedding party. After a seemingly interminable wait, a proud father escorts the beaming bride down the aisle. The eyes of groom and bride meet and their hearts beat a little faster. The hour of their long-awaited marriage has arrived. They are to become one in the eyes of God and men. The preacher makes a few appropriate remarks. The bride is given to the groom by her devoted parents. This is the greatest human gift they could confer upon this fortunate young man. They are entrusting her future happiness and lifelong security into his hands. The preacher shares what God has to say concerning the majesty of marriage and the royal character of the realm the couple is now entering. Then come the important parts of the ceremony: the exchange of mutual vows and rings, and the pronouncement of their being husband and wife. From this moment onward they are Mr. and Mrs.

From the time this young man says "I do" and hears his bride respond with the same magnificent duet, his life will never be the same. Other than his use of these words when he confesses his faith in Christ, no other words will be filled with such comprehensive meaning. Before these words were spoken he was single. Now he is married. Before his chief thoughts may have been built around the "I" complex. Now there must be a change of pronouns. It is no longer "I" and "me" but now it is "we" and "us." Previous to this he was known as a single unit. Now he will live in the framework of a double unit. Previously his decisions affected primarily himself. Now they affect two people. What are some of the great responsibilities he assumes as he begins a new and exciting chapter in his life?

HE IS TO SHOW HIMSELF A MAN

When he was a child it was proper for him to act as a child. When he was immature he was not expected to function in the framework of maturity. However, with the coming of marriage and home responsibilities he is expected to act as a man. Marriage is no place for the two mates to behave as children. Children do not concern themselves with their daily needs. Their shelter, food, clothing, medical needs, and educational requirements are provided by parents. A young man who has become a husband cannot ignore his new responsibilities as head, leader, and provider. Such leadership demands maturity. He is to exert maturity in fulfilling the new roles of breadwinner and provider. This is no realm for the immature who could care less about meeting this week's grocery bill or from where money for monthly utility bills and the rent will come. When children come to that home he is to manifest maturity as father, guide, and head. Again, this is no role for the immature. Decisions vitally affecting an entire family will be his to make and immaturity is an exceedingly poor foundation from which to make them. Becoming a husband and later experiencing fatherhood demands maturity in men.

THE HEAD OF THE WIFE

Marriage forms an institution and establishes an organization. Each institution or organization must have a head if it is to function properly. Such leadership is imperative for a home — the most basic unit of human society. Jehovah could have made the wife the head, but He did not do so. He could have left the home without leadership until the arrival of children who could then ascend the throne and rule the household, but He did not do so. He could have directed the parents of the new married couple to head the new household, but He did not do so. He chose the man to be the head and authorized this headship to rest on principles of right. Each function as head must be built on the foundation of true love. When the family members submit to a headship that rests on right, truth, and love, then God is pleased with that family and its leadership.

Now let us go "to the law and the testimony" and see what the Bible says on this point (Isa. 8:20). Let us follow a principle given by our blessed Lord, "What is written in the law? how readest thou?" (Luke 10:26). Man's headship over the wife and home goes back to the very first marriage. Before Adam and Eve left Eden Jehovah God said to the woman, just after their sin, "I will greatly multiply thy sorrow and thy conception; in sorrow thou shalt bring forth children; and thy desire shall be to thy husband, and he shall rule over thee" (Gen. 3:16). Man's headship of the wife and home is amply set forth throughout the Patriarchal Dispensation. The significant name given to this age refers to the leadership of the father. The word *patriarch* means father. God spoke to Noah in Genesis 6 and expected him to convey heaven's will to his wife and family. Noah was the head of his home. Jehovah spoke to Abraham in several chapters of Genesis. Sarah, an ancient worthy, highly esteemed her husband. Peter in the New Testament highly commends her obedience and recognition of him as head and lord of the home (I Peter 3:6). Christian women today can be daughters of Sarah only by the same hearty submissiveness. Abraham was head of his home. The same can be stated concerning his distinguished descendents such as Isaac, Jacob, Joseph, and a host of others. These men were the heads of their wives. Peter sums up the attitude of those early women: "For after this manner in the old time the holy women also, who trusted in God, adorned themselves, being in subjection unto their own husbands" (I Peter 3:5).

The New Testament repeats and even amplifies the injunction concerning leadership which must be accepted by husbands and respected by wives. I Corinthians 11:3 provides the general framework of headship in various realms. This verse constitutes God's vertical ladder of authority. The passage reads, "But I would have you know, that the head of every man is Christ; and the head of the woman is the man; and the head of Christ is God." God, Christ, man, and woman in that order is Paul's teaching. Is it a dishonor for Christ to recognize and abide by God's authority over Him? No! He never thought so. Statements in John 4:34; 6:38; 8:29, and 17:4 fully declare Christ's joy in doing the Father's will. Is it a dishonor for man to recognize and be respectful to Christ's headship over him? No! Man comes into his greatest happiness and projects his greatest usefulness in life when he serves acceptably under his head — the Lord Jesus Christ. Why should any woman feel it is a signal dishonor for her to recognize the general headship man sustains over her? Man's headship over the woman is not confined exclusively to the home situation. First Timothy 2:12 and 3:1-7 speak of man's leadership and headship in church relationships as well. The wife who delights in being submissive to her husband in the home is not the type who would be rebellious to the eldership that God placed over her in the church. Obedience to divine law in one realm is conducive to obedience in other realms.

Paul clearly establishes the husband's headship over the wife and home in Ephesians 5. "Wives, submit yourselves unto your own husbands, as unto the Lord. For the husband is the head of the wife, even as Christ is the head of the church: and he is the saviour of the body. Therefore as the church is subject unto Christ, so let the wives be to their own husbands in every thing" (Eph. 5:22-24). The spirit of submission which the church extends to Christ its head should be the type of submission the wife extends her head — her husband. It would be out of place for the spiritual head, Christ, to be submissive to the church. This would be a reversal of what divine wisdom teaches. It would also be a reversal of the divinely ordered roles in the home for the wife to become the head and the husband to be placed in the position of submission to her. Paul closes this beautiful chapter by suggesting, "and the wife see that she reverence her husband" (Eph. 5:33). This reverence or godly respect cannot grow and thrive in the framework of domination by the wife. It can thrive as she manifests a spirit of submission. Changing God's will along this line will not produce harmony and happiness in the marital realm but rather will lead to only disharmony and sorrow.

Peter also convincingly establishes the husband as head of the wife. The Christian wife who was married to an unbelieving husband owed him submission. Marriage laws of God apply when both partners are Christians. The same laws apply in mixed marriages when one partner is a Christian and the other is not. The same laws apply when neither marriage partner is a Christian. Marriage goes back to the very beginning of human history. Marriage is as old as the human race. Listen to what Peter says regarding wifely submissiveness. "Likewise, ye wives, be in subjection to your own husbands; that, if any obey not the word, they also may without the word be won by the conversation of the wives; While they behold your chaste conversation coupled with fear. Whose adorning let it not be that outward adorning of plaiting the hair, and of wearing of gold, or of putting on of apparel; But let it be the hidden man of the heart, in that which is not corruptible, even the ornament of a meek and quiet spirit, which is in the sight of God of great price. For after this manner in the old time the holy women also, who trusted in God, adorned themselves, being in subjection unto their own husbands: Even as Sarah obeyed Abraham, calling him lord: whose daughters ye are, as long as ye do well, and are not afraid with any amazement" (I Peter 3:1-6). The Christian wife is to be submissive to her non-Christian mate. Only in a matter of conflict between his desires and divine law should she be disobedient to his precepts and obedient to God's higher law. Only in cases where he might seek to block her performance of religious obligations should she exercise the privilege of pursuing allegiance to a more demanding law. The principle then should be placed in operation that Peter and his fellow apostles followed when religious and civil laws conflicted, "We ought to obey God rather than men" (Acts 5:29). The non-Christian wife is to be submissive to her Christian husband. The non-Christian wife also owes submissive allegiance to her non-Christian husband. The headship of the husband over the wife is in effect whether both parties are in the Lord's church or outside the Lord's church.

Christ in the home will guarantee that the husband will seek to discharge the responsibilities which a wise God has placed upon his shoulders. With Jesus at the helm of the home the wife will joyfully respond in the beautiful spirit of submissive reverence, reverence for Jesus and respect for her husband. No husband can ignore his responsibilities without a serious deviation from duty. Such a deviation is sin, manifests dislike for God's arrangement, and strikes at the successful functioning of the home. No real man will be derelict here. His manhood is at stake. The happiness of his marriage begins or ends with this very point.

I have often preached and lectured on the home. On occasion after a sermon about these Bible principles I have had Christian wives who wanted to do the right thing ask, "What can I do? My husband just will not assume the headship of our home. I desperately wish he would." There is only one thing she can do. Certainly she cannot turn over the headship to her children. That would only create an additional problem and would be highly detrimental to the welfare of the children. She then has to do the same thing in this area that a widow does: assume the headship herself. She should continue to pray that her husband will soon see his own responsibility. Until he does the home has to have a head. Every husband derelict in this should be reminded that he is failing to honor God's law, placing an undue hardship upon his wife, leaving himself open for unkind remarks from those who know the situation, and doing irreparable damage to his children. They will grow up in a home environment that has deviated from heaven's pattern. Such situations may well make it impossible for his sons and daughters to grow up with a proper respect and healthy attitude toward husband and father as head and wife and mother in the role of submission. Let it be emphasized that any sin in the home is going to affect adversely all other relationships. We need to do what God said to do, how He said to do it, and to do it for the very purpose He established. This surely includes the husband and father being head of the home and other members being submissive to this authority.

THE HUSBAND IS TO LOVE HIS WIFE

When preaching or lecturing on the home I always prefer to connect the husband's headship over the home with the divine directive that he love his wife. Paul did the same. He writes of the wife being submissive in Ephesians 5:22. He establishes the husband's headship of the wife in Ephesians 5:23 and compares it to the Lord's leadership of His church. He tells the wife to practice the spirit of subjection even as the church does toward her holy head, Christ (Eph. 5:24). Then in strikingly beautiful language Paul says, "Husbands, love your wives, even as Christ also loved the church, and gave himself for it; That he might sanctify and cleanse it with the washing of water by the word, That he might present it to himself a glorious church, not having spot, or wrinkle, or any such thing; but that it should be holy and without blemish" (Eph. 5:25-27). Never in the annals of marital counsel has a husband's obligation of love for his wife been so clearly stated as here. Paul did not choose the kind of love that Jacob had for Rachel, Boaz had for Ruth, Elkanah had for Hannah, or Joseph had for Mary to serve as the standard for marital affection between husband and wife. Paul knew of all these deep loves of the Hebrew past. He did not even single out the great love he had seen between Aquila and Priscilla and which was known firsthand by the Ephesians (Acts 18:18-26). Paul chose a love that transcended all other love as the standard toward which he directed every husband for a sincere and diligent imitation. He chose the love of Christ for the church. What kind of love did that Groom confer upon His Bride? It was a giving love. Christ loved and Christ gave. These verbs vibrate with deep beauty and real meaning. The two verbs *love* and *gave,* or their derivatives, are frequently connected with deity's attitude toward fallen humanity. What has been aptly designated as "The Golden Text of the Bible" says, "For God so *loved* the world, that he *gave* his only begotten Son, that whosoever believeth in him should not perish, but have everlasting life" (John 3:16, emphasis added). In Ephesians 5:2 we read, "And walk in love, as Christ also hath *loved* us, and *hath given* himself for us an offering and a sacrifice to God for a sweetsmelling savour" (emphasis supplied).

Deity loves and deity gives. One may give without loving but it is impossible to love without the beautiful accompaniment of giving. Love cannot be shut up in a vacuum. It will manifest iself. The love of Christ was a giving love. So must be the love of husband for wife.

Jesus' love was a pure love. He desired the best for His church on earth. He proposes a heavenly hereafter as her ultimate destiny. He desired her to be a glorious church. He desired every spot and wrinkle to be removed. Without blemish is another of His supreme desires for her spiritual condition. The husband must have a pure love for his wife. For her he seeks the best. Upon her he confers his deepest love, humanly speaking.

The love of Jesus for the church was a sacrificial love. So great was His love for the church that the cruelties of Calvary were not sufficient obstacles to keep Him from His avowed purpose of redeeming mankind. The love of husband for wife must be a sacrificial love. His life with her and for her should be a real "labor of love." The love of Jesus was an undying love. John 13:1 relates, "Now before the feast of the passover, when Jesus knew that his hour was come that he should depart out of this world unto the Father, having loved his own which were in the world, *he loved them unto the end*" (emphasis added). Often it does not take much to quench our love. This was not true with Jesus' love. The eleven apostles forsook Him in Gethsemane but He still loved them. Peter followed Him afar off but Jesus still loved and prayed for Peter that his faith fail not (Luke 22:31-33). Even when the lips of the pressured Peter were denying any knowledge or acquaintance with the condemned Christ, Jesus was planning to die for Peter's sins and for the transgressions of the whole world. The love of husbands for wives should be an undying love. As I listen to words of hate and bitterness expressed by alienated husbands and wives it often seems that it takes such a little to quench the glow of their love. Let there be a love between husband and wife that is unquenchable and the divorce courts can close their doors permanently.

The love of Jesus is a forgiving love. He braved the horrors of Calvary to make possible man's forgiveness. Jesus and His Father have never withheld pardon from offending humanity when the necessary stipulations have been met. One of the marvelous messages which left the lips of the crucified Christ was, "Father, forgive them; for they know not what they do" (Luke 23:34). This petition received an answer when some of His murderers repented and were baptized on Pentecost (Acts 2). Marriage must be built on the foundation of forgiveness. I have seen marriage break that could have been saved had the forgiving love of Jesus been present in the heart of the offended mate. But it was not there and the marriage ended. Nothing the offending mate could say would bring pardon from the offended. Because husbands and wives are imperfect there will frequently be an exchange of expressions such as "I am sorry; I have sinned. Please forgive me." Forgiveness must not then be withheld by any husband or wife who loves the Lord and also his marriage partner with the kind of love Jesus has for His church.

Paul chose the world's most wonderful type of love to be a model for husbands to emulate. An extension of this type of love from every husband and a grateful reception of it by every wife could make safe and secure the homes of the world. A reciprocation of this type of love on the part of the wife would make our homes the paradises of marital happiness which the Father intended.

Paul did not erect just one standard of love in Ephesians 5. He pointed to a second standard. "So ought men to love their wives as their own bodies. He that loveth his wife loveth himself. For no man ever yet hated his own flesh, but nourisheth and cherisheth it, even as the Lord the church: For we are members of his body, of his flesh, and of his bones" (Eph. 5:28-30). No sane man will mistreat his own body. He will spare no expense in keeping it healthy and seeking to restore it when ailing. He will not injure his body. It is precious to him. He seeks to protect it from all harm. Husbands should treat their wives with this type of care and concern. No wife would ever have nursed bruises on her body had her husband been following Paul's sage counsel. A man who loves his wife as he loves himself will not use his brute strength in a fit of uncontrollable anger to crush her. A husband who would mistreat his wife is, in my judgment, one of the cruelest people on earth. He does not deserve to be called a man. Real manhood will not deal with womanhood in such a cruel framework. A man's real character is accurately indexed by his attitude toward women in general and his own wife specifically. Let him love his wife as he does his own flesh. He does not betray the best interests of his own flesh. Neither should he betray the best interests of his wife.

Proper love for her will work for harmony in the home. He will deal with her gently. Love will sparkle in his eye as he beholds her from day to day. Genuine affection will form the guidelines of his every attitude toward her. She will hold the key to his heart. Kindness will form the wings upon which his daily words will be conveyed to her. Because he loves her he will work for the success of their home. Because he loves her his eyes will not become filled with lust for another fleshly companion. His love for God and wife will constrain him to do as the ancient sage of Uz did: "I made a covenant with mine eyes; why then should I think upon a maid?" (Job. 31:1). He will not have "eyes full of adultery, and that cannot cease from sin" as some did in Peter's day (II Peter 2:14). Because he loves her he will eagerly await the hours that he can be in her company again. Because he loves her they will work together, worship together, and play together. Because he loves her he will recognize that together they make a team. When separated, as they will be from time to time, he will recognize that the most important human being on earth is his beloved wife. Because he loves her his home will be his haven on earth. They will be "heirs together of the grace of life" (I Peter 3:7). Because he loves her a separation or divorce is the last thing he wants on earth. Because he loves her he wishes to spend the remainder of his days as her loyal and affectionate husband. He desires a full reciprocation of all these marital attitudes.

Christ in the home will insure that the right kind of love exists in a man's heart for his wife. The more a man allows Jesus to rule his life, the more successfully will he function as a good husband. Husbands, lift up Christ and His word in your homes and thereby enhance your role as husband and head of the home.

THE HUSBAND IS TO PROVIDE FOR THE WIFE

The husband as breadwinner is an outgrowth of his dual roles which have been previously discussed. Laziness toward this divinely imparted obligation seriously impairs the husband's role as head and casts a big question mark on the reality of his love for the wife. It is the height of injustice and the epitome of unfairness for a man to take a woman from her parents' home where she has had the security of food, shelter, clothing, and spiritual provisions and to place her in a home where there is little or no security. This man may soon put a little baby in her arms. He may be shiftless and irresponsible about providing for them. She may not know from week to week whether or not there will be support from him. She may not have money for the baby's next formula. She may not have money for this month's utility bills, the next grocery buying day, or for the next time the rent is due. *Christ in the home* will make for industry on the part of the breadwinner. There may be times when he will be out of work. There may be times when sickness will seriously impair his earning power. But the Christian breadwinner will not deliberately be out of work. He will not be content to walk the pathway of laziness.

From the very beginning God intended the man to provide for the wife and later his children. By nature man is better able to battle the elements of the soil or to face the frustrations of the complex business world. That Jehovah expected the first man to work for himself and wife seems to find expression in Genesis 3: 19, "In the sweat of thy face shalt thou eat bread, till thou return unto the ground; for out of it wast thou taken; for dust thou art, and unto dust shalt thou return."

This same concept is repeated in the writings of Paul. He instructed that "younger women marry, bear children, guide the house, give none occasion to the adversary to speak reproachfully" (I Tim. 5:14). That the woman was to guide the house lends emphasis to the idea that the husband should be the breadwinner. In Titus 2:4-5 Paul states that older women were to "teach the young women to be sober, to love their husbands, to love their children, To be discreet, chaste, *keepers at home,* good, obedient to their own husbands, that the word of God be not blasphemed" (emphasis added). The husband is the breadwinner. In dealing with children's responsibility to their aged mothers and grandmothers Paul says, "But if any provide not for his own, and specially for those of his own house, he hath denied the faith, and is worse than an infidel" (I Tim. 5:8). If a grown child fails to support his needy widowed mother or grandmother then he has denied Christianity and sinks to a lower level than that occupied by infidels. Even unbelievers may be diligent in taking care of their aged relatives who are in need. Previous chapters in this study have already clearly established the fact that marriage demands supreme loyalty, of a human nature, to the wife. These principles therefore suggest that a man who would not take care of his wife and children has denied the faith and is worse than an infidel. If he is obligated to those who begat him, parents and grandparents, then he also is obligated to those whom he has begotten as well as to the wife through whom they were begotten. As husband and father he will take seriously and conscientiously his role as breadwinner. He cannot be successful either as husband or father if in the role of breadwinner he is a deliberate failure.

"RENDER UNTO THE WIFE DUE BENEVOLENCE"

Knowledgeable students of the Bible will recognize this precept as constituting part of Paul's marital injunctions in I Corinthians 7:

3-5. Paul writes, "Let the husband render unto the wife due benevolence: and likewise also the wife unto the husband. The wife hath not power of her own body, but the husband: and likewise also the husband hath not power of his own body, but the wife. Defraud ye not one the other, except it be with consent for a time, that ye may give yourselves to fasting and prayer; and come together again, that Satan tempt you not for your incontinency."

Paul here is setting forth God's law touching the physical relationship. The husband is to be always mindful of the physical needs of his wife. His body is no longer his. By marriage there has been a transfer of ownership. His wife has every right in the world to expect that he will do his best to reward her with a happy life in the realm of sex. Fulfillment in this realm will cast a strong vote for a long, happy, and useful life together. Failure in this realm will cast a question mark over real marital happiness in other aspects. Disinterest in the role of the physical relationship has prompted more than one rejected wife to seek physical gratification with a man other than her husband. This, of course, constitutes sin on both her part and that of the consenting male. The wife has become guilty of adultery but her unconcerned husband has been a major contributor to this marital delinquency. Paul was aware that when marriage mates forego this part of their marriage for too long one or both may become easily seduced by Satan and seek a physical companion elsewhere. Paul sought to avoid this by a wise admonition.

No normal husband should withhold this privilege from his wife. Her normal bodily appetites call for fulfillment. She entered marriage to him in anticipation of this as one of the beautiful rewards of the marital union. When he defrauds her he sins against the God who strongly prohibits such selfishness. When he defrauds her he sins against his wife and fails to fulfill his part of their marital responsibilities. He is placing before her the temptation to seek illicit companionship elsewhere. He may even drive her toward seeking a divorce which will release her and permit her to enter a second marriage as far as state law is concerned. It is no exaggeration to suggest that happy marriages are largely contingent upon the respective fulfillment of the marital mates in the area of sex. Any veteran of marriage counseling could offer sufficient case testimony to substantiate this contention.

If the reader has thought that only husbands have been defrauded in this matter and that no such problem exists among wives, he has little knowledge of marital problems. Ann Landers perhaps has the widest reading audience of almost any newspaper columnist dealing with the personal problems of people. Her readers number into the tens of millions. Through the years she has received and reviewed letters from both husbands and wives who feel they have been deliberately defrauded in this area of their marriage. These lines were written shortly after she devoted an entire column to letters written from wives who were starved for physical attention from their husbands. Such dereliction can create mammoth problems in a marriage.

Marriage partners should be keenly aware of the injunctions in I Corinthians 7:3-5. *Christ in the home* means there should be an intense desire on the part of the husband to filfill this role of his marriage. Let the husband be faithful to his wife. Let him deeply sense at all times that she is the only one with whom he may cohabit in an approved framework. Let him also be keenly aware that he is the only one with whom she may cohabit. Doing the right thing in this area, as in all the facets of marriage, is imperative for a happy and harmonious home. Following Jesus makes for right actions.

"BE YE KIND"

I am aware that we have already considered Ephesians 4:32 in connection with Christ's Golden Rule in Matthew 7:12. But no one will ever emphasize too much the need for kindness to be expressed in human relationships. Hall L. Calhoun is quoted as having said, "There are three rules for learning. They are repetition, repetition, repetition!" The message of kindness needs constant emphasis in our age of anger and world of wrath. There is no area where kindness is more needed than in our homes. Here it is all too frequently a total stranger. Some husbands and wives practice kindness to all others but not to their marriage partner. Human kindness should find its greatest expression in the tender and intimate bonds of holy wedlock. Let us look again at these rules for happiness: "And be ye kind one to another, tenderhearted, forgiving one another, even as God for Christ's sake hath forgiven you" (Eph. 4:32). "Therefore all things whatsoever ye would that men should do to you, do ye even so to them: for this is the law and the prophets" (Matt. 7:12).

These precepts are not addressed exclusively to husbands but husbands are included. Let the husband be kind to his wife in thought. What he would have her think of him let him think of her. Let the husband manifest kindness in communication. Whatever he would have her show him in the verbal department let him show her in the way of words. Let him be gentle and kind in deeds. Kind words can be heard; kind deeds can be seen. Let there be an abundnace of both. Whatever kindness he would like to receive from her in daily deeds let him give to her. Why should a husband be kind to his wife? She has left loving parents to be joined with him. She chose his proposition of marriage over many others she possibly had. She has taken his name. She proudly displays that ring that he lovingly placed on her finger before the marriage altar. She has gone into the valley of the shadow of death to give birth to his children. She has lovingly performed a thousand deeds to make their life happy and their home cozy. The preparation of his meals, the running of his errands, the keeping of his house, the aid she extends to him in his chosen work or profession, the proper keeping of his wardrobe, the training she gives his children, and the love she generously proffers in moments of tender intimacy are among the strongest incentives for kindness. Diligent practice of Christ's counsel in Matthew 7:12 and Paul's precept in Ephesians 4:32 by husbands everywhere could infuse a dynamic degree of happiness into the hearts of wives. *Christ in the home* means following the Golden Rule. It means "be ye kind."

GIVING HONOR UNTO THE WEAKER VESSEL

In the opening six verses of I Peter 3 the apostle gives counsel to wives. Then he proceeds to offer some sage advice to husbands. It never fails to amaze me as to how much wisdom can be crowded into one verse of Scripture. First Peter 3:7 is an excellent example. Peter presents a comprehensive list of imperatives for husbands. "Likewise, ye husbands, dwell with them according to knowledge, giving honour unto the wife, as unto the weaker vessel, and as being heirs together of the grace of life; that your prayers be not hindered."

An analysis of this verse can be an exceedingly fruitful study for every husband. Diligent practice of the commandments in this verse can make a man the kind of husband the Lord intends and that every good wife richly deserves. It is true that in the preceding passage Peter talked of Christian wives being married to unbelievers and the relationships involved in that situation. However, in this passage the implication is clear that the husbands addressed are Christians and their wives are also Christians. This is logically deducted from the final part of the verse which pictures them as "being heirs together of the grace of life; that your prayers be not hindered." They could not be heirs together unless they were both

Christians. They would not form a marital unit which stood on praying grounds and enjoyed pleading terms with the majesty on high unless they were Christians. Such considerations prompted that great and able expositor of Scripture, Guy N. Woods, to say, "Wives might occasionally obey the gospel without their husbands, but not likely would husbands become Christians without their wives." (*A Commentary on the New Testament Epistles,* Vol. VII, Nashville: Gospel Advocate Company, 1954, p. 92).

Husbands are to dwell with their wives. Brother Woods observes that *dwell* is "translated from a term which denotes domestic association, [and] sums up the relationships of the marriage state." This dwelling is founded upon knowledge. Men should seek a "due understanding of the nature of the marital relation. . . ." Too many men assume the relationship of husband for most of their life but never make a serious attempt to understand their wife. Women are of a mold different from men. Their characteristics are different. They usually react differently to a given situation. Let there be diligent attempts made on the part of husbands to understand their wives and vice versa and many heartaches associated with ignorant wedlock can be avoided. This knowledge will not come during the honeymoon or even the first months of marriage. It is acquired through years of living with each other and learning about each other. This can be one of the real challenges of marriage.

The husband is to honor his wife. Brother Woods says that *honor* in this text "is the rendering of the same word translated *precious*" as found in I Peter 1:19. In that passage Peter spoke of "the *precious blood of Christ,* as of a lamb without blemish and without spot . . ." (Emphasis added). Brother Woods continues to shed helpful light on the meaning of this marital injunction. "Christian husbands are to regard their faithful wives as precious and to assign to them the honor that is their due" (Woods, p. 93). What if every husband would be a Christian husband to his wife? What if every husband would consider his wife as the most precious human possession of his life? Such attitudes would cause many of the problems standing at the thresholds of many homes to evaporate. Is your wife precious to you? Do you let her know by words and deeds just how precious she is to you? Why not take her in your strong embrace today and tell her that her price is "truly above rubies" (Prov. 31:10)? It will brighten her whole day to know that no price tag can ever be placed on her worth in the heart of her husband. Again Brother Woods says, "The woman is called a 'weaker vessel' not because of moral or intellectual weaknesses, but solely from the fact that she lacks the physical prowess commonly characteristic of man. The husband is exhorted to dwell with his wife in due consideration of the fact that she is physically weaker; and to regard her always as a fellow heir of the grace of life — life eternal — which awaits all of the faithful (I John 17:3). In styling the wife as the weaker vessel the implication is that man is also a vessel — both the husband and wife being instruments which God uses in his service." (Woods, p. 93). No right-thinking husband will ever use his stronger physical strength to abuse or mistreat his wife. He promised at the marital altar to protect her — not persecute her.

I have always been impressed with the beautiful thought of husband and wife being partners together and heirs on their way to heaven. They study together. As a harmonious unity they read and reverence God's word together. They pray as a team. They head in the same direction for worship. What a tragedy when the wife goes one direction and the husband goes another for worship. What a tragedy when the wife goes to worship but the husband stays at home. She is seeking the Christ; his interest is directed toward earthly affairs. While she seeks the bread of life he thinks about the life of bread. While she seeks to strengthen her faith in the Lord he may be out on a lake seeking fish. This is not what Peter had in mind. He visualized both marital partners as Christians with another world kept prominently in view. In dating it is so much better that a Christian boy or girl date a fellow heir of life. It is so much better if both marital partners are "joint heirs of the grace of life" rather than being religiously alienated from each other and God.

Peter counseled the foregoing partly to the end "that your prayers be not hindered" (I Peter 3:7). I have always been deeply impressed by Guy N. Woods' comments on this verse, "The word *hindered* is the rendering of a word which means literally to cut in, to interrupt. Where strife and discord obtain in a home, prayer is cut into and interrupted — the message to heaven is short-circuited! Bitterness, division, and bickering are opposed to the spirit of prayer and operate to terminate all efforts in that respect. Only where peace and harmony prevail can the husband and wife join their efforts in united prayer to the throne of grace" (Woods, p. 93). Husbands have enough sufficient counsel here to keep them busy for life. This Christian counsel should be the major concern of every marriage partner. No husband can afford to ignore these precepts if he wants to be the kind of husband envisioned herein. *Christ in the home* will insure constant and conscientious cultivation of these imperatives for every husband.

When husbands lift up the Bible in the home the Bible will lift up husbands in the home.

QUESTIONS FOR DISCUSSION

1. Why are the words "I do" in the marriage ceremony so meaningful? What changes will they make in a young man's life?
2. Why should a person who has just taken a wife show himself a man? Why will marriage fail if both display immaturity?
3. In what ways should the husband show himself a man?
4. Whom could God have made the head of the home? Whom did He choose? Upon what is the headship of the husband to rest?
5. List and discuss the texts which establish man as head of the wife and home.
6. Discuss the husband who refuses to be head of the wife and his home. How does he hurt his home? What should the wife then do?
7. The husband's headship should always be connected with which apostolic directive? Discuss Paul's connection of these two in Ephesians 5:23, 25.
8. Discuss in detail the kind of love Jesus had for the church. Tell how each facet of this love has meaning for the husband's relationship with the wife.
9. What second standard of love for husbands to practice did Paul erect in Ephesians 5? If practiced by each husband, list some things it would prohibit him doing to the wife. Also list some things it would prompt in his behavior toward her.
10. How will proper love for the wife work for harmony in the home? List some of its negative and positive fruits.
11. Discuss in detail the role of the husband as breadwinner and provider.
12. Read and discuss I Corinthians 7:3-5.
13. Against whom does a husband sin when he defrauds the wife in the physical relationship? What can be some of the consequences of this act of defrauding?
14. Why is kindness such a necessary ingredient for a truly happy home? Why do you think it is so frequently missing in homes of today?
15. List several reasons why husbands should be kind to their wives.
16. Memorize I Peter 3:7 and analyze each admonition it contains.

6

Portraits of Bible Husbands

An example is a very powerful thing. A good example has the power to make us seek its emulation. A bad example has the power to warn us from a downward and wicked course of life that will end in certain sorrow and sure destruction. Our study of husbands can perhaps be brought to its best conclusion by considering the type of husbands not needed and those that are needed. We shall approach this portrait-type study in that order, the negative first and the positive last. This will permit us to close with a positive emphasis.

THE KIND OF HUSBANDS NOT NEEDED

We do not need husbands like the churlish Nabal. His story is told in I Samuel 25. David was fleeing from the wrath of Saul, the maddened monarch of the land. David and his men had helped Nabal's shepherds and given them protection. Now David asks the wealthy shepherd for food. Nabal refuses. Notice the strong contrast between Nabal and his wife presented in verse 3: "Now the name of the man was Nabal; and the name of his wife Abigail: and she was a woman of good understanding, and of a beautiful countenance: but the man was churlish and evil in his doings; and he was of the house of Caleb." Later the chapter presents an appraisal of Nabal by one of his own servants who said to Abigail, "Now therefore know and consider what thou wilt do; for evil is determined against our master, and against all his household: for he is such a son of Belial, that a man cannot speak to him" (I Sam. 25:17). Abigail recognized the gravity of the situation. She took matters into her own hands and took food to David. When she came to David she said, "Let not my lord, I pray thee, regard this man of Belial, even Nabal: for as his name is, so is he; Nabal is his name, and folly is with him: but I thine handmaid saw not the young men of my lord, whom thou didst send" (I Sam. 25:25). David recognized the wisdom of her counsel and changed his plans to exterminate Nabal's whole house. Another revealing glimpse of Nabal is given in I Samuel 25:36. There at a feast, the kind that kings held, Nabal's heart "was merry within him, for he was very drunken. . . ." Abigail told him nothing of her own proceedings until his sobriety returned. Perhaps she had learned through bitter experience that there can be no reasoning with a drunken husband. Many wives can so testify who live with husbands and strong drink. When Abigail told Nabal what she had done, "his heart died within him, and he became as a stone. And it came to pass about ten days after, that the Lord smote Nabal, that he died" (I Sam. 25:37-38).

The contrast between this husband and wife who lived some three thousand years ago is about as wide as any other mentioned in the Bible. What he was she was not. What she was in character and wisdom he totally lacked. She had good sense; he was a fool. She was a good woman; he was evil, wicked, and worthless. She could be reasoned with; he was not open to counsel from any source. She would share the great wealth they possessed; he would selfishly hoard every particle of their abundance. She was a peacemaker; he was a breaker of the peace. He was a drunkard; every indication is that she was not. He felt the wrath of the Lord; she was blessed of the Lord. He came to a tragic end; she later became David's wife. Nabal was everything a husband and man should not be. We do not need husbands of his kind.

We do not need husbands like Ahasuerus mentioned in Esther 1. This Persian monarch was hosting a bountiful banquet in his palace at Shushan. The royal wine (wine of the kingdom — marginal reference) flowed in abundance. The king became filled with this fiery liquid and under its influence rashly issued a directive "To bring Vashti the queen before the king with the crown royal, to shew the people and the princes her beauty: for she was fair to look on" (Esther 1:11). Queen Vashti became known as an ancient example of modesty and chastity. She refused to obey the drunken king. "But the queen Vashti refused to come at the king's commandment by his chamberlains: therefore was the king very wroth, and his anger burned in him" (Esther 1:12). No right-thinking husband would want his wife to parade her beauty before the lustful eyes of other men. Yet this man did. He became very angry when she refused to become a participant in this royal banquet. Husbands today who approve of their wives going provocatively dressed into public places where roving male eyes will lustfully survey every gesture and movement of their partially clad bodies breathe far more of Ahasuerus' spirit than they do the spirit of Christian virtue and modesty. We need husbands who will protect their wife's modesty and forbid the display of her body for the viewing of those whose eyes are filled with lust (II Peter 2:14). It is difficult to separate strong drink and immodesty in speech and action. Liquor and immorality seem to have a natural affinity for each other. They are bosom bedfellows in scenes of sin.

We do not need husbands like those pictured in the closing book of the Old Testament. Those unholy husbands were dealing treacherously against the wives of their youth. God's prophet, Malachi, thundered against this great evil of his time: "Yet ye say, Wherefore? Because the Lord hath been witness between thee and the wife of thy youth, against whom thou hast dealt treacherously: yet is she thy companion, and the wife of thy covenant. And did not he make one? Yet had he the residue of the spirit. And wherefore one? That he might seek a godly seed. Therefore take heed to your spirit, and let none deal treacherously against the wife of his youth. For the Lord, the God of Israel, saith that he hateth putting away: for one covereth violence with his garment, saith the Lord of hosts: therefore take heed to your spirit, that ye deal not treacherously" (Mal. 2:14-16). Over one thousand years separate Moses, the first writer of the Old Testament, and Malachi, the concluding penman of that section of Holy Writ. Marriage standards deteriorated, if anything, during this millennium. Because of the hardness of men's hearts Moses made provision for husbands to seek writings of divorcement and to put away their wives (Deut. 24:1-4). In Malachi's day men were dealing treacherously against their wives. That these wives had been their companions from youth and were their partners in binding covenant relationships meant nothing to these wife-haters. The Lord was witness between them and their wives but this did not change their harsh treatment of their wives. God was gravely concerned; they were glibly unconcerned. God hated the divorce system; they favored it and employed it to put away their unwanted companions.

Genesis 2 tells the beautiful story of marriage as it begins in the Old Testament. Malachi 2 tells the sordid story of broken marriages. Genesis 2 has marriage in the framework of majesty; Malachi 2 has it in the framework of misery. In Genesis 2 love is the glue that binds marriage partners together; in Malachi 2 hatred is the disrupting element that tears marriage bonds and wedlock covenants asunder. In Genesis 2 marriage had God for its head; in Malachi 2 marriage had Satan for its head. There is a wide contrast between the beauty of marriage in Genesis 2 and the ugliness of divorce in Malachi 2. Love and gentleness reign in Genesis 2; hatred and treachery are the prominent characteristics of Malachi 2. Today we need husbands who will build marriages with their wives upon the standards of Genesis 2. We do not need husbands who will act as did those in Malachi 2. Jehovah smiled upon marriage in Genesis 2; he frowned upon broken marriages in Malachi 2. As a husband are you closer to the spirit of Genesis 2 or Malachi 2? *Christ in the home* will bind you to the spirit of Genesis 2 and will forever fortify you against the ugly spirit of Malachi 2. Much can be learned about marriage from a thorough study of these two chapters.

We do not need husbands as were those who came to Jesus in Matthew 19 with the question, "Is it lawful for a man to put away his wife for every cause?" (Matt. 19:3). It appears that those husbands had been listening to some of their recent rabbis such as Hillel who taught the putting away of one's wife for almost any trivial excuse. Jesus directed them back to the very beginning of marriage as set forth in Genesis 2. The Lord said, "Have ye not read, that he which made them at the beginning made them male and female . . ." (Matt. 19:4). There were husbands in the first century who could see no glue at all in the marriage contract. Marriages could be broken for every whim of disgruntled husbands. Thus many marriages could be contracted during a man's lifetime. It seems that these lax laws had even affected the disciples' thinking to some extent. When Jesus explained the lifetime glue that God intends to hold a marriage together, the disciples said, "If the case of the man be so with his wife, it is not good to marry" (Matt. 19:10). Jesus dealt further with these matters in Matthew 19:11-12. Today we have both husbands and wives who likewise see little glue in the marriage union. Most anything can turn their minds away from the permanency of marriage toward the direction of divorce. In multitudes of cases today it takes but very little to quench marital love. The easy divorce laws which have been enacted by those who do not fear God or regard the eternal interests of humanity have made the putting asunder of marriage mates into a thriving daily business. We do not need husbands who think of ending marriages but who will do all in their power to hold their homes together. Following Jesus did not prompt the query of Matthew 19:3. Those husbands asked the question because they had not been following what Jesus taught in Matthew 5:31-32 and were ignorant of the original laws of marriage in Genesis 2. Had they been interested in following Jesus they would not have sought to trap Him. Had they been interested in following Jesus they would not have set Jesus against Moses. Had they been interested in following the Lord Jesus they would never have raised a question relative to the advisability of divorcing one's companion for trivial excuses.

We do not need husbands today who will steal the affections of another's wife. David did this in II Samuel 11. That story is the blackest chapter in the king's otherwise illustrious life. While taking a night walk on the roof of his palace the idle monarch saw a beautiful woman washing herself. David lusted after her. He inquired into her identity. His growing lust was not quenched in the least when he learned that she was married and that her husband at that very hour was serving in David's army and was risking his life daily for the king's cause against the Ammonites. David sent for her. Adultery was the next link in that unfortunate chain of events. The first two links were an idle moment and a look of lust from a man. Bathsheba soon sent word of her being with child. David vainly sought to pass off the paternity of the child to the woman's husband but utterly failed in this cowardly maneuver. Finally, as a last resort to cover his crime, the desperate monarch had the innocent Hittite slain in battle. Uriah conveyed his own death summons to Joab, the king's battle line commander. After Uriah's death David took the beautiful Bathsheba for his own wife. Second Samuel 11 records the development of David's lust which culminated in a malicious murder. The chapter ends with the appraisal of David's sin. The Bible says, "But the thing that David had done displeased the Lord" (II Sam. 11:27). The marginal reference here for displeasure has that it "was evil in the eyes of" the Lord. By this act David sinned against the Lord, his kingdom, his wives and children, and gave "great occasion to the enemies of the Lord to blaspheme" (II Sam. 12:14). By this action David despised both the Lord and His commandment (II Sam. 12:9-10). Masses of men today are not content with their own wives. They desire to steal temporarily the affections of other married women. Thus a chain of events is set in order that may possibly break up two homes before the last link is added. We do not need husbands that will seek affection from other women. Let husbands be satisfied with their own wives and not be mislead by the enticing theory that "stolen waters are sweet" (Prov. 9:17). The final taste of unlawful flesh cannot help but be extremely bitter to every male transgressor when full recompense is dispensed.

Herod Antipas and Felix also committed adultery. Quickly I would point out that by listing these two Roman rulers as being guilty of the same crime as that committed by King David we are not placing all three characters on the same level. What David did was clearly out of character for a righteous man and David was a righteous man. But Herod Antipas and Felix were acting like the sinners they were when they engaged in the theft of wives. Their actions were in full harmony with their habitual life of crime, sin, and degradation. Herod Antipas was a son of Herod the Great. He had a brother named Philip who lived as a private citizen in Rome. Herod went to Rome and visited Philip. Philip was married to Herodias who was a granddaughter of Herod the Great and thus a niece of both Philip and Herod Antipas. Herod Antipas repaid Philip's hospitality by taking Herodias back with him to Galilee. The fearless preacher, John the Baptist, told the wicked monarch, "It is not lawful for thee to have thy brother's wife" (Mark 6:18). Herod Antipas had acted in a most unbecoming way. He had sinned. Herodias had sinned. Both were now living in adultery. Herod was already married to the daughter of Aretas, an Arabian king or emir. Two homes were broken up by this wife theft. We do not need husbands today who will do such despicable deeds. A popular song of some years back offered the wise counsel of "Don't rob another man's castle, the Bible says 'thou shalt not steal.' It may be a shack, down by the tracks, but everything in it's his own." Herod robbed his brother's castle. He took what belonged to another. We do not need husbands of his kind.

Felix, the unprincipled Judean governor during the middle of the first century was also guilty of wife theft. There seemed to be nothing off limits in his attempt to obtain the object of his devilish desires. When his lustful eyes fell upon the beautiful Drusilla, daughter of Herod Agrippa I, sister of Agrippa II and Bernice, and great-granddaughter of Herod the Great, Felix felt Drusilla must be his. The fact that she already belonged to another man meant nothing to this brash ruler. Through the help of a sorcerer, who acted as a go-between, Felix managed to persuade Drusilla to leave her husband and become his wife. Being the wife of a Roman procurator offered so much more than her present position as wife of an insignificant ruler. Deceitful Drusilla left her husband and entered an adulterous union with Felix. They were living in arrogant adultery when their paths crossed with that of Paul. He was given the opportunity to preach "the faith in Christ" to them while imprisoned for two years at

Caesarea (Acts 24:24). Paul was not a man pleaser. His discourse was not diplomatic. He was not there "to win friends and influence people" by ignoring the needs of the listeners and making them feel good with pleasing phrases, complimentary clauses, and soothing sentences. They were comfortable in their sins. Paul appeared there to afflict the comfortable. Luke does not record the words Paul used for the dynamic discourse but does mention the three headings of the message: "And as he reasoned of righteousness, temperance, and judgment to come, Felix trembled, and answered, Go thy way for this time; when I have a convenient season, I will call for thee" (Acts 24:25). As Paul reasoned so brilliantly and penetratingly concerning right doing and self-control, did not the governor's mind recall all his crimson crimes? Did not he recall the wife theft of which he had earlier been guilty? The fleshly spoils of that notorious theft sat by his very side as this scorching sermon settled upon their evil hearts. We do not need men who will steal another's wife and enter into an immoral relationship with her. We need men today who will respect the sanctity of the home. We need men today who will respect what belongs to another man. Wife theft is an enormous transgression.

Christ in the home will constantly act as a powerful deterrent in keeping men from being the wrong kind of husbands today.

THE KIND OF HUSBANDS WE NEED

We need husbands today who will consider the wife as "bone of my bones, and flesh of my flesh" (Gen. 2:23). She will then be considered precious in the sight of the husband. Consideration will prompt the kind of gentle affection necessary for a wholesome and contented union between husband and wife.

We need the type of love in hearts of husbands that Jacob felt for his beloved Rachel when he was working seven years for her hand in marriage. The Bible says, "And Jacob loved Rachel; and said, "I will serve thee seven years for Rachel thy younger daughter. And Laban said, It is better that I give her to thee, than that I should give her to another man: abide with me. And Jacob served seven years for Rachel; and they seemed unto him but a few days, for the love he had to her" (Gen. 29:18-20). We have frequently heard that love makes burdens light and service easy. Jacob found this to be true. Those seven years were actually as long as any seven years in Jacob's life. Yet they seemed so short. There were daily toils to pursue and burdens to be lifted constantly for the accounts we read of Laban's do not allow us to think that he was a lenient lord over

Jacob. Yet every burden the toiling Jacob lifted and every task he accomplished was worth the anticipated reward of the lovely Rachel as wife. We need husbands with this kind of love for their wives. We usually see this type of love manifested more frequently during courtship than after the marriage ceremony. This should not be. It takes love to woo and win; it requires love also to retain and rejoice in a wife all the days of a man's life. We need more husbands possessing the kind of love Jacob felt for Rachel.

We need husbands of honor like Boaz. The wealthy Bethlehemite treated the youthful widow Ruth with gentleness and tenderness. Boaz showed Ruth much kindness when she first went among his maidens to glean the barley grain during the Palestinian spring harvest (Ruth 2:5-23). If the world were filled with men such as noble Boaz our wives and daughters would be safe from assault day or night. Boaz belonged to that part of the human race which so often has been cruel and aggressive toward the fairer sex. But Boaz was not of this disposition. Ruth's honor was safe in his company. The events of Ruth 3 make this plain. He recognized that Ruth the Moabitess had real character. He said, "for all the city of my people doth know that thou art a virtuous woman" (Ruth 3:11). With dispatch he performed the part of a near kinsman toward her. There was a nearer kinsman than was he. He allowed this nearer kinsman to decide what he would first do about the piece of property in question and the marriage to Ruth. The man said no and relinquished the right of Ruth to Boaz. Boaz became the husband to Ruth. A beautiful romance budded into marriage. We have no doubts but what it was a beautiful marriage for beautiful courtships encourage beautiful and rewarding marriages.

We need more husbands such as Elkanah was to Hannah. In I Samuel 1:8 he asked her, "am not I better to thee than ten sons?" Ten was a number of completeness or perfection among the Hebrews. Elkanah chose this unique number and coupled it with the love that properly trained sons would show their mother to portray how good he was to Hannah. What if every husband would seek to be as good to his wife as ten sons are to their esteemed mother?

We need husbands who, along with their wives, will form a team of workers for the Lord. Luke 1 presents the beautiful team which Zacharias and Elisabeth formed as the New Testament Age was about to dawn. Luke says, "And they were both righteous before God, walking in all the commandments and ordinances of the Lord blameless" (Luke 1:6). There is the beautiful story of Joseph and Mary as they together obeyed God's will. There is something very precious about how diligent Joseph was in doing the Lord's will in the events leading up to the birth of the Babe of Bethlehem, their rapid exit into Egypt, their return to Nazareth, and the trip the family took to Jerusalem when Jesus was twelve (Matt. 2; Luke 2). Aquilla and Priscilla are mentioned some six times in the Bible. Neither is ever mentioned separately. They were a team when Paul first met them at Corinth in Acts 18:2-3. They were a team as they journeyed with Paul and remained at Ephesus while he traveled on to the Holy Land and Antioch in Syria (Acts 18:18-19). They were a husband and wife team as they taught the deficient Apollos more perfectly God's way (Acts 18:26). They were still a team when they risked their lives for Paul's safety (Rom. 16:3-4). They were a team when they had the church meeting in their house at Rome (Rom. 16:5) and at Ephesus (I Cor. 16:19). The last mention of them is made by Paul in II Timothy 4:19. They were still a team of fervent Christian workers. Divorce and a broken home are never thought of when Bible students remember the names of Aquilla and Priscilla. We need more Christian husbands who will emulate Aquilla and more Christian wives who will imitate Priscilla.

CONCLUSION

In this portrait-type study we have noted the kind of husbands men should and should not imitate. *Christ in the home* will provide the correct concepts that every husband needs to follow fervently. Men who will lift up the Bible and the Christ thereof will find their roles as husbands and later as fathers greatly enhanced.

QUESTIONS FOR DISCUSSION

1. Discuss the power of an example.
2. What power lies in a good example?
3. What power lies in a bad example?
4. Tell the story of the churlish Nabal. Why do we not need husbands of his kind?
5. Why do we not need husbands like the Persian king Ahasuerus in Esther 1?
6. Why do we not need the kind of husbands pictured in Malachi 2?
7. Contrast Genesis 2 and Malachi 2 as far as marriage attitudes and dispositions are concerned.
8. Why do we not need husbands like those who came to Jesus in Matthew 19?

9. Why do we not need husbands like David when he stole the affections of another man's wife? Discuss the many ramifications of this sordid story.
10. Discuss Herod Antipas and why we do not need husbands of his kind.
11. Discuss Felix and why we do not need husbands of his kind.
12. Why do we need husbands that will feel toward their wives as Adam did toward Eve in Genesis 2:23?
13. Why do we need husbands with the kind of love that Jacob had for Rachel?
14. Describe Boaz in his relationship with Ruth and discuss why we need husbands of his kind today.
15. What kind of love did Elkanah have for Hannah? Why is such love needed today?
16. Describe Zacharias and Elisabeth as a righteous team.
17. Describe Joseph and Mary as a team of workers for the Lord.
18. Discuss Aquilla and Priscilla in each of the New Testament references to them.
19. Are you and your wife seeking to be a modern example of such a working partnership for the Lord?
20. Make a list of the things husbands and wives can do together to serve Christ.

7

The Wife in the Home

A beautiful bride stands beside her proud father in the foyer of the church building where she has attended public worship since infancy. It was in this building that she obeyed the gospel as a teenager. Here she has learned so much about the Lord, His church, and what the home ought to be. Now this building is to be the scene of her marriage. The people who mean most to her are assembled for this great event. Her family is there. Her closest companions have come to be a part of her long-awaited day. In a moment she and her father will march down the aisle. All eyes will rest upon her beaming countenance. But she has eyes for just one person in the auditorium — that handsome young man who has wooed, won, and now awaits to claim her hand and heart in marriage. Their courtship has been clean and Christian. Their dating has been directed by principles of purity. They have fallen deeply in love with each other. Voluntarily they have agreed to enter into the blessed estate of matrimony. Now the moment has arrived. Down the aisle she gracefully walks. Each step brings her closer to him and holy wedlock. The preacher says some preliminary words. In response to his question, "Who gives this woman in marriage?" the father says, "Her mother and I do." The preacher continues. Several divine injunctions concerning marriage are enumerated. Upon completion of this part of the ceremony the couple joins right hands. There is the exchange of vows. The ring ceremony comes next. There is the pronouncement of their now being husband and wife. The prayer is uttered for the happiness of their home and the success of their marriage. The lips of husband and wife touch for the bridal kiss. They have now entered a new and exciting relationship. From this moment on this young lady will have a completely different type of life. Before she was a daughter living at home. Now she is a wife with a home of her own to help manage. Before she was single; now she is a part of a unit. Her responsibilities will increase for now she is an important part of society's most basic unit. What obligations and responsibilities are placed on her as she enters into matrimony?

SHE MUST SHOW HERSELF A WOMAN

In a previous chapter we established that the boy must now show himself a man. The same applies in the case of the girl. She must show herself a woman. She is no longer living in a world of dolls. She is no longer living in a world of school parties, slumber parties, and so forth. Now she is married. There will be the normal adjustments that all couples face as they settle down to the routines of establishing a home, building a happy and harmonious marriage, and preparing to rear a family. There will be meal preparation, grocery buying, the keeping of a neat home, perhaps the continuation of a job, and a host of other responsibilities. The practice of stretching each dollar and making every penny count becomes very important in keeping themselves financially solvent. All of these responsibilities call for womanhood. Immaturity will fail in these roles. This is exactly why marriage is for mature people and not for immature boys and girls. Problems will arise. Decisions will have to be made. Because marriage partners are not perfect, disagreements will arise and must be settled. Maturity will travel a long distance in helping the newly married couple to meet these problems and to make the proper adjustments. Where there is no maturity, trouble will soon loom larger and larger. The role of wife demands a woman — not a girl who is still acting as a child. Many marriages have failed to survive that first very important year because the two mates refused to grow up and to face their problems maturely.

THE WIFE IS TO BE SUBMISSIVE

Wifely submission to the husband began with Eve. Jehovah said to her, "I will greatly multiply thy sorrow and thy conception; in sorrow thou shalt bring forth children; and thy desire shall be to thy husband, and he shall rule over thee" (Gen. 3:16). Wifely submission continued throughout the Old Testament era. The patriarch was head of the wife and the family. Peter surveyed the worthy women of the Old Testament and said, "For after this manner in the old time the holy women also, who trusted in God, adorned themselves, being in subjection unto their own husbands: Even as Sarah obeyed Abraham, calling him lord: whose daughters ye are, as long as ye do well, and are not afraid with any amazement" (I Peter 3:5-6). The apostle Peter recognized that wifely submission had been practiced by God's noble women of the past. Christian women were counseled to do the same. They could enter the coveted roles of being modern daughters of the saintly Sarah by showing the proper respect for their husbands. The clear implication is that they could not become the adopted daughters of Sarah if they refused the spirit of submission. Peter earlier had written, "Likewise, ye wives, be in subjection to your own husbands; that, if any obey not the word, they also may without the word be won by the conversation of the wives . . ." (I Peter 3:1). Paul had this to say about wifely submission, "Wives, submit yourselves unto your own husbands, as unto the Lord. For the husband is the head of the wife, even as Christ is the head of the church: and he is the saviour of the body. Therefore as the church is subject unto Christ, so let the wives be to their own husbands in everything" (Eph. 5:22-24).

These texts substantiate the role of the husband as head of the home and call upon the wife to be submissive. For the wife to rebel against this principle would show disrespect for both God and her husband. Samuel was rejected by Israel in his declining days when the nation sought to copy the customs of neighboring nations. It appears that the aged prophet thought the action was just a rejection of him. However, Jehovah informed the prophet that "they have not rejected thee, but they have rejected me, that I should not reign over them" (I Sam. 8:7). When the Israelites clamored for a king they rejected more than a human judge — they rejected God as their real leader. When a wife rejects the rulership of the husband in the home she has rejected more than her husband — she has rejected God. There is no logical way to avoid this inescapable conclusion. Following Jesus will provide the incentive for every Christian wife to be truly submissive to her husband. Regard for God's law and love for her husband will provide no other alternative for godly wives. The choice narrows down to whether the wife wishes to obey God and honor her husband in this matter or to disobey Jehovah and dishonor the man whose name she has taken. Disrespect at this point can permanently disrupt the happiness and harmony of any home.

Jesus Christ never attempted to remove Himself from the Father's authority. Had He done so He would not have been our perfect Redeemer. His greatest happiness was found in being submissive to the Father's will. Man has often attempted to remove himself from Christ's dominion. When that occurs it does nothing for a man except to bring him misery. When woman decides that she should liberate herself from any and all submission to man she is asking for trouble. I claim no prophetic powers but I see no ultimate good coming to God's cause, the good of man, the betterment of woman, or the strengthening of the home as a result of the current women's liberation movement. A woman gains much by being submissive in every realm commanded by God and this includes submission to the husband in the home.

THE WIFE IS TO LOVE HER HUSBAND

Through Titus Paul gave exhortation that older women teach the younger "women to be sober, to love their husbands, to love their children, To be discreet, chaste, keepers at home, good, obedient to their own husbands, that the word of God be not blasphemed" (Titus 2:4-5). Love demands loyalty, kindness, and gentleness to him in thought, words, and deeds. Love will keep her from constantly nagging him. Nagging is a sure way to drive him away from home. Love will keep her from demeaning him before her friends. Some wives cannot find a single good thing to say to or about their husbands. Such wives need some pointed reminders about the one who picked their husbands in the first place! Has it not occurred to these wives that they are publicly advertising the fact that they showed exceedingly poor judgment in their choice of a husband? Genuine love will prompt the wife to help the husband with his problems. She will encourage him to make good in his chosen profession. Every advancement he makes will delight her heart and thrill her spirit. Every defeat he suffers will be a blow to her. Envy and jealousy have no place between a husband and wife. Real love will continue steadily in adversity as well as in the fine hours of success and prosperity. Real love will keep alive her confidence in him when others become skeptical. Real love will make her happy to be his Mrs. It will prompt her to do her best to be a good wife. Other than her responsibility as a Christian no other interest will occupy comparable ground as that of being a Christian wife and later a Christian mother. *Christ in the home* will insure the kind of love that a wife should manifest toward her husband.

THE WIFE IS TO RESPECT HER HUSBAND

Ephesians 5:33 says, "Nevertheless let every one of you in particular so love his wife even as himself; and the wife see that she reverence [respect] her husband." Respect is important in all human relationships. It is imperative in marriage. A girl should not date a young man if she does not respect him. Should she date him, she may later marry him and if respect is lacking, there is little likelihood that the marriage can survive. There must always be a deep bond of respect between the marital mates if happiness is to be achieved. No young lady should ever contemplate marriage to a young man whom she does not fully respect. If there is no respect at the marriage altar, it is doubtful that there will be respect subsequently in the home. The wife should respect her husband as a man, as head, as breadwinner, and later as the father of her children. Of course the husband is not passive in this important role of creating and maintaining respect. He must assume his roles in the home if the wife is going to have a firm foundation upon which to build her respect for him. The man who lives up to the Scriptural standards which were discussed in the preceding chapters will be the kind of man for whom the wife can develop genuine and lasting respect. When the *Christ in the home* philosophy permeates the marriage there will be the type of genuine respect that God expects to exist between husband and wife. It is amazing how every obligation in the home can be successfully discharged if the Lord lives and reigns in the hearts and lives of each member of the family.

THE WIFE IS NOT TO DEFRAUD THE HUSBAND

I am aware that some of these Scriptural principles are being repeated. This is done deliberately. Today especially we need to stress the Scriptural precepts touching home and marital relationships.

Paul's great chapter on marriage is I Corinthians 7. I believe it is the only chapter in the Bible that is dedicated almost exclusively to questions and observations relative to marriage. The Corinthians needed this material for the lax times in which they lived; we desperately need it today. Multitudes of people today possess far more of the Corinthian spirit of freedom in sexual relationships between those not married to each other than they do of the Christian spirit which absolutely limits this relationship exclusively to marriage. It seems that even God's sanctified people in Corinth were subject to these grave errors. Paul tells how purity may be maintained between the sexes. "Now concerning the things whereof ye wrote unto me:

It is good for a man not to touch a woman. Nevertheless, to avoid fornication, let every man have his own wife, and let every woman have her own husband. Let the husband render unto the wife due benevolence: and likewise also the wife unto the husband. The wife hath not power of her own body, but the husband: and likewise also the husband hath not power of his own body, but the wife. Defraud ye not one the other, except it be with consent for a time, that ye may give yourselves to fasting and prayer; and come together again, that Satan tempt you not for your incontinency" (I Cor. 7: 1-5). In verse one Paul states that remaining single is right and permissible. Some can live lives of purity without entrance into the marital state; others cannot. They are constituted differently and cannot live virtuously without companionship from the opposite sex. For this latter class there are two alternatives open: a life of fornication which is solidly condemned throughout Holy Writ or entrance into marriage which is the honorable way to fulfill these strong urges of the human heart (Heb. 13:4). Verse two deals with this very situation. Paul talks of only one way that the physical relationship can be right and honorable. That is through marriage. To avoid fornication every man is to have his own wife and cohabit with her and her only. To avoid fornication every woman is to have her own husband and cohabit with him and him alone.

Advocates of the "new morality" and proponents of "situation ethics" tell us that the physical relationship between the unmarried can be beautiful if both are consenting adults, if no one will be hurt, and if the situation is right for such behavior. The Bible teaches the very opposite. God says that such a relationship is sinful and will damn eternal souls if persisted in as a way of life and if forgiveness is never sought and achieved (I Cor. 6:9-10; Gal. 5:19-21; Rev. 21:8; 22:15). God has not left it entirely to consenting adults to practice this act with what they call sophisticated discretion. He is the maker of their bodies and has a right to be considered in any decision involving their bodies. There is no such thing as harmless fornication or innocent adultery. David found this to be true. He discovered that adultery is an enormous sin in the eyes of Jehovah God (II Sam. 11:27). David's moving confession in the penitential fifty-first psalm expresses a correct appraisal of this crime: "Have mercy upon me, O God, according to thy lovingkindness: according unto the multitude of thy tender mercies blot out my *transgressions.* Wash me thoroughly from mine *iniquity,* and cleanse me from my *sin.* For I acknowledge my *transgressions*: and my *sin* is ever before me. Against thee, thee only, have I *sinned,* and done this *evil* in thy sight: that thou mightest be justified when thou speakest, and be clear when thou judgest" (Psalm 51:1-4, emphasis added). Religious leaders who advocate the advisability of sexual relations outside marriage whether they be premarital or extramarital are either ignorant or infidels (cf. II Sam. 11; Ps. 51; I Cor. 7:2; Heb. 13:4). There is never a situation outside of marriage where the sexual relationship can be experienced without sin. It is marriage and then sex; not sex and then marriage. Situations do not change sin into purity.

The wife is commanded by Paul to render "due benevolence" toward her husband. Health permitting she should be sensitive to his needs and eager to respond lovingly. She cannot afford to ignore his needs. That would invite a serious rupture in their marital harmony. Sex was a part of his anticipated reward when he made her his at the marriage altar. She has no right to renege on this part of their marriage. That would encourage him to seek satisfaction with another and would be sin on his part. She would become an accessory to the sin because of her persistent refusals to meet his needs in this area. Paul declares that at the beginning of a marriage there is a transfer of ownership. Before marriage the woman's body was her own possession. After marriage the husband possesses power over her body. She in turn possesses power over his body. This has already been discussed in a previous chapter directed to husbands. Unless her health will not permit or his demands along this line are totally unreasonable she should not withhold this pleasant privilege from him. Practicing blackmail in this area of their marriage can seriously damage marital permanence and happiness. In verse five Paul says the foregoing of such privileges for a certain season should not be practiced unless there be mutual consent. Paul advises that the abstaining period not be long lest Satan tempt one or both partners to seek satisfaction elsewhere.

Christ in the home will fortify the wife against defrauding her husband in this important realm of their marriage. Keep him happy at home and he is not likely to think seriously of fulfilling his personal needs with someone else. Every wife needs to remember that the salvation of her husband's soul may be at stake here. If she deliberately defrauds him in this aspect of their marriage, he may seek illegal cohabitation with another. That would be sin on his part. He cannot go to heaven if he is an adulterer (Gal. 5:19-21; I Cor. 6:9-10).

SHE SHOULD BE A CHRISTIAN WIFE

A non-Christian woman might possibly become a wife of a Christian man. But it is my deep-seated conviction that she cannot

be the kind of wife he needs unless she is a Christian. He may not
be strong spiritually himself. A non-Christian companion might possibly forever quench the little spark of spirituality he possessed
when he first entered marriage. Had she been a Christian she may
have led him to devout discipleship. On the other hand, a husband
may not be a Christian. If the wife is a Christian, then she may do
for him the very thing Peter had in mind in I Peter 3:1. "Likewise,
ye wives, be in subjection to your own husbands; that, if any obey
not the word, they also may without the word be won by the conversation of the wives. . . ." Peter here portrays the Christian wife
winning her unbelieving husband by her daily demeanor. Her
words to him about Christianity may not avail but her daily loving
deeds speak with a power which he may be unable to ignore and
resist. She cannot win him by compromise. She cannot encourage
his conversion if she is not a Christian in her speech habits and
daily practices. Her manner of life has to be pure and chaste. Peter
says, "While they behold your chaste conversation [manner of life]
coupled with fear" (I Peter 3:2). She cannot win his soul for Christ
if all available moments of the day are spent with the external
adornment of her person. Peter, by way of wise admonition, said,
"Whose adorning let it not be that outward adorning of plaiting the
hair, and of wearing of gold, or of putting on of apparel; But let it
be the hidden man of the heart, in that which is not corruptible,
even the ornament of a meek and quiet spirit, which is in the sight of
God of great price" (I Peter 3:3-4). Peter is exhorting Christian
wives to recognize which things in life are really important. The
main allegiance is not toward external adornment. Worldly women
hope to keep their husbands by sporting elaborate hairstyles, displaying costly jewelry, and wearing the latest fashions. The Christian wife will dress in a becoming manner but will recognize that
adorning her spirit is far more important than an elaborate hair-
style, rare jewels, or a closet full of expensive clothes. Possession of a
meek and quiet spirit is of great price in God's sight. The Christian
wife recognizes that this is the area where she should major. Spiritual beauty is much more important to her than is physical beauty.

    When a woman comes to death's door it will be far more impor-
tant that she has been a Christian wife to her husband, a Christian
mother to her children, and a Christian neighbor to her friends than
any or all attainments her worldly sisters may have achieved. Beautiful faces and fine figures are coveted by worldly women. God's
woman knows that in the long run a beautiful heart and a lovely
disposition will pay far greater dividends. The beauty of a face and
the striking features of a fine figure will ultimately fade while the

beauty of a meek and quiet spirit will endure and yield eternal rewards. *Christ in the home* can make a woman into the kind of Christian wife she ought to be.

A TRIO OF WIFELY VIRTUES

"And be ye *kind* one to another, *tenderhearted, forgiving* one another, even as God for Christ's sake hath forgiven you" (Eph. 4:32, emphasis added). This advice is not pointed toward wives exclusively but it surely includes them. They cannot afford to ignore it. Here are three attitudes that can work wonders in marital relationships.

The wife should be kind. The Bible's most beautiful portrayal of womanhood is in Proverbs 31:10-31. One of the lovely gems which sparkles so brilliantly in this tribute to the virtuous woman is in verse 26: "She openeth her mouth with wisdom; and in her tongue is the law of kindness." The attitude of kindness toward that man whose name she bears should be indelibly inscribed upon the mind, tongue, and hands of every wife. She should be kind in her thoughts of him. Kindness originates in the thinking processes. Then it is translated into speech patterns and daily life. Let every wife be kind in thought and actions.

The tongue can bless or curse. It can make a home happy or sad. Angry words must be avoided. This is certainly true in that most intimate of human relationships — marriage. The deeper the love the husband has for his wife, the more cutting will be the unkind and angry words which an angry wife may hurl at him. Kind words and nagging expressions usually do not flow from the same set of lips. Where there is the one there will be the absence of the other. No husband wants a wife who constantly nags. Dean J. P. Sanders told of a story which came out of the Korean conflict. This young man grew so tired of receiving the nagging letters from his wife back home that he wrote in desperation, "I wish you would stop nagging me so I could fight this war in peace!" A man can face and endure almost any problem more easily than he can listen to a nagging wife. Nagging can very quickly kill a marriage. A kind wife will not nag.

Kindness must manifest itself. Love has to be manifested. So does kindness. Kindness in thought, motive, and word will exhibit its true colors in deeds. Every day the wife has many opportunities to display kindness. Every kind deed she performs adds a little more glue to their marriage. The heart of any right-thinking husband will be deeply touched by the kindness which she manifests in her daily deeds toward him. The question: Does real kindness prompt this deed? is an excellent guideline in the formation of daily habits toward marital mates. The bitter enemies of marital happiness such as anger, wrath, malice, and harshness should be ousted in order that kindness may take its rightful place upon the throne in controlling marital relations. *Christ in the home* brings kindness. Jesus is the personification of kindness. He will not reside in a home where kindness is never manifested in thought, motive, word, and deed.

The wife needs to be tenderhearted. Hard hearts do not make for harmony in any human relationship. This is paramountly true in marriage. The hearts of both husband and wife should be tender and sensitive. Tender hearts cannot and will not wound the feelings of each other without a quick demonstration of genuine regret, a confession of the wrong, and a sincere request for forgiveness. A hard heart will not mind inflicting wounds without cause. Neither will it be very easily wounded. A tender heart will not deliberately wound. A tender heart is sensitive and can be hurt easily. Our concept of God is of one who has a heart of tenderness. This aspect of His character will not permit Him to be unkind. The heart of God can be grieved by the disobedience and irreverence of His people. Jehovah was frequently grieved with Israel in the wilderness. "When your fathers tempted me, proved me, and saw my works forty years. Wherefore I was grieved with that generation, and said, They do alway err in their heart; and they have not known my ways . . . But with whom was he grieved forty years? was it not with them that had sinned, whose carcases fell in the wilderness?" (Heb. 3:9, 10, 17). Jesus is tenderhearted. His whole sojourn upon God's green footstool was a demonstration of tenderhearted attitudes and actions toward ruined and wrecked humanity. If we are going to emulate this divine characteristic of our lovely Lord, then we will have to be tenderhearted. The tender heart does not wish to inflict unnecessary pain and it does not wish to be pained. Tenderhearted treatment of marital mates is an imperative. Let the wife be tenderhearted to her husband. Let him be the same to her.

The day I wrote this chapter I also preached a sermon on I John 4:8. This majestic verse tells us that God is love. There were five points in the message relative to the divine characteristics of God's love. His is a giving love, a forgiving love, a revealed love, a sacrificial love, and an enduring love. God's love for man made Him a God of forgiveness. The more love that exists in a marriage, the deeper determination there will be to practice forgiveness. The wife is not perfect. Neither is the husband. They will make mistakes. Mistakes call for repentance, confession, and forgiveness. Contrary to a statement that has been prominently used to advertise a current movie, "Love means never having to say you're sorry!" real love means a confession of wrong committed, an earnest expression of regret, and a sincere request for forgiveness. When the wife does wrong she expects forgiveness from her husband. When he does wrong she should be willing to cover his sins with the majestic mantle of forgiving love. Of course it is understood that forgiveness comes after the offender meets the demands necessary for receiving forgiveness. As long as the offending mate habitually commits a certain sin and remains impenitent toward those sins, I do not believe the innocent mate is obligated to extend forgiveness. Jehovah does not do so and I know of no Scripture verse where He authorizes us to do so either. Jehovah stands ready to extend forgiveness just as soon as an offender meets the proper stipulations. So should every marital mate.

Christ in the home means the wife will major in kindness, extend tenderhearted treatment, and practice the blessed and heavenly spirit of full forgiveness toward her husband. This trio of Christian virtues cannot be emphasized too much in our age of anger, era of evil treatment, and time of trouble.

THE WIFE AS HOMEMAKER

The wife will determine the tone of the home. This is the sphere in which she reigns as queen. She can make the home clean and cheery or leave it dingy and dull. She can readily radiate a spirit that will make her husband long for home every time he is away or she can display a disposition that will make home anything but a place of pleasure to him. She should major in keeping the home attractive. I have visited homes where there was marital trouble and I was asked to counsel with the partners. Occasionally I have sensed on the first visit that an industrious wife and a tidy home would do as much as anything to help the situation. Where there is no wifely interest in the preparation of nourishing meals and the keeping of a clean house trouble will come sooner or later — and it usually comes sooner than later. A husband who came from a home where his mother was an excellent cook and a tidy and well organized homemaker is not going to be pleased to have the very opposite in a wife. Wives need to wake up at this point and major in homemaking attainments. They cannot afford to be inefficient very long in these roles as cook and housekeeper. Again following the principles of Jesus will make for household industry in these domestic duties.

WHEN THE WIFE WORKS

There was a time when few women left the home for outside employment. When our nation was young and made up principally of people in rural sections, about the only work women did outside the home was in the field by the side of their husband and children. But with the coming of the industrial revolution the tenor of the times drastically changed. America ceased to be primarily a land of people who worked the soil for sustenance. We became a nation of city and suburban dwellers. Men began to flock to factories seeking employment. Soon their wives followed. Within the last twenty or thirty years millions of homes have sent forth two daily wage earners instead of the husband as the principal breadwinner. The pressures of inflation and a desire for more material things than one salary can afford have prompted many wives to seek employment outside the home. That such a trend has disrupted the homes of many cannot be denied. Every marriage counselor lists this as one of the problems faced by many husbands and wives. When there are children and both parents are away from home most of the day the problems can become even more acute.

I recently read that 55 percent of American wives work outside the home. No doubt this percentage will climb even higher in years that lie ahead. When the wife works forty hours or more per week it is only proper that the husband join her in the work of cooking and keeping the house. If she is expected to make half the living wage of the family, it is only fair that he help with half the house work. It is totally unfair for him to think that he has no responsibilities at home when the four o'clock bell rings but the wife has another day of work awaiting her upon arrival at home. Even when the wife works only at home it will do him good to help from time to time. Then he will not be helpless if sudden illness were to hospitalize her or serious sickness of a near relative demanded her temporary presence away from home duties. But when he expects her to help him make the living she has every right to expect joint efforts on his part toward performing domestic duties. Any husband that really cares about his wife is already doing his share and gladly. *Christ in the home* will prompt mutual help in keeping attractive the home of the two wage earners.

When the wife lifts up the Bible in the home, the Bible will lift up wifehood in the home. This will follow as surely as night follows day.

QUESTIONS FOR DISCUSSION

1. Describe the beauty of a marriage ceremony for a young Christian girl.
2. In what ways must the young bride show herself to be a woman?
3. Why is marriage not for the immature?
4. Read each of the Biblical quotations which indicate that the wife should be submissive and discuss the significance of each.
5. Discuss the seriousness of a wife refusing to be submissive to her husband. Whom did the Israelites really reject when they turned from Samuel? Now apply these principles to the wife who refuses to be submissive.
6. Discuss the current liberation movement among some women of our day. Did Jesus ever seek to liberate Himself from the Father's authority? What happens when man seeks to liberate himself from Christ's authority? What about women who seek to liberate themselves from the authority of men over them?
7. Discuss the kind of love the wife should have for the husband. What did Paul say regarding this matter? What will real love prompt? What will it prohibit?
8. Why is it so important that a wife respect her husband? In what ways should she respect him?
9. How must the husband help in building up and maintaining this respect?
10. Is there a value in repetition? How does repetition fit into the overall design of these lessons on the home? In your judgment have we repeated God's instructions about the home as much as we should have? Why, or why not?
11. Read and briefly discuss 1 Corinthians 7
12. How can there be purity in sex relationships? Discuss the wisdom of God in restricting this relationship to marriage and marriage only.
13. Discuss the great contrast between Biblical morality and the new morality. Discuss the arguments given by new morality advocates which would permit sexual relations between two consenting adults, if no one will be hurt and the situation is right.
14. Discuss II Samuel 11:27 and Psalm 51:1-4 in the light of what the new morality advocates.
15. Why should the wife never deliberately defraud the husband in matters pertaining to the physical aspects of their marital union?
16. Discuss the importance of the wife being a Christian.

17. Discuss in detail I Peter 3:1-4.
18. Memorize Ephesians 4:32. What are the three lovely virtues set forth? Take each one and discuss each in detail as far as wives are concerned.
19. What are five characteristics of God's love? Tell why each should be practiced in the romantic realm of marital love.
20. What is wrong with the statement, "Love means never having to say you're sorry"?
21. Discuss the wife as a homemaker.
22. Discuss the wife who works outside the home.
23. What obligations should the husband shoulder when the wife works?
24. When the wife lifts up the Bible in the home what will the Bible do for wifehood in the home?

8

Portraits of Bible Wives

Vice is a very ugly thing even when viewed merely in the abstract. However its character is much more vivid when it is practiced by a human being. Then vice stands out in all its hideous ugliness. Virtue is a very beautiful thing when discussed in the abstract. However its beauty becomes far more resplendent when observed in the lives of people. Look at how much greater is our understanding of faith, patience, courage, purity, and total sacrifice to a cause when we view respectively the personifications of these virtues in Abraham, Job, David, Joseph, and our blessed Lord. This is exactly why illustrations are so powerful in the realm of teaching. This is exactly why biographical studies are a favorite with nearly all people. Jehovah recognized this and filled His Book with living examples of both the unholy and the holy. Let us now apply this to wives.

THE KIND OF WIVES NOT NEEDED

Our concluding chapter on husbands closed with a negative and positive look at husbands. We shall follow the same plan in our study of wives. The Bible paints the portraits of wives who failed to measure up and of others whose price was really above rubies (Prov. 31:10).

We do not need wives like the one Lot possessed. The Lord did not want us to forget this woman. He said tersely, "Remember

Lot's wife" (Luke 17:32). Neither Moses who talks of her in Genesis 19 nor Jesus who speaks of her in Luke 17 chose to reveal her name. She is simply designated as Lot's wife. She and her husband had lived in sinful Sodom for quite some time. Lot had "pitched his tent toward Sodom" (Gen. 13:12). Soon he was living in its very midst. The corrupt sinners of Sodom "vexed his righteous soul from day to day with their unlawful deeds" (II Peter 2:8). Lot never became accustomed to the enormity of their constant iniquity. What reaction Mrs. Lot may have had toward the sin and vice around her is not revealed. Payday for sin finally dawned for the grievous sinners that inhabited the lustful cities of the Jordan plain. Lot and his family were to be spared provided they vacated the doomed city. Genesis 19:16 describes their reluctance in leaving the city. The clear implication of the chapter is that some of their children preferred to stay. This may account for their lingering. The angels hasten their departure from sin-cursed Sodom. Strict instructions were given about their reaching the place of safety. They were absolutely forbidden to cast a backward glance at the burning city. Their eyes were to be kept ahead. Lot's wife disobeyed this clear injunction. "But his wife looked back from behind him, and she became a pillar of salt" (Gen. 19:26). She died in disobedience. The pillar of salt is not the end of this story. Had Lot's wife obeyed and lived it is highly doubtful that the heinous crime of incest which a drinking Lot and his two desperate daughters later practiced would have occurred. The two daughters said they wanted to preserve their father's seed upon the earth (Gen. 19:32). Had their mother been alive at the time this thought would possibly never have crossed their mind. They succeeded in getting their father under the iniquitous influence of diabolical drink in order that each might conceive by him and bear a child. Moab and Ben-am-mi were the sons born as a result of these two episodes. These boys fathered the Moabites and the Ammonites who proved to be thorns in Israel's side in future generations (Gen. 19:37-38). Little did this disobedient wife realize what evil would result from that backward glance of disobedience. We do not need wives today who will disobey God's will as did Lot's wife. We need wives who will look ahead, not behind to some Sodom of their past, if such be a part of their personal history.

We do not need wives like Jezebel was to Ahab and Athaliah was to Jehoram. These two women were a mother-and-daughter team. They run close competition in deciding who is the most wicked woman, wife, and mother that ever disgraced a home. Jezebel became the wife of Ahab in I Kings 16:31. "And it came to pass, as if it had been a light thing for him [Ahab] to walk in the sins of Jeroboam the son of Nebat, that he took to wife Jezebel the daughter of Ethbaal king of the Zidonians, and went and served Baal, and worshipped him." Possibly nobody before him ever made a worse choice for a wife than did Ahab. The Bible tells us, "But there was none like unto Ahab, which did sell himself to work wickedness in the sight of the Lord, whom Jezebel his wife stirred [incited — marginal reference] up" (I Kings 21:25). Ahab sold his soul to the devil and Jezebel helped him write up the bill of sale! Some men are rather weak. They are controlled by the dominant personalities that surround them. How they fare in life is largely determined by the character of the person whose magnetic powers are greatest over them. Ahab was caught between a righteous magnet, Elijah, and an unrighteous magnet, Jezebel. When Ahab was with the colorful Tishbite, the easily swayed monarch treaded higher ground. But for the most part he was under the iniquitous influence of the strong-willed Phoenician princess whom he had foolishly married. She led him down the treacherous trail to rampant idolatry. Had this eighth king of the Northern Kingdom had a good wife the story of his life might read differently. Without debate we do not need women of Jezebel's kind to fill the roles of modern wives. Look at what Jezebel's own foolish daughter did. Athaliah was an able successor to her mother on the infamous throne of feminine wickedness. The Bible says, "Jehoram was thirty and two years old when he began to reign, and he reigned eight years in Jerusalem. And he walked in the way of the kings of Israel, like as did the house of Ahab: for he had the daughter of Ahab to wife: and he wrought that which was evil in the eyes of the Lord" (II Chron. 21:5-6). Jehoram led "the inhabitants of Jerusalem to commit fornication, and compelled Judah thereto" (II Chron. 21:11). He prompted the inhabitants of his capital city to adopt the "whoredoms of the house of Ahab" (II Chron. 21:13). He murdered his own brothers who were better men than was he. The closing verses of this chapter relate how he was punished for his enormous transgressions. He died a miserable death and made his earthly exit "without being desired" (II Chron. 21:20). He was denied a burial place "in the sepulchres of the kings" (II Chron. 21:20). Jehoram had a righteous father as predecessor but a bad wife as a companion. He chose to follow the manner of conduct which she had learned in the home of her infamous parents, Ahab and Jezebel, instead of walking in the ways of his father, the just Jehoshaphat. Athaliah did Jehoram evil all the days of their marriage. She was the opposite of the worthy woman of Proverbs 31:10-12. We do not need wives like Athaliah.

We do not need wives like those that the sons of God married. "And it came to pass, when men began to multiply on the face of the earth, and daughters were born unto them, That the sons of God saw the daughters of men that they were fair; and they took them wives of all which they chose" (Gen. 6:1-2). There is a very fanciful theory that the "sons of God" mentioned in this chapter referred to angelic beings. The daughters of men would refer to women on earth. According to the theory there was cohabitation of angelic beings and women. The union of such, the theory propounds, led to the birth of children who became giants in the earth, mighty men, men of renown (Gen. 6:4). Our Lord's statement in Matthew 22:30 that angels are sexless beings would refute this theory once and for all. The sons of God in this passage were righteous men. The daughters of men were worldly and wicked. It seems safe to assert that the men were decendants of righteous Seth while the daughters were descendants of wicked Cain. When marriages were made between the sons of God and the daughters of men a highly degenerate set of descendants resulted. Righteousness almost evaporated from the earth in those days. Except for Noah and his family there were no righteous people left. This Old Testament example offers strong and convincing testimony about the grave risks involved when the righteous team up with the wicked in matrimony. The sons of God evidently fell in love with the physical beauty of these worldly daughters that were available for marriage unions. The physical took precedence over the spiritual in these marital ties. The result was almost total ruin for the human family. Today sons of God do not need daughters of men (worldly, wicked women) for their companions.

Men today do not need the type of wives that Solomon had. The quantity and quality of his wives combined to work for his spiritual downfall. He multipled unto himself wives even though the Mosaic economy under which he lived and reigned specifically and strictly forbade such a transgression on the **part** of the king. "Neither shall he [the king] multiply wives to himself, that his heart turn not away: neither shall he greatly multiply to himself silver and gold (Deut. 17:17). The quantity was mistake number one for the Israelite monarch. The quality was mistake number two. First Kings informs us what Solomon's wives succeeded in doing to the greatly blessed monarch. "For it came to pass, when Solomon was old, that his wives turned away his heart after other gods: and his heart was not perfect with the Lord his God, as was the heart of David his father" (I Kings 11:4). Succeeding verses picture his building places of worship for the idolatrous gods worshiped and served by his heathen companions (I Kings 11:5-8). The youthful wise ruler of I Kings 3 became an old and foolish king who would no longer be admonished in behalf of right and truth. "Better is a poor and a wise child than an old and foolish king, who will no more be admonished" (Eccles. 4:13). Nehemiah lived several centuries later. The closing chapter of his short book calls to remembrance the sinister influences Solomon's wives held over the once illustrious king of Israel. "Did not Solomon king of Israel sin by these things? yet among many nations was there no king like him, who was beloved of his God, and God made him king over all Israel: nevertheless even him did outlandish women cause to sin" (Neh. 13:26). To a very great extent a man's eternal destiny rests on the type of wife he marries. She has the power to lift him higher or to drag him lower. It takes a mighty strong man to go to heaven with a wicked wife at his side. She will be a millstone around his neck all the days of his life. That is precisely why we do not need wives like those of Solomon. I feel very confident that the sequel to Solomon's story would have been far different had there been just one queen in his life who was a righteous worshiper of Almighty God. The multiplication of wives led to the multiplication of wickedness.

We do not need wives such as Mrs. Job was during the days of Job's grievous afflictions. The totally unexpected avalanche of adversities which descended so suddenly upon the Uzzean patriarch tested not only the mettle of his character but served to evaluate the lack of real character possessed by his wife. The first chapter of Job reveals the loss of their vast wealth and the destruction of all their children. Unknown to either Job or his wife, Satan had gained permission to try Job's faith. Satan had stated that Job served Jehovah because of what heaven had conferred upon him in the form of material comforts and worldly riches. Satan said in Jehovah's presence, "Doth Job fear God for nought? Hast not thou made an hedge about him, and about his house, and about all that he hath on every side? thou hast blessed the work of his hands, and his substance is increased in the land. But put forth thine hand now, and touch all that he hath, and he will curse thee to thy face" (Job 1:9-11). Satan was given power to touch Job with the loss of his family and possessions but was restricted from touching his person (Job 1:12). Satan was proved wrong in this contention. The chapter ends by stating, "In all this Job sinned not, nor charged God foolishly" (Job 1:22). In chapter two Jehovah reminds Satan of Job's greatness, goodness, and loyalty even though he had been persecuted "without cause" (Job 2:3). Satan had another maneuver that he was sure would bring about Job's downfall and destruction. He said, "Skin for skin, yea, all that a man hath will he give for his life. But put forth thine hand now, and touch his bone and his flesh, and he will curse thee to thy face. And the Lord said unto Satan, Behold, he is in thine hand; but save his life" (Job 2:4-6). Satan then "smote Job with sore boils from the sole of his foot unto his crown. And he took him a potsherd to scrape himself withal; and he sat down among the ashes" (Job 2:7-8). If Satan had been predicting how Job's wife would react to these unexpected reversals in their family fortune, he would have been much more accurate. The loss of their family, their wealth, and Job's health was just too much for her continued faith in God's goodness. Her own words reveal her real character. Notice Job's instant response to them. "Dost thou still retain thine integrity? curse God, and die. But he said unto her, Thou speakest as one of the foolish women speaketh. What? shall we receive good at the hand of God, and shall we not receive evil? In all this did not Job sin with his lips" (Job 2:9-10). Regardless of what men may face in life they do not need foolish wives who will offer unwise counsel as did Job's wife. His burdens would have been easier to bear had she loyally stood by his side with unflinching help. How cutting to his pained heart and troubled spirit this remark of hers must have been. We do not need wives like this today.

We do not need wives like Herodias and Drusilla. Both of these women left former husbands to enter into adulterous unions. Herodias left her husband Philip in Rome to come back to Galilee as the wife of Herod Antipas, Philip's own brother. Drusilla left her first husband to become the wife of the notorious Roman governor, Felix. When John the Baptist pointed out the adulterous nature of the marriage of Herod Antipas and Herodias the inflamed wife "had a quarrel against him, and would have killed him; but she could not" (Mark 6:19). However, her unquenchable thirst for John's blood was not abated. She maneuvered maliciously, when her husband rashly vowed to give the shameless Salome anything she would choose even to the half of his kingdom (Mark 6:21-23). Salome was a totally submissive puppet in the hands of her infamous mother, so she asked for John's head (Mark 6:24). Herod Antipas lacked the spine to buck her request. He recognized the binding nature of his oath and couldn't face the laughter that would surely come from his birthday companions if he refused to fulfil his promise. He sent a guard away to do the evil deed. A wicked wife, a malicious mother, a dancing daughter, a silly oath, and a henpecked husband all paved the way for the demise of one of the best men who ever lived. We do not need wives like Herodias.

Neither do we need wives like the daring Drusilla. Her stunning beauty captured the fancy of Felix. Though married to another man at the time, this presented no real obstacle to her. She left him for the added luster and glamour of being the wife of a Roman governor. Many a woman has turned her back on marriage vows and home responsibilities because another man with better looks, more money, added glamour, or a finer house sought her companionship. A woman who would do this is a living example of the passage in Jeremiah 17:9, "The heart is deceitful above all things, and desperately wicked: who can know it?" It takes a very deceitful heart to do with marriage vows what Herodias and Drusilla did. We do not need their counterparts as wives today. Such women must have been in the mind of Solomon as he offered the following counsel, "Hearken unto me now therefore, O ye children, and attend to the words of my mouth. Let not thine heart decline to her ways, go not astray in her paths. For she hath cast down many wounded: yea, many strong men have been slain by her. Her house is the way to hell, going down to the chambers of death" (Prov. 7:24-27). There is no surer way for a man to go to hell than by treading the route of wicked women.

Solomon had much to say about wicked women in his inspired work of Proverbs. Let us note a few of his observations because such women do not make for worthy wives or marvelous mothers. We do not need women for wives and mothers who fit the description of Proverbs 5:3-8, "For the lips of a strange woman drop as an honeycomb, and her mouth is smoother than oil: But her end is bitter as wormwood, sharp as a twoedged sword. Her feet go down to death; her steps take hold on hell. Lest thou shouldest ponder the path of life, her ways are moveable, that thou canst not know them. Hear me now therefore, O ye children, and depart not from the words of my mouth. Remove thy way far from her, and come not nigh the door of her house. . . ." Later in the chapter the wise man says, "And why wilt thou, my son, be ravished with a strange woman, and embrace the bosom of a stranger? For the ways of man are before the eyes of the Lord, and he pondereth all his goings" (Prov. 5:20:21). The evil woman described in Proverbs 6:24-35 is a constant threat to the good of society and the sanctity of marital fidelity. Jehovah's laws are designed "To keep thee from the evil woman, from the flattery of the tongue of a strange woman. Lust not after her beauty in thine heart; neither let her take thee with her eyelids. For by means of a whorish woman a man is brought to a piece of bread: and the adulteress will hunt for the precious life. Can a man take fire in his bosom, and his clothes not be burned? Can one go upon hot coals, and his feet not be burned? So he that goeth in to his neighbour's wife; whosoever toucheth her shall not be innocent. Men do not despise a thief, if he steal to satisfy his soul when he is hungry; But if he be found, he shall restore sevenfold; he shall give all the substance of his house. But whoso committeth adultery with a woman lacketh understanding: he that doeth it destroyeth his own soul. A wound and dishonour shall he get; and his reproach shall not be wiped away. For jealousy is the rage of a man: therefore he will not spare in the day of vengeance. He will not regard any ransom; neither will he rest content, though thou givest many gifts." Though this counsel is addressed to men it is a good description of the kind of women who destroy homes and disrupt society. Those women while they live in such a fleshly environment cannot ever be good wives and mothers in a home. Homes of today have no greater enemies than these women and the foolish men whom they seduce. The lewd woman with the display of her impudent actions toward a naive man void of moral understanding is portrayed by Solomon in Proverbs 7:6-27. She evidently is married but her husband is away from home for a specified period. She is an aggressive adulteress while he is away. Such a woman cannot be the kind of wife a man needs. Yet if the Kinsey report is accurate there are millions of wives in our nation who practice what was described in Proverbs three thousand years ago. Solomon observed another kind of problem when he said, "It is better to dwell in the wilderness, than with a contentious and an angry woman" (Prov. 21:19). "It is better to dwell in the corner of the housetop, than with a brawling woman and in a wide house" (Prov. 25:24). "A continual dropping in a very rainy day and a contentious woman are alike" (Prov. 27:15). "A foolish son is the calamity of his father: and the contentions of a wife are a continual dropping" (Prov. 19:13). This type of woman also will not make for worthy wives and needed motherhood. *Christ in the home* can help every wife to avoid falling into these dishonorable roles of womanhood. We do not need any more of the wrong kind of wives. The world is already too full of this type of woman. We need many wives who will seek to be the right kind of mates to their husbands.

THE KIND OF WIVES NEEDED

We need women to enter marriages who have practiced purity and retain their treasured virginity when they stand at the marriage altar. Rebekah was a virgin when arrangements were made for her to leave the land of her nativity and become wife to Isaac in Canaan. The Bible says of her, "And the damsel was very fair to look upon, a virgin, neither had any man known her: and she went down to the well, and filled her pitcher, and came up" (Gen. 24: 16). Virginity should be a most desirable ingredient that every Christian girl takes with her to the marriage altar. She should enter marriage with the determination that her husband will be the only man who will ever touch her body. (Of course if he should die, then she could well enter into another marriage.) A young woman who has been wild and promiscuous prior to marriage may pursue the same type of life afterwards. Her premarital past then becomes the extramarital present. If anything, this latter kind of life is a degree worse for before she at least was not sinning against a husband and children except in anticipated fashion. We need wives characterized by sexual purity. In view of the alarming statistics of our day this is truly one of the great imperatives of our day. Jimmy Allen says, "A well-known protestant preacher has estimated that in 85 percent of the marriages, where both parties are still in high school, pregnancy is a factor. Incidentally, 60 percent of teenage marriages fail. In a number of our metropolitan communities, one out of eight births is illegitimate. One of every five women who marry in our country is already expecting a child by her prospective husband . . . According to the Kinsey reports, the majority of American men and at least half the women have had premarital sexual experience." (*The American Crisis*, pp. 12-13.)

We need wives who will honor, cherish, and love their husbands. Peter said, "For after this manner in the old time the holy women also, who trusted in God, adorned themselves, being in subjection unto their own husbands: Even as Sarah obeyed Abraham, calling him lord: whose daughters ye are, as long as ye do well, and are not afraid with any amazement" (I Peter 3:5-6). These worthy women of the ancient past established a tone of fidelity, honor, respect, submission, and love for their husbands that calls for a continuous repeat in our times.

We need wives such as Ruth was to Mahlon first and then to Boaz. Little is said about her first marriage. However, it seems safe to assert that she was a dutiful wife to Naomi's son else the aged mother-in-law would hardly have been so full of love and

affection for the widowed daughter-in-law. Her romance of purity
and marriage with honor to the wealthy Boaz of Bethlehem are
well-known stories to all Old Testament students. It was my
privilege to visit the fields of Boaz, or at least what is pointed out to
modern tourists as having belonged to this ancient Bethlehemite,
in February of 1970. My mind traveled back more than three
thousand years. I sought to visualize the industrious Moabitess as
she went to glean grain in these or nearby fields (Ruth 2:1-3).
Ruth soon earned a reputation among the Hebrew people for being
a virtuous or worthy woman (Ruth 3:11). A beautiful romance
budded between the former maiden of Moab and Boaz the Bethlehemite. Soon it blossomed into the honorable estate of holy
matrimony. From that union came the two illustrious descendants
— David and the Messiah (Ruth 4:21-22; Matt. 1:5-6). Ruth
possessed the necessary ingredients that make for a successful wife.
She had stability of character, persistence, industry toward daily
duties, and a sense of love, honor, and integrity seldom par-
alleled in our day. These qualities will always be of tremendous
help in making a woman into a worthy wife. May Jehovah God
give us more women like Ruth to serve as wives and later as mothers
of precious children.

We need wives with the determination to preserve their modesty
like that of the Persian queen Vashti. Her husband, King Ahasuerus,
made an ungodly demand of her. He wanted her to expose her
striking beauty before the lusty eyes of men who were high on
strong drink (Esther 1:10-11). Vashti valued her modesty more
highly than the honor of remaining a Persian queen. The Bible
says, "But the queen Vashti refused to come at the king's commandment by his chamberlains . . ." (Esther 1:12). There are
some things that a husband, even a king, is powerless to control.
Vashti would not compromise her convictions to please a drunken
king. No man has the right to exploit his wife as Ahasuerus sought
to do. We need desperately wives and mothers who cherish modesty
and chastity. Those women could quickly change the tone of
immodesty that characterizes so much of the world in which we live.
For her splendid act Vashti has earned the respect of millions of
Bible readers.

We need wives who are of the mold suggested by Solomon.
"Whoso findeth a wife findeth a good thing, and obtaineth favour
of the Lord" (Prov. 18:22). A good man wants a good wife to
wear his name, bear his children, guide his home, and share in
the building of a worthwhile life together. With these factors in
mind a good man will seek for a suitable mate. Fortunate is any

woman to have made this type of impression upon the man whom she loves. By her future behavior as wife she will either confirm his impression of her or bitterly disappoint him. It is largely up to her as to whether five, ten, twenty, or fifty years after their marriage was entered he can still feel that he made a good choice of a wife. Solomon said, "House and riches are the inheritance of fathers: and a prudent wife is from the Lord" (Prov. 19:14). A father may bequeath to a son houses and riches by means of the family inheritance. However, the original source of a prudent wife is the Lord. A man who has a wife with wisdom, good sense, and understanding should thank the Lord daily for such a treasured gift. Heaven conferred her upon him.

This chapter would be incomplete if I omitted reference to the most beautiful portrait of womashood the world has ever read (Proverbs 31:10-31). There a woman is pictured as wife and mother. "Who can find a virtuous woman? for her price is far above rubies. The heart of her husband doth safely trust in her, so that he shall have no need of spoil. She will do him good and not evil all the days of her life. She seeketh wool, and flax, and worketh willingly with her hands. She is like the merchants' ships; she bringeth her food from afar. She riseth also while it is yet night, and giveth meat to her household, and a portion to her maidens. She considereth a field, and buyeth it: with the fruit of her hands she planteth a vineyard. She girdeth her loins with strength, and strengtheneth her arms. She perceiveth that her merchandise is good: her candle goeth not out by night. She layeth her hands to the spindle, and her hands hold the distaff. She stretcheth out her hand to the poor; yea, she reacheth forth her hands to the needy. She is not afraid of the snow for her household: for all her household are clothed with scarlet. She maketh herself coverings of tapesty; her clothing is silk and purple. Her husband is known in the gates, when he sitteth among the elders of the land. She maketh fine linen, and selleth it; and delivereth girdles unto the merchant. Strength and honour are her clothing; and she shall rejoice in time to come. She openeth her mouth with wisdom; and in her tongue is the law of kindness. She looketh well to the ways of her household, and eateth not the bread of idleness. Her children arise up, and call her blessed; her husband also, and he praiseth her. Many daughters have done virtuously, but thou excellest them all. Favour is deceitful, and beauty is vain: but a woman that feareth the Lord, she shall be praised. Give her of the fruit of her hands; and let her own works praise her in the gates." An abundance of such women to serve as wives and mothers in the homes of the world today could change the direction of human society in one short generation. We need wives like this worthy woman. *Christ in the home* could make this possible.

We need wives who will join hands with their righteous husbands in doing the Lord's work as a team. Elisabeth joined hands with Zacharias as together they served the Lord. Luke 1:6 says, "And they were *both* righteous before God, walking in all the commandments and ordinances of the Lord blameless" (emphasis added). Such a consecrated couple became Jehovah's choice to bring John, the messianic harbinger, into the world.

There is a particular beauty about Joseph and Mary. They both loved the Lord. Together they take Christ into Egypt (Matt. 2: 13-15). Together they make an exit from Egypt to Nazareth (Matt. 2:19-23). Together they make the trip from Nazareth to Jerusalem to worship. "Now *his parents* [not just one of them] went to Jerusalem *every year* at the feast of the passover" (Luke 2:41 emphasis added). Together they were seeking the twelve-year-old Jesus when they found Him in the temple. "Son, why hast thou thus dealt with us? behold, *thy father and I* have sought thee sorrowing" (Luke 2:48 emphasis added). Together they reared him and toward both He manifested the spirit of childlike submissiveness. The Bible says He was "subject unto *them* . . ." (Luke 2:51 emphasis added). Together they watched Jesus increase "in wisdom and stature, and in favour with God and man" (Luke 2:52). Joseph and Mary were greatly blessed all these years because Christ was the divine guest in their home. They knew from firsthand experience what it was like to have *Christ in the home.*

Priscilla must have been a model wife indeed. Each time she is mentioned it is in connection with her husband, Aquilla. That she helped him in the making of a living seems to be definitely implied in Acts 18:2-3. As a Christian team they traveled with Paul to Ephesus. They remained there to lay the groundwork for the establishment of Christ's cause in that thriving Asiatic metropolis (Acts 19:18-19). As a team they teach the eloquent but deficient Apollos "the way of God more perfectly" (Acts 18:26). Together they served as Paul's "helpers in Christ Jesus" (Rom. 16:3). Together they risked their own lives for Paul's safety. Their loving service prompted eternal gratitude from Paul and all the Gentile churches (Rom. 16:4). Together they made room in their home for the church to assemble for its work and worship. Paul mentions the church meeting in their house in Romans 16:5 and I Corinthians 16:19. The final mention which the Bible makes of them is recorded in II Timothy 4. They are still a team. We need more wives like Priscilla.

The information available about the wives of married apostles and the Lord's physical brothers is quite scarce indeed. Peter's mother-in-law is mentioned in Mark 1:29-31 and Luke 4:38-39. This means Peter had a wife. Paul supplies us with another insight. He writes, "Have we not power to lead about a sister, a wife, as well as other apostles, and as the brethren of the Lord, and Cephas?" (I Cor. 9:5). On their evangelistic journeys their devoted wives accompanied them. This is another instance of wives joining their husbands in the furtherance of the Lord's cause. We need wives who will hold up the hands of their husbands as they preach the gospel, teach the Bible, lead the singing, oversee the work as elders, or serve in the capacity of deacons. One of the most delightful of all spiritual scenes is the picture of Christian husbands and wives who have joined hands for life and together are promoting with ardor, faith, love, and conviction the work of the Lord. *Christ in the home* is the real secret of such a beautiful combination.

When women lift up the Bible in the home the Bible will lift them up as wives and mothers. *Christ in the home* is the key that will open the door of success to every woman who chooses to excel as the worthy wife of a good man. May the Lord bless richly every woman who has chosen this to be one of the three majors of her life. The others would be her roles as a faithful Christian and as good mother to her children.

QUESTIONS FOR DISCUSSION

1. Discuss Lot's wife in the light of Genesis 19 and Luke 17:32. What lessons would the Lord have us remember about her?
2. What kind of wife was Jezebel to Ahab? Why do we not need her kind today?
3. Describe Athaliah as a wife. After whom was she patterning her life?
4. Identify the daughters of men in Genesis 6:1-2 and tell why they were bad choices as wives for the sons of God.
5. Discuss Solomon's wives both as to quantity and quality. How did he make grievous mistakes in both of these areas? What did these wives lead him to do?
6. What did Job's wife admonish him to do in Job 2:9? What was wrong with her counsel? Why do we not need wives like her today?
7. Who was Herodias? Why do we not need wives like her today?

8. Describe Drusilla. Why is the captivating beauty of a wicked woman such a dangerous thing?
9. Discuss some of the statements Solomon made in Proverbs about the ways of wicked women over weak men.
10. Tell what Solomon said about women who are contentious in the home. Why does this disposition not make for good and worthy wives?
11. Which virtue did Rebekah bring to the marriage altar? Discuss this in light of the multitudes of nonvirgins who come to the marriage altar today.
12. Discuss Sarah as wife in view of the teaching of I Peter 3:6.
13. What necessary ingredients for a good wife did the righteous Ruth possess?
14. Which virtue did Vashti possess that is greatly despised by so many women today?
15. Why is the discovery of a wife a good thing? What must the wife do to make sure her husband continues to believe he found in her a good thing? From where does the prudent wife come?
16. Discuss in detail Proverbs 31:10-31.
17. Discuss Elisabeth as a member of the righteous team mentioned in Luke 1.
18. Discuss Mary (the Lord's mother) and Joseph as a team of workers for the Lord.
19. Describe Priscilla as the wife of Aquilla in the work of the Lord.
20. Tell about the wives of the apostles and those married to the Lord's brethren.

9

The Father in the Home

When Jesus Christ as the divine guest enters our homes He gives a new meaning and dimension to fatherhood and motherhood. Christianity bestows an elevating and purifying influence upon each of these relationships. This chapter and the next three will deal with parenthood in the home. It is my sincere desire to portray the type of parenthood we desperately need today and the kind we will have when *Christ in the home* philosophy permeates the family framework. I will be as firm as truth demands and as kind as love will permit. My purpose is not to harm but to help; not to discourage but to inspire every father and mother to aim at faithful parenthood. Godly fatherhood coupled with noble motherhood will always add up to righteous parenthood. The triangle for success in rearing good children has these sides: God, righteous fathers, and godly mothers. Surround children with these purifying influences and tomorrow's generation will show marked improvement. The Bible and common sense testify to the correctness of this affirmation.

SOME THOUGHT-PROVOKING QUESTIONS

Are you the kind of father that Jehovah and His Son desire you to be? Are you the kind of father your children really need? If your son grows up to be the kind of man you are right *now*, what manner of man will he be? Could you be justly and truly proud of him? When he matures will he bless society if he becomes like his father? Will he be on his way to heaven on his twenty-first birthday if he emulates you? Exactly what do you mean to your family? Are you the real head and the noble leader of society's most basic unit? Is your home happier when you are present or when you are away? Does sadness descend or vanish when you are there? Each of these questions should provoke serious intro-spection by every current or potential father.

MARRIAGE FIRST, FATHERHOOD NEXT

From the very beginning Jehovah God fully intended that a man be a husband before he becomes an expectant father. Divine wis-dom decreed that marriage is to precede expectant parenthood. God has a one-, two-, and three-step procedure along this line. He does not intend for men and women or boys and girls to deviate from the order dictated by His wisdom. Marriage is to be first. The sexual relationship is to be next. Then in course of time is to come the conception and birth of a child. Many couples do not follow this wise divine order. While unmarried to each other they engage freely in the sexual relationship. Conception is frequently the result of such illegal unions. Then the couple thinks in terms of marriage. They have totally rearranged God's clearly revealed order. With them it is sex first, expectant parenthood next, and then marriage. By so doing they have seriously transgressed God's law. All that the advocates of the "new morality" or the practitioners of "situa-tion ethics" may say in defense of such glaring transgressions will not undo the great harm that has occurred in the lives of such a couple. Scars have been inflicted upon their emotional framework that a lifetime will not fully erase. Forgiveness can be attained but scars of the sure consequences will remain. The guilt of the sin can be removed by meeting God's requirements but the fact of fornication and the conception of a child out of wedlock will always be there. These cannot be erased totally from lingering memories that will surely remain. God intends for a man to be a husband before he engages in the act that may make him an expectant father. So-phistication will never be able to delete sin from premarital sex.

Adam and Eve were husband and wife before there was a Cain or Abel on the way toward birth (Gen. 2, 4). Abraham and Sarah were husband and wife many years before Isaac became the pre-cious fruit of their marital union (Gen. 11:29-30; 21:1-3). Isaac and Rebekah were husband and wife many years before Esau and Jacob were conceived and came to birth (Gen. 24:67; 25:20-26). Jacob was husband to Leah and Rachel, his primary wives, and to

Bilhah and Zilpah, his secondary wives, before any of his twelve sons or the one daughter were expected (Gen. 29, 30). Amram and Jochebed were husband and wife before the conception of Miriam, Aaron, or Moses (Exod. 2:1ff). Joseph was married to Asenath before Manasseh and Ephraim were on their respective ways toward birth in the land of Egypt (Gen. 41:45, 50-52). Moses and Zipporah were married before Gershom was expected (Exod. 2: 21-22). Elkanah and Hannah were husband and wife long before the birth of any of their six children beginning with Samuel (I Sam. 1:19-20; 2:20-21). Boaz and Ruth were firmly situated in holy wedlock before Obed was on his way (Ruth 4:9-10; 13-17). Zacharias and Elisabeth were married many years before the birth of John (Luke 1).

Marriage and then the physical relationship with the conception of children always occurring in wedlock and not out of it constitute God's divine order. When boys and girls seek to rearrange this order, trouble of the deepest kind is inevitable. "The way of transgressors is hard" is a Scriptural affirmation that knows no refutation (Prov. 13:15). Moral transgressions committed in the dating game produce a sure harvest of bitter fruits. I have counseled with enough young to know whereof I speak.

FIRST FEELINGS OF FATHERHOOD

A husband takes his wife to the doctor. They both are fairly confident that she has conceived and that parenthood looms upon their horizon. The doctor's examination confirms their expectation and raises even higher their anticipation. Now their marriage will bear the precious fruit of a child. They both are happy. The child was conceived in wedlock. It will be born to parents who love each other. For the next several months they seek to prepare for the baby's coming. Each passing day brings them closer to the coveted role of parenthood.

Then the hour arrives when the husband takes his wife to the hospital for the delivery of their eagerly awaited baby. Modern medical science will cooperate with God in the safe delivery of the child. After a few slow hours of prayerful interest and anxious waiting doctor emerges to tell the concerned husband that he and wife are now parents of a healthy child. Both mother and child are doing well. Within a few moments the new father will be permitted that first glimpse of the child that a gracious God has given him and his wife. Directions are given and he walks to the specified corridor for the first glimpse of his darling baby. Feelings never before experienced and responsibilities never felt hitherto crowd into the happy heart of the relieved husband.

Whether this young man is a Christian or a non-Christian will determine the type of questions which will now challenge him regarding his child's future. The new non-Christian father will tentatively lay plans for the child which will be circumscribed only by earthly interests and considerations. The devout Christian father will naturally manifest zealous interest in the child's earthly life but the Christian framework of his own life will project his thinking toward the child's eternal future. The eternal salvation of that little child will be of far greater importance to that father than any matter that is purely earthly in nature. What kind of person that child has for a father at birth, what kind of man he will be the next eighteen years, and the type of teaching imparted from parent to child will be mighty factors in determining the direction of that child's future. The mature young Christian who becomes a father will realize more keenly with each day's passing how weighty with eternal responsibilities his new role in life really is. When the mother and child are brought home a new era in their lives dawns. The next eighteen or twenty years can be majestic or miserable. To a very great extent the father and mother decide which tone will be dominant.

SCRIPTURAL IMPERATIVES FOR FATHERHOOD

Jesus Christ brings the fear of God and a diligent determination to keep heaven's will into the hearts of fathers. They should be Christian fathers. They should have heard the gospel (Rom. 10:17), believed in the deity of Jesus (John 8:24), repented of their sins (Acts 17:30), sweetened their lips with a courageous confession of Jesus as Christ and Son of God (Rom. 10:9-10) and have been baptized for the remission of sins (Acts 2:38). It is always ideal if the child has a Christian father from birth onward. My father was baptized thirteen years before my birth. It has been an inestimable blessing to have had a Christian father from infancy onward. My father gave me an excellent example to follow: hard work, honest toil, Bible study, prayer, church attendance, and a deep interest in the gospel of Jesus Christ. The times my father and I have worshiped and studied the Bible together are legion. I cherish the hope that my children can say the same of me when they reach maturity and reflect on what their father has meant to them.

A good father will recognize man's supreme duty in life. "Let us hear the conclusion of the whole matter: Fear God, and keep his commandments: for this is the whole duty of man" (Eccles. 12: 13). He will recognize the importance of being strong, showing himself a man, and keeping the charge of God (I Kings 2:2-3). He will seek to follow the wise counsel of Micah, "He hath shewed thee, O man, what is good; and what doth the Lord require of thee, but to do justly, and to love mercy, and to walk humbly with thy God?" (Mic. 6:8). A good father will recognize that his main mission in life is love for God and man. Jesus said it this way, "Thou shalt love the Lord thy God with all thy heart, and with all thy soul, and with all thy mind. This is the first and great commandment. And the second is like unto it, Thou shalt love thy neighbour as thyself. On these two commandments hang all the law and the prophets" (Matt. 22:37-40). Real fathers will be men of deep faith. To this faith they will add or supply "virtue; and to virtue knowledge; And to knowledge temperance; and to temperance patience; and to patience godliness; And to godliness brotherly kindness; and to brotherly kindness charity" (II Peter 1:5-7). Diligent cultivation of these sacred principles cannot help but make the men of our age into the type of fathers that all little boys and girls need as they grow to maturity in the home. Such blessings are worth far more to children than if their fathers could bequeath to them vast property holdings or great sums of money.

REAL FATHERS AND FAITHLESS HUSBANDS

Somehow people have gotten the idea that there is no connection between fatherhood and a man's faithfulness to his marriage vows. It has been stated in my presence, "He is a good father to his children even though he is faithless to his wife who is their mother." I do not buy this for one moment. I deny emphatically that a man can be faithful as a father and faithless as a husband. I do not believe that a faithful father and a faithless husband come wrapped up in the same human personality. How can anyone imagine that he can be the right kind of a father to his children and care nothing for the mother that brought them into the world? The man who seeks to fill these highly contradictory roles may deceive his children for a few years but the day will ultimately come when the children discover that Daddy is not the man they believed him to be. It is one of the most tragic days in a child's life when he discovers that Daddy does not love Mommy but loves other women. That child will never again have the same feelings or the deep respect for that father which he once had. A father can die in a boy's heart many years before that father answers the final summons.

A man cannot love his children and mistreat their mother. If his love is divided between her and other women, there is really no love there. Real love cannot be divided in such fashion. A man cannot disobey Paul's injunctions that he love his wife as Christ loved the church and as he loves his own body and be the type of father God demands and his children surely deserve (Eph. 5: 25, 28). A man cannot renege on the marriage vows he voluntarily made and at the same time be a real father to his children. A disregard for his marriage vows will bring grief to the wife he has deserted. Such desertion will keep her from being the happy and contented mother that children must have if they are to become well adjusted. A child that grows up in a home where his father does not love his mother and is unfaithful to her is deprived of life's most cherished blessings in the home. Such a background may be two strikes against the child one day having a happy home of his own. It is difficult for a child to have correct concepts of the home if he has been reared in a framework of a faithless husband as his father and a rejected wife as his mother. My heart goes out to every precious child that grows up in a home where the man whom he calls father is unfaithful to his mother.

John sets forth a principle about our relationship to God and fellow Christians. "Whosoever believeth that Jesus is the Christ is born of God: and every one that loveth him that begat loveth him also that is begotten of him" (I John 5:1). If we love him that did the begetting (God) we must also love those that are begotten of him, that is, Christians. Love for God demands love for all Christians. Love for Christians also demands love for God. We cannot love God and hate His children. Likewise we cannot love children of God and hate the Father of those children. The same principle in modified form exists in the home. A man who really loves his wife will love the children that are begotten as a result of the marital union. A man who loves his children the way he should is going to love the mother that gave them birth.

Real fathers and faithful husbands meet and merge in the same male personality. *Christ in the home* will prompt a man to be faithful and loving to his wife and dutiful and devoted to his children. A faithless husband and a faithful father are not found in the same man. The two roles are totally incompatible, mutually exclusive, and self-contradictory.

THE FATHER IS HEAD OF THE HOME

In Ephesians 5:23 Paul establishes the husband as head of the wife. "For the husband is the head of the wife, even as Christ is the head of the church: and he is the saviour of the body." Though speaking primarily of the husband and wife relationship, the inspired apostle in the same breath established the father as head and ruler over his children. Paul tells the wife to be submissive to the husband (Eph. 5:22). It is certain that if the wife is to be submissive to the husband that the submissive spirit is also expected of children toward their father. The wife is to be subject to her husband even as the church voluntarily maintains the spirit of subjection to Christ her head. It is therefore certain that children should be in subjection to their father as ruler. Children who refuse the rulership of their fathers are as much out of place as is the church when it refuses to be in subjection to its ruling head. Ephesians 6:1-3 makes it decisively clear that children are to be submissive.

The rulership of husband and father is not established upon a dictatorial, tyrannical, harsh, or selfish kind of domination. Instead it envisions a husband who loves his wife as Christ loves the church. It envisions a father who loves his children as God loves His sons and daughters. When man's leadership of his family is built upon this type of foundation, he assumes a role that God fully intended him to fill. Fathers who through lack of interest or insufficient courage fail to assume this position are falling down in one of the paramount responsibilities of true fatherhood. The good father will work in close cooperation with the mother of his children and, if wise, will depend to a great extent upon consultation with her as together they form the framework of family policies. Entirely too frequently today husbands and wives have abdicated their positions as head (Eph. 5:23) and guide (1 Tim. 5:14) of home policy-making and allowed their children to become little kings and queens in running the family. It is always a deep disappointment to visit a home where parents cater to every childish whim and fancy. The Bible never says, "Parents, obey your children in the Lord for this is right." That philosophy came from Satan and has been meekly accepted by fearful parents today. Immeasurable harm will result when parents do not assume their rightful roles of authority in the home. It is completely unfair to allow children to assume positions of authority and leadership for which they have neither the experience nor wisdom. Since the father is God's choice to rule by love the family, it is his imperative duty and royal right to make absolutely sure that he and his wife remain as the supervisors of the family. They should never delegate this important task to anyone else. God did not choose a child or an in-law to head the home; he chose the husband to do it. *Christ in the home* prompts a diligent determination from every father to perform well this important task.

THE FATHER MUST BE A PROVIDER

Children enter this world as creatures wholly dependent upon someone else. Several years elapse between birth and self-sufficiency for the child. This dependency introduces another cardinal duty which fathers must assume — financial support. Every day of the child's life will find him in need of food, clothing, and shelter. He will need medical attention when ill. Several years of expensive education lie before him as he grows to maturity. The child must also be taught about the needs of his soul. He deserves to learn not only how a living may be made but also how to make a life. These are imperatives in successful child-rearing. Thoughtful parents in a position to do so will also evidence an interest in providing little extras which gladden the heart of every boy and girl. Rearing children involves money but also countless hours of personal attention both from father and mother. Fathers cannot provide by proxy the personal attention their sons and daughters deserve and need. Rearing children is not a task belonging exclusively to the mother.

The father is God's choice to be the family breadwinner, though unavoidable circumstances such as unemployment, illness, disease, or death may cause variation here. He may be unable to make a living for a large family without breadwinning aid from his wife. An able father will gladly labor for those whom he has helped to bring into the world. Twin concepts of real love are: (1) it makes service easy, and (2) it thinks in terms of others first. Laboring for a wife and children makes any job easier to perform. Real love will prompt any father to think of the family's basic needs before concern is focused on his own needs. A fishing or hunting trip will always be canceled if an emergency bill for wife or children calls for that money instead. He may have practically no spending money left for himself when all the bills are paid but ample provision for the family's needs will be a rich reward in itself.

Any person who will help to bring a child into the world and will not turn the first hand toward its support is not worthy of being called either father or a man. Paul says, "But if any provide not for his own, and specially for those of his own house, he hath denied the faith, and is worse than an infidel" (I Tim. 5:8). I recognize that the context speaks of the care and attention children are to extend their aged mothers and grandmothers when they are unable to care for themselves. If the son or daughter is obligated to care for aged parents because they cannot care for themselves, they surely are obligated to care for the very children whom they have brought into the world. Failure at this point is equivalent to a denial of the holy faith. It is to sink below the level maintained by infidels. Unbelievers who love their children do not renege at this self-imposed duty. Believers should perform such duties with even greater industry. Paul refers to the well-known principle of parental provision to teach the careless Corinthians a needed lesson. "Behold, the third time I am ready to come to you; and I will not be burdensome to you: for I seek not yours, but you: for the children ought not to lay up for the parents, but the parents for the children" (II Cor. 12:14). Paul was not interested in the possessions of the Corinthians but in the Corinthians themselves. He was not advocating that they provide for him. As their father in the gospel he was interested in providing for their spiritual needs. For them he would spend and be spent (II Cor. 12:15). The same principles hold true for the physical father. He seeks not the child's possessions but is interested in the child. He does not think about what the child owes him by way of recompense but what he owes the child. I once heard a husband of a childless marriage say that he and his wife ought to adopt one or more children in order that they might be taken care of in their older days. That type of reasoning is a failure to recognize the selfless nature of *giving* parenthood. That man thought too much of getting and not enough of giving.

The person who fails to provide for his own when he is able to provide for them has failed as a father. No other virtue of a father will compensate for failure here. *Christ in the home* will not tolerate a deliberate side-stepping of this weighty responsibility of a father.

THE FATHER AND MODESTY

That many young girls and older women have abandoned modest attire is no longer open to debate. This is the age of the low-cut blouse, the mini skirt, skin-tight pants, and even "see through" garments. The beaches and swimming pools have been turned into a semi-nudist resort. Both sexes wear practically nothing. Such scanty garb for public attire characterizes even many Christian young girls and older women. Some women have lost their ability to blush regardless of how little they wear.

I, for one, do not buy the argument that *all* women are so naive as to be totally unaware of the effect their immodest attire has upon men. Some may be, but others are not. Be that as it may, I can say that every normal husband and father without exception knows what goes on in the minds of men when women appear in public in immodest attire. This is an area where the Christian husband and father should do some strict legislating. He should see to it that his wife and daughter are modestly attired when the eyes of the public observe them. If his wife and daughter are lacking decency at this point, he should inject some of his standards of decency into their choice of what to wear in public. Jesus said, "Ye have heard that it was said by them of old time, Thou shalt not commit adultery: But I say unto you, That whosoever looketh on a woman to lust after her hath committed adultery with her already in his heart" (Matt. 5:27-28). Any husband or father who possesses holiness of heart and innocency of intent should desire to make doubly certain that neither his wife nor daughter should ever dress in a provocative or seductive fashion. Paul wrote, "In like manner also, that women adorn themselves in modest apparel, with shamefacedness and sobriety; not with braided hair, or gold, or pearls, or costly array" (I Tim. 2:9). If wives and daughters who profess Christianity show a reluctance to listen to apostolic authority, it seems that its is past time for the family head to exert some needed pressure to bring about conformity to this Scriptural injunction. Even if the wife and daughter wear modest attire under protest and because of the family head's strong directive instead of their own choice, they will not be tempting some man's roving eyes to lust after them. This is an area where husbands and fathers should begin to take notice and do something to correct immediately the growing malady of immodest dress. Of course, that the husband and father should be modestly dressed when he appears in public is an absolute prerequisite to his being effective in helping to solve the problem.

It has always seemed highly inconsistent for a father to become irate with a young man who makes an aggressive pass at his daughter on a date when that very father forked over the money to buy her thigh-revealing skirts, low-cut blouses, or skimpy bikini and permitted her to wear such flimsy garb on the date with that young man. It is naive for a father to think that his daughter would be safe with any and every young man when she advertises her bodily charms so openly and invitingly. *Christ in the home* will induce a Christian father to act consistently in father-daughter relationships.

FATHERS AND LONG-HAIRED SONS

Some fathers apparently do not care what their sons do nor what they look like. But I cannot imagine a Christian father being unconcerned when his son becomes effeminate and begins to grow a head of hair like a woman. I have recently met young people of Christian friends and until introduced I hardly knew whether they were sons or daughters! As a father I would count it a reflection on me if people could not tell whether my child is a boy or a girl. Paul said, "Doth not even nature itself teach you, that, if a man have long hair, it is a shame unto him?" (I Cor. 11:14). It is a shame for men or boys to have long hair. It likewise is a shame for fathers to have such little control over their sons still living at home that the sons successfully defy their fathers at hair-cutting time! Has all backbone been removed from such fathers? Is there no spine left at all? Here is another area where Christian fathers in the early seventies are derelict in their duty.

THE FATHER AS SPIRITUAL LEADER

Many fathers have a totally materialistic concept of their role in the home. They believe that the husband constitutes part of the biological unit that makes possible the conception of the child. Nine months later he becomes a father to a little boy or girl. He takes seriously his role as a breadwinner. He brings home the weekly check that provides shelter, clothing, food, medical attention, and educational needs for the child during its first eighteen years. When he works his forty hours a week and spends a little time with the child he feels he is a good father and has fully discharged his responsibility in this role. There are no promptings of heart or urgings of conscience to lead him toward a much more important role of fatherhood, that of being the spiritual leader in his home. He never instills the fear of God into the pliable hearts of his children. He never reads the Bible to them. Prayer is not a part of his life. Only when company is present will he ever give thanks for a meal and then he often asks someone else to lead in prayer. A church building witnesses his presence only at a funeral or a wedding and then he is quite uncomfortable in this strange environment. The years speed by and each child is now grown and just as irreligious as is the father. This man is a *signal failure* as a father. He has been derelict in that most far-reaching of fatherhood roles, that of being the spiritual leader. Nothing that he has provided in the material realm will compensate for negligence in this vital area of parental activity.

Jehovah God has given fathers the weighty responsibility of properly training their children as they grow to maturity. The Bible speaks with both clarity and emphasis about this cardinal task. Solomon, to whom heaven gave an unparalleled degree of wisdom, counseled those rearing children to "Train up a child in the way he should go: and when he is old, he will not depart from it" (Prov. 22:6). Some fathers apparently wish this passage were addressed exclusively to mothers for that would leave fathers totally free of any obligations toward the exercise of spiritual leadership. Failure as a father in this realm of responsibility could cost the salvation of precious children. It could also mean the father is lost. A man who takes no interest in teaching his children the will of the Lord is not very interested in going to heaven himself. He does not have much fear of going to hell else he would tread a different trail of activity both for himself and his children. Judgment will be severe for a man who fails to train his children. If there are children still at home, fathers had better be diligent practitioners of this wise counsel. Solomon clearly admonished that children should be trained in the way they should go. Children, as they grow to maturity, will travel either the high road that leads to God, Christ, and the new Jerusalem, or the low road that leads to sin, shame, degradation, and ultimately a devil's hell. The type of training they receive in youth, how effectively it is instilled into their pliable hearts and impressionable minds, and how well parents live their own religious convictions before them will be determining factors in selecting the route children will ultimately travel.

In parallel passages directed respectively to the Ephesians and the Colossians Paul wrote, "And, ye fathers, provoke not your children to wrath: but bring them up in the nurture and admonition of the Lord" (Eph. 6:4). "Fathers, provoke not your children to anger, lest they be discouraged" (Col. 3:21). God's love for the little children of the world will not allow fathers to ignore these apostolic precepts with impunity. No father can escape these words calling for parental counsel by turning the spiritual leadership over to the child's mother. Fathers should make sure that Bible reading and prayer are a part of family activities. Fathers should make sure that church-going comes before sports and pleasures. School events are important but one's relationship to God takes precedence. Such decisions will be made quite naturally by the father and accepted without question by the child if the whole family's past has been built upon the principle of Matthew 6:33. *Christ in the home* means that husband and father is at the helm as spiritual leader and captain.

THE FATHER AS AN EXAMPLE

Words from a father's lips will not mean much to a child if there is a serious gap between what Dad says and what Dad does. Dad cannot impress purity upon a son if he himself is impure. He cannot point a child to Jesus if the direction of his own life is contrary to the counsels of Christianity. He cannot expect the child to use decent speech if his own speech patterns are filled with profanity. My father told the story of a man and his son who were doing some work for him many years ago. Something went wrong and the son let out a string of curse words. His father reminded the boy that the lady of the house was nearby and that he should be careful of his language. A few minutes later something else went wrong and this time it happened to the father. He likewise let out a string of curse words. Quickly, the son reminded him of the nearness of the lady and that he too should be careful about his speech! Need we suggest the possible source of the young man's brand of language? A father cannot teach honesty to a son if his own life is built on dishonesty, cheating, and deception. Actions speak louder than words. A father cannot teach his son to behave when he is with the opposite sex if the father misbehaves with other women. A father who is shiftless and refuses to accept responsibility seriously should not think he can impress industry and responsibility on his children. A father who smokes, drinks, and gambles should not think that he can influence his children to shy away from such undesirable practices. A father who has never mastered his own temper will not be much of an influence in building a boy that can control his temper. A father who never reads the Bible, never prays, never attends church, and never shows any inclination toward a religious life is not the kind of father who will rear sons and daughters in that faith that is most holy, that hope that anchors our future aspirations, and that love which surpasses all other virtues. I Corinthians 13:13 demands that fathers demonstrate these virtues before their children.

We need fathers today who are themselves Christians. We need fathers who will be good examples. Such fathers can effectively teach and direct their boys and girls to make an honorable living here and to live a successful life which enriches the present and prepares for the future. *Christ in the home* is again the answer for this much-needed area of a father's responsibilities.

When fathers lift up the Bible in the home the Bible will lift up fatherhood in the home.

QUESTIONS FOR DISCUSSION

1. What are the components in the triangular formula of child-rearing success?
2. What are some of the thought-provoking questions every father should face?
3. Why should marriage precede expectant fatherhood? What is God's one-, two-, and three-step plan along this line? How have many couples rearranged this wise divine order and with what disastrous consequences?
4. List some Bible couples that faithfully followed the divine arrangement of marriage first, then the physical act, and then the conception and birth of children.
5. How does Proverbs 13:15 fit in with dating indiscretions?
6. Describe some of the first feelings of fatherhood. How will these feelings differ between a Christian father and a non-Christian father?
7. List some Scriptural imperatives for fatherhood.
8. Can men who are unfaithful to their wives be faithful as fathers? Why, or why not?
9. Discuss the concept of man as the head of the home. What happens when children rule the home?
10. Discuss the area of the father as the provider for the family.
11. List and discuss the twin concepts of real love.
12. Discuss Paul's care and concern for his spiritual children. Apply these principles in the parent-child relationship.
13. Discuss fathers and the modest appearance of their wives and and daughters. If mothers refuse to take the lead in choosing modest dress for themselves and their daughters, what actions should Christian husbands and fathers take?
14. Discuss a father's responsibility toward his son and the long-hair fad.
15. Discuss the father as a spiritual leader in his home. What totally different concept of this role do many men possess?
16. Discuss how texts such as Proverbs 22:6, Ephesians 6:4, and Colossians 3:21 touch the task of the man's spiritual leadership.
17. Discuss the great need for fathers to be examples to their children.
18. What kind of fathers do we need today?
19. When fathers lift up the Bible in the home what will the Bible do for fatherhood in the home?

10

Portraits of Bible Fathers

From many years of experience I have learned that it is well to state a principle, give its Biblical proof, and then illustrate it with an example. That is what I am attempting to do as I speak about the husband, wife, father, mother, and child relationships in the home. Humanly speaking, these constitute the heart of home relationships. I am stating some rather obvious truths about each. Biblical proof is then submitted. Finally, I intend to paint some portraits of those who failed to measure up and those who did measure up to Jehovah's standards. Though a place for the negative is frequently denied by the worshipers of a total positive approach I believe man needs to know what God has said by way of negative warnings as well as by positive admonitions. It is my purpose to note both sides of the picture. As we have done in previous studies we shall look first of all at portraits of men who failed as fathers. Then we shall look at portraits of men who reaped golden success in the realm of fatherhood. I prefer to present the negative first and close with the positive.

THE KIND OF FATHERS NOT NEEDED

We do not need fathers today who will pitch their tents toward Sodom as did ancient Lot. When the time came for a separation between Abraham and his youthful nephew, the younger man made a choice that clearly indicated materialism was the dominant factor.

The magnanimous patriarch gave Lot his choice (Gen. 13:9). Gratitude toward his benevolent uncle and a vision of wisdom for the future welfare of his family were not decisive factors in the choice Lot made. The Bible says, "And Lot lifted up his eyes, and beheld all the plain of Jordan, that it was well watered every where, before the Lord destroyed Sodom and Gomorrah, even as the garden of the Lord, like the land of Egypt, as thou comest unto Zoar. Then Lot chose him all the plain of Jordan; and Lot journeyed east: and they separated themselves the one from the other. Abram dwelled in the land of Canaan, and Lot dwelled in the cities of the plain, and pitched his tent toward Sodom. But the men of Sodom were wicked and sinners before the Lord exceedingly" (Gen. 13:10-13). Lot pitched his tent *toward* Sodom. Soon he was living in the *midst* of these sinful Sodomites. Sodom was not a proper environment for the rearing of a family. Peter lets us know that even the righteous Lot had his soul vexed from day to day with the "filthy conversation of the wicked" and seeing and hearing "their unlawful deeds" day by day (II Peter 2:7-8). If righteous Lot had his soul vexed daily with what he saw and heard in sinful Sodom, it is hardly likely that his family could escape serious environmental influences that would work toward the wreck and ruin of their souls. A thorough study of Genesis 19 implies that some of Lot's children chose to remain behind and not to accompany the quartet that left Sodom. Lot's wife perished on the way to safety. The heinous crimes of strong drink and incest involving Lot and his two surviving daughters occupy the last verses of this chapter. Beyond doubt these are some of the saddest and most sordid stories to be found anywhere.

Many modern fathers have made many of life's decisions with materialism as a dominant factor. A job advancement in another city may be eagerly accepted with no thought beforehand as to how such a move may affect the family spiritually. There may not be a Lord's church in or nearby the new community. Instead of establishing a new work for the Lord in the new town the family may stop attending church. Thus the children may be reared with little or no Bible training, no worship periods conducted after the New Testament order, and no Christian young people for fellowship and association. An entire family may be lost to the cause of Christ. Many fathers and mothers look toward the glitter of gold instead of the guidance of God when major decisions are made.

The principle of pitching the tent toward Sodom operates to a very great extent in the choice of college educations. Too many parents make the choice of where to send their children on the basis of materialism. The state school is cheaper. Perhaps it is much closer. The children can get more of the kind of courses they need for a chosen career. But is it cheaper if they decide to accept the evolutionary dogma there? Is it closer in the real sense of the term if the parents lose them forever to a life of immorality learned on a campus where "free love" is the "in" practice? Do they have access to the courses that really matter? Christian schools have two added pluses to offer, Christian training and Christian fellowship. Parents who do send their boys and girls to a non-religious school should seek one out where an active work is carried out by the church on or near the campus. That can be a tremendous aid in keeping that son's or daughter's faith fed and healthy while he is pursuing higher education. Basil Overton has well said that students must feed their faith while they are in school. I fully concur. Parents must make sure that there are opportunities for the feeding of their young people's faith.

Fathers today can encourage their sons to pitch their tents toward Sodom by inducing them to take up a profession or career that will be centered in money-making but will be no contribution at all toward being faithful to God or rendering a needed service to humanity.

We do not need fathers who will be permissive as Eli. Eli was a good man himself and did a superb work in the training of youthful Samuel. But he was a permissive parent with his own children. First Samuel 2:12 says, "Now the sons of Eli were sons of Belial; they knew not the Lord." They committed grievous sins concerning the sacrifices and caused men to abhor "the offering of the Lord" (I Sam. 2:17). They turned the tabernacle area into a camp of immorality. Women trooped to the area and these sons of Eli committed adultery with them (I Sam. 2:22). Eli mildly rebuked their heinous actions with some weak words. He said, "Why do ye such things? for I hear of your evil dealings by all this people. Nay, my sons; for it is no good report that I hear: ye make the Lord's people to transgress. If one man sin against another, the judge shall judge him: but if a man sin against the Lord, who shall entreat for him?" (I Sam. 2:23-25). God's attitude toward Eli's inexcusable permissiveness is set forth in the following words: "For I have told him that I will judge his house for ever for the iniquity which he knoweth; because his sons made themselves vile, and he restrained them not" (I Sam. 3:13). The marginal references for *vile* and *restrained* are "accursed" and "frowned not upon them." Hophi and Phinehas smiled upon wickedness but their grievous sins brought forth no frowns from their permissive parent. The curses of an aroused heaven were about to descend on this family but Eli still made no real effort to curb his sons' sins. Three forms of authority over these boys met and merged in Eli. (1) He was their father. (2) He was their priest. (3) He was their judge. Domestic, religious, and civil authority converged in his hands and yet he used none of the three powers to curb his wicked sons.

Ours is a permissive age. Many boys and girls grow up and never see Daddy set a boundary line for their actions. They never hear him say a no to their demands. They never feel his weight behind corporal punishment for he believes in rearing children "the John Dewey" way. Fathers who have this philosophy should take a long look at themselves in the mirror of I Samuel 2 and 3. Eli tried permissiveness and it did not work. It never has worked. It never will. Parents who are permissive are among the greatest enemies a child has. Solomon said it this way, "The rod and reproof give wisdom: but a child left to himself bringeth his mother to shame" (Prov. 29:15). "Correct thy son, and he shall give thee rest; yea, he shall give delight unto thy soul" (Prov. 29:17). The converse of this last statement would read, "Withhold correction from thy son and he shall give thee pain; yea, he shall deliver misery unto thy soul." Permissive parents produce permissive children and permissiveness will wreck human society. *Christ in the home* will not allow the deadly sin of permissiveness to prevail. This grievous sin needs to be eradicated from every home in the land. Christian homes should lead the way in the eradication.

We do not need fathers who practice theft, deception, and dishonesty as did Achan in Joshua's day. The children of Israel have just crossed the swollen Jordan River. Plans are made for the capture of Jericho. Jehovah God made it plain that all the spoils of the city belonged to Him. Jericho's riches were to flow into His treasury with no exceptions allowed (Josh. 6:17-19). Secretly one of the Israelites trespassed this law. Due to this infraction of Jehovah's law the anticipated easy capture of nearby Ai was thoroughly thwarted. Joshua and the people were filled with fear. Jehovah revealed the facts that sin was in the camp and proper punishment must be meted out if heaven's frowns upon the entire nation were to be translated into smiles of approval. With dispatch Joshua began to seek out the guilty party who had "transgressed the covenant of the Lord," the one who had "wrought folly in Israel" (Josh. 7: 15). The search narrowed to the tribe of Judah and ultimately Achan was found to be the troubler. The conquering warrior of Palestine said to the exposed thief, "My son, give, I pray thee, glory to the Lord God of Israel, and make confession unto him; and tell me now what thou hast done; hide it not from me. And Achan answered Joshua, and said, Indeed I have sinned against the Lord God of Israel, and thus and thus have I done: When I saw among the spoils a goodly Babylonish garment, and two hundred shekels of silver, and a wedge of gold of fifty shekels weight, then I coveted them, and took them; and, behold, they are hid in the earth in the midst of my tent, and the silver under it" (Josh. 7: 19-21). Joshua sent messengers immediately and the stolen goods were found. Achan apparently was not alone in the committal of this crime. It appears that his family members were accessories to the crime. The thief and his family were brought to the valley of Achor for the pronouncing of the sentence. Mention is expressly made of "his sons, and his daughters" (Josh. 7:24). Acting as judge, Joshua said, "Why hast thou troubled us? the Lord shall trouble thee this day" (Josh. 7:25). The troubler and his consenting family were stoned and burned in the valley of Achor. A heap of stones was raised to serve as a reminder of Achan's folly. The name *Achor,* according to the margin, means Trouble.

The practice of dishonesty marches rampantly through the land today. How can fathers who practice dishonesty be good fathers? How can they be an influence for good in rearing truthful and honest sons and daughters? They cannot. When little boys know that nearly all the tools in Daddy's tool box really belong to his company and he has brought them home one by one, the boys are going to be influenced. When little boys and girls hear parents brag about illegal income deductions turned in annually on April 15, they will be influenced. When little boys and girls hear parents brag about how they short-changed the local merchant and got away with it, they will be influenced. When little children use towels that have been collected from every motel and hotel in which their parents have ever stayed, they will be influenced. One guest in a certain house asked the lady if her maiden name might have been Hilton. This was the name that appeared on every towel he used while there! You know the source of those towels! We do not need parents today who will practice dishonesty. Achan led his family to destruction by his covetous desire for that which belonged to another. Fathers who are dishonest today are leading their sons and daughters in the wrong way. *Christ in the home* will not allow for the practice of deception in words and deeds in the lives of fathers.

We do not need fathers such as Jeroboam was to Nadab. Jeroboam was the first of nineteen kings of the Northern Kingdom, or Israel. This nation lasted for about two hundred and fifty years.

Jeroboam had the opportunity of setting a righteous tone for his government and for his successors, one of whom would be his son Nadab. But in this he miserably failed. He chose to walk in the ways outlined by his own sinful stubbornness. His sinful substitutions of God's will chronicled in I Kings 13 read somewhat like a modern manual or confessional of faith devised by religious leaders today who are dissatisfied with God's Book. Jeroboam was not faithful any of the twenty-two years he spent upon the throne of Israel. Of his son who succeeded him we read, "And Nadab the son of Jeroboam began to reign over Israel in the second year of Asa king of Judah, and reigned over Israel two years. And he did evil in the sight of the Lord, and *walked in the way of his father, and in his sin* wherewith he made Israel to sin" (I Kings 15:25-26, emphasis added). Nadab did not have a righteous father to emulate. His father authored an apostate system of religion for citizens of the Northern Kingdom and established a tone of stubborn rebellion that each of his successors foolishly followed. Of most of them the Bible records this or a similar statement, "And he did evil in the sight of the Lord, and walked in the way of Jeroboam, and in his sin wherewith he made Israel to sin" (I Kings 15:34). We do not need fathers like Jeroboam.

We do not need fathers who rear their children to speak Ashdodic language. Such was the case in Nehemiah's day. He observes, "In those days also saw I Jews that had married wives of Ashdod, of Ammon, and of Moab: And their children spake half in the speech of Ashdod, and could not speak in the Jews' language, but according to the language of each people" (Neh. 13:23-24). The root of this problem among Jewish men lay in their wrong choice of women for wives and ultimately for the mothers of their children. When half the marital unit is Ashdodic, it will not be surprising that children born to that union will speak the language of Ashdod. We are getting further removed all the time from the language of sound doctrine. Many of our young people do not know how to converse intelligently about religious realities without using language that is filled with Ashdodic terms. Much of the Ashdodic problem could be eliminated if both fathers and mothers were well acquainted with Biblical language. But a Christian father and a non-Christian mother, or vice versa, do not make for the development in the home of a vocabulary filled with the language of sound doctrine.

We do not need fathers who teach their little boys to curse. A little fellow was once using one curse term right after another on a farm where several men were working. One of the men asked him where he learned such language. Proudly he said, "From my Daddy." His father was a poor example in this realm.

We do not need irreligious fathers today. A lady in a certain community had the practice of regularly inviting all the neighborhood children to her home for refreshments and while they were there she would tell them a Bible story. One day a new boy came with the other children. She told them the Bible story for that day would be about Jesus. Upon mention of this name the little fellow who was there for the first time became very frightened and began to cry. Looking into the matter later the lady learned why. This little lad came from a home that was totally irreligious in nature. The only time he ever heard the name of Jesus was when his parents were deeply angry and engaged in a tirade of profanity. He had associated the highest and holiest of all names with an enraged mother and irate father. How tragic for children to grow up in homes where God and Christ are only used as expressions of profanity. A grown man nearly fifty years of age once told me that he was nearly eighteen years old before he ever heard the name Jesus used in his home by his parents. What a tragedy!

We do not need fathers today who prefer fishing on Sunday to worshiping in God's house. We do not need fathers who would rather read comics than listen to the words of Christ on Sunday morning. We do not need fathers today who would rather be at a lakeside than have the Lord by their side in a worship assembly. We do not need fathers today who prefer golf over God. We do not need husbands and fathers today who will discourage their wives from the practice of Christianity and will make fun of their sons and daughters who desire to obey the gospel. We do not need fathers today who will stand in the way of their children's obedience to the gospel of Christ. I have assisted a number of young people who had to obey the gospel without their father's knowledge or else he would have stopped the entire process. Children who will risk their father's strong displeasure and maybe even physical punishment to obey the gospel are to be greatly admired. We think the smiles of approving heaven must surely rest upon them. But think of the terrible consequences awaiting every father who seeks to be an obstacle in the way of his children's obedience to the gospel of Christ. Unless such fathers repent severe judgment will be indeed upon them.

We do not need fathers who will encourage their sons and daughters to sow a crop of wild oats in youth. I once heard of a father that encouraged his son to be prepared to "go all the way" on dates with his girl friends. Boys have enough temptations to face without a father's encouragement being extended toward the practice of immorality. We do not need fathers who make available alcoholic beverages in the home. This is precisely where many children learn to drink. They emulate their parents in drinking to a definite degree. In Utah, a survey was made among high school students some years back. Of the girls surveyed it was discovered that 79 percent of them did not drink at all. A check was made among their mothers and exactly 79 percent of them were not alcoholic imbibers. The survey further revealed that 56 percent of the boys never drank. Significantly, 56 percent of their fathers never drank. These statistics also revealed that 21 percent of the girls drank and 21 percent of their mothers drank. Among the boys 44 percent of them drank and 44 percent of their fathers drank. I would quickly affirm that there exists here more than a mere coincidence. Children are definitely influenced by the drinking or non-drinking habits and practices of their parents.

In 1963 *The Commercial Appeal* of Memphis, Tennessee, presented a series of articles titled "Pitfalls of Youth." The eighth article in that series dealt with the drinking habits of the nation's youth. Several pertinent quotations were made by Dr. Herman D. Goldberg, Chairman of the Psychology Department of Hofstra College in New York. At the time Dr. Goldberg had conducted one of the most exhaustive surveys ever made into the drinking habits of young people. He concluded from his studies that many young people begin to drink at the very tender age of thirteen. He tersely asked, "And who tempts them into drinking in the first place? Their parents!" The psychology professor states that "where parents are heavy drinkers, the children become heavy drinkers, where the parents drink in moderation, the children will do the same, and where parents drink very little and are strict about drinking rules, the children usually abide by them."

An interesting article appeared in *The Commercial Appeal,* March 5, 1963. According to the Memphis Police Department's juvenile squad most young people begin to drink at home. Members of this squad told of a teen-age boy whom they questioned. He had been left alone at home for an entire week. "We went out to question him in connection with a vandalism case and found him passed out on the sofa. He had gotten the *liquor out of the cabinet at home."* (Emphasis mine — R.R.T.) This article further pointed out "that a common argument from youngsters for drinking and smoking [the article joined these two undesirable habits together] is 'Mother and Daddy drink it, why can't I?'" Some years ago a father gave up both smoking and drinking. He said, "If they see me drinking, they'll figure they ought to be able to do it."

Perhaps we have all heard the story of the father who learned of the automobile accident in which his youthful daughter and her boy friend were involved. Liquor had been responsible for the accident. The father vowed to find the man who sold them the liquor and deal with him accordingly. To steady his nerves he went to the place where he kept his own liquor. It was gone! The awful truth then struck him that his daughter must have taken along the bottle of liquor on that date. He was the man responsible for supplying them the fiery liquid of death for their date.

Edgar Allan Poe was a brilliant young writer. He died at a young age. He is reported to have been an alcoholic at death. He once stated that he learned to love the taste of good wine at his *father's table*. A drinking father may feel certain that alcohol will never become his tyrannical master and he its duped servant. Perhaps he will never be a heavy drinker or an alcoholic. But he has no assurance that his children will escape alcoholism. The drinking father may live to see a son or daughter a confirmed alcoholic. What a tragedy to pay for imbibing the devilish liquid and thus making it available for his children. Currently one out of every two adults in our nation drinks alcoholic beverages. The number of alcoholic consumers in our nation is now about eighty to ninety millions.

We need fathers who will not smoke. An article in *The Commercial Appeal,* February 27, 1963, says, "Inevitably, the children of parents who are smokers are more likely to become smokers themselves. Seventy percent of the smoking teen-agers said they had obtained parental permission about a year after they had begun to smoke regularly." Some time back the American Cancer Society put out a little tract titled "The Great Imitators." The whole purpose of the tract was to warn smoking parents that their example will have a definite effect upon their children. They suggest that where both parents smoke 44 percent of the boys and 37 percent of the girls will take up the habit. If only one parent smokes, 37 percent and 29 percent respectively of the boys and girls will smoke. If neither parent smokes, only 29 percent of the boys and 16 percent of the girls take up the habit. Each day in our country about 4,500 boys and girls take up smoking. As a smoking father do you really think your example will be of no consequence to your impressionable boys and girls? You *can* break the habit. We urge you to do it without delay.

Christ in the home can keep fathers from being the wrong kinds of examples for their children.

THE KIND OF FATHERS WE NEED

In the area of unrighteousness or righteousness the power of an example is undisputed. In this section I propose to take a long look at some men of the past who raised fatherhood to higher levels. Our own concepts of fatherhood can be greatly raised by looking at these men and learning from them. Concepts which are clothed in human flesh are much easier to imitate than are ideals which are merely abstractly stated.

We need fathers today who will emulate Enoch, the seventh from Adam. The Bible has painted his portrait by using only a few brief verses. However, everything stated about this ancient worthy is commendable. The author of the Pentateuch wrote, "And Enoch lived sixty and five years, and begat Methuselah: And Enoch walked with God after he begat Methuselah three hundred years, and begat sons and daughters: And all the days of Enoch were three hundred sixty and five years: And Enoch walked with God: and he was not; for God took him" (Gen. 5:21-24). The author of Hebrews wrote, "By faith Enoch was translated that he should not see death; and was not found, because God had translated him: for before his translation he had this testimony, that he pleased God" (Heb. 11:5). Jude wrote, "And Enoch also, the seventh from Adam, prophesied of these, saying, Behold, the Lord cometh with ten thousands of his saints, To execute judgment upon all, and to convince all that are ungodly among them of all their ungodly deeds which they have ungodly committed, and of all their hard speeches which ungodly sinners have spoken against him" (Jude 14-15). These verses picture Enoch as a father, one who walked with God, a man who was translated and allowed to escape death, a man of faith, one who pleased God, and as a courageous prophet who feared not to set forth God's prophetic will toward ungodly speech and ungodly conduct. Methuselah had a father of faith. He and his father Enoch lived side by side for three centuries. Methuselah could never recall any period of his life but what his righteous father was pleasing to the heavenly Father and walking with this Divine Being. Methuselah outlived his father on earth by 669 years. During these centuries he had the precious memory of a father who walked with God. How many sons reading these words today have fathers who walk daily with Jehovah God? If your father is gone, is one of your precious memories of him that of a man who lived close to God and walked daily with Him through life? Some of the sons who read this possibly cannot ever remember a day but what their fathers in the flesh were walking with Jehovah. Others are so unfortunate as never remembering a day when their fathers *did* walk with Jehovah God. How many of the fathers who read this are seeking to make it possible that your sons may have fathers who walk with God? As the father of your children you are the only person on earth who can make it possible for your sons and daughters to have a father such as Enoch was to Methuselah. Sons and daughters today desperately need fathers who will seek to emulate Enoch. *Christ in the home* will help today's fathers to be fathers like Enoch.

Our world stands in desperate need of fathers who will emulate noble Noah. The heroes of faith chapter, Hebrews 11, describes him, "By faith Noah, being warned of God of things not seen as yet, moved with fear, prepared an ark to the saving of his house; by the which he condemned the world, and became heir of the righteousness which is by faith" (Heb. 11:7). Peter calls Moses a "preacher of righteousness" in II Peter 2:5. Moses said, "But Noah found grace in the eyes of the Lord. These are the generations of Noah: Noah was a just man and perfect in his generations, and Noah walked with God" (Gen. 6:8-9). According to the language of Genesis 6 there was not another father in Noah's day who shared Noah's faith in Jehovah God. The stark fact that other fathers were deeply entrenched in sin and wickedness did not drive the faithful patriarch into damning unbelief and utter despair in seeking salvation both for himself and his family. Noah believed God's word regarding the impending flood. He and his family would share in the pronounced doom unless he moved with dispatch and in harmony with God's instructions. We do not find Noah in the passive role of spiritual lethargy. Instead he is mightily engaged in diligent preparation for family survival. Building the gigantic ark to heaven's specifications must have loomed as an enormous task yet his family's salvation depended upon its successful completion. Finally the ark was ready and when the forty days of rain came Noah and family were secure in the ark of safety. The same waters that destroyed their infamous contemporaries became the instrument of their physical salvation.

Noah reared his children in an atmosphere where universal evil prevailed. The satanically strong and persistent influences of such wickedness did not detour Noah and his wife from instilling Jehovah's fear into the hearts of their three sons. If Noah could rear his children in such a way that they were counted worthy to enter the ark and be saved from the universal deluge, let us take renewed courage in rearing our children in our crooked and perverse generation. When Christian fathers become as concerned about saving

their children from the eternal lake of fire as Noah was in saving
his sons from the universal lake of water, we will have many more
children safely housed in the ark of Christian safety, the church
of Jesus Christ. Some have classed this ancient "preacher of righteousness" a failure since he saved only himself and seven others.
They greatly err who lay this criticism at the feet of this ancient
"preacher of righteousness." Any father who can save himself plus
all of his immediate family deserves unstinted praise. Surely the
Just Judge at the last great day will see that such men are properly
praised and richly rewarded. God give us more fathers with an un-
daunted faith, a godly fear, a righteous heart, and a dynamic determination to move mightily toward the salvation of themselves and
their families. We need millions of men who will seek to become
modern Noahs to their families.

There is a great need for men today to fill honorably and successfully the role of fatherhood as did the saintly Abraham nearly
four millenniums ago. This former citizen of Ur and sojourner in
Canaan was truly one of the most remarkable men who ever honored God with a loyal life, a fervent faith, and a holy heart. This
ancient patriarch deserves credit for many things, and Biblical
writers have not been slow in so honoring him. "Father of all them
that believe," "father of us all," and "father of many nations" are
a few descriptive terms employed by Paul in Romans 4:11, 16, 18
to designate the worthy patriarch and the relationship we sustain
toward him.

Abraham not only proved himself to be an ideal father to youthful Isaac but also set a splendid example for the millions of physical and spiritual descendants who trace their fleshly or spiritual
lineage back to that Hebrew patriarch. Not only have great and
good men honored him as a faithful father but the God of heaven
paid him the same compliment. Jehovah chose to reveal to Abraham His plans for Sodom's destruction, and gives His reasons for
that revelation in one of the grandest commendations ever given
Abraham. God said of him, "For I know him, that he will command his children and his household after him, and they shall
keep the way of the Lord, to do justice and judgment; that the Lord
may bring upon Abraham that which he hath spoken of him (Gen.
18:19). God knew that Abraham would point the feet of his children toward the pathway of patience, loyalty, and truth. Abraham
was already training his children "in the way they should go" nine
centuries before Solomon penned the words of Proverbs 22:6. Abraham was bringing up his children in the nurture and admonition of
the Lord nineteen centuries before Paul penned the exhortation of

Ephesians 6:4. What kind of confidence can the Father above place in us as fathers regarding our future success in the correct rearing of our precious children? I fear that not many of us as fathers deserve to have said of us what God said of Abraham as father in Genesis 18:19.

Abraham thus furnishes an excellent model for Christian fathers and his pattern of child-rearing must be duplicated in all homes today. Abraham proved that God's confidence in his ability as a father was not misplaced. Isaac's peaceful and patient pilgrimage which stretched across 180 years is a moving tribute to the faithful training he received at the feet of father Abraham. Children in Abraham's day were trained to be what they were then exactly as children are trained to be what they are now. If Abraham had failed as a father, it is doubtful he would have ever acquired the designation "father of the faithful." Failure in fatherhood would have kept the designation "the God of Abraham, Isaac, and Jacob" from ever becoming a meaningful expression. The placement of Isaac and Jacob in this expressive term demanded that Abraham teach his first and second generations about Jehovah. Isaac had his illustrious father for seventy-five years. Jacob was fifteen when his famous grandfather died. These must have been rich and rewarding years indeed for Isaac and Jacob as they enjoyed firsthand the beautiful fruits of Abraham's faithfulness. Before Abraham entered the coveted circle of fatherhood he was first a man of God, a person of unparalleled faith for his generation, and one who had a hold upon Jehovah God few men have ever experienced. These excellent background ingredients enabled him to transmit his fervent faith, uncommon goodness, and abiding loyalty to his son of promise and to an uncounted multitude who affectionately refer to him as "father Abraham." Fathers today who have a strong hold upon God can be much more successful in helping their children clasp the hand of deity. When we have more modern day Abrahams to head Christian homes we will have more children rising up to "keep the way of the Lord, to do justice and judgment" (Gen. 18:19).

We need fathers today who will emulate the just Joshua. The name of this man is usually held to be synonymous with military genius. Under God's directions he led the people across the swollen Jordan on dry ground and conquered the strongholds of the heathen nations that controlled Western Palestine. Mention of his name usually arouses the mental image of a faithful spy, a successful general, or the man who prompted God to lengthen a day so a decisive battle could be won for the Israelite army. Near the end of the book that bears his name we see his portrait as a father.

These words of Joshua should penetrate deeply into every father's heart today. "And if it seem evil unto you to serve the Lord, choose you this day whom ye will serve; whether the gods which your fathers served that were on the other side of the flood, or the gods of the Amorites, in whose land ye dwell: but as for me and my house, we will serve the Lord" (Josh. 24:15). The Israelite leader thus placed a challenging choice before his hearers. He recognized that service to God begins with a voluntary decision. He would not force them into a godly framework of spiritual service. The choice had to be theirs. No matter what course their consciences might dictate, the aged leader spoke nobly for himself and the members of his household: My family and I will stand on Jehovah's side; we will be His people. Joshua's courageous report as one of the two faithful spies, his leadership in conquering Western Palestine, his command for the sun to stand still, and his wise parceling of the land to the remaining nine and one-half tribes stand as no greater tribute to his character as a man than does the royal resolution of Joshua 24:15. His dynamic determination to have a God-serving family is most inspiring. If every Jewish father had been of like mind, the history of the Jewish people would have been written with a far different stroke of the inspired pen than what we find in the six books of I and II Samuel, I and II Kings and I and II Chronicles. Instead of the Book of Judges containing the "Dark Ages of Hebrew History," as it certainly does, that book could have been called the "Golden Days of Hebrew History."

If every father who reads these lines would determine to serve faithfully and loyally the God of heaven and strive to lead his family into like attitudes and practices, the current direction of most families on earth would be drastically altered. As a father what decision have you made to serve Him? Have you determined to rear your family for His service or have you decided to be a completely passive parent in the important realm of spiritual leadership? Can you live with an easy conscience as a father if you deliberately allow your children's future to be shaped by any of the prevailing winds that might be blowing at the time? Joshua's God is still in heaven. He awaits your decision as a father. Failure to line up by the side of faithful Joshua in a similar choice will mean the left hand in judgment for you and may mean the same side for your children unless someone else influences them for the right. We need more fathers of the caliber of just Joshua. The *Christ in the home* concept leads to this noble type of fatherhood.

The far-reaching influence of a good father's teaching and example is vividly portrayed in Jeremiah 35. Pots full of wine and cups were set before the Rechabites with the command extended, "Drink ye wine." Can you imagine with what rapidity this invitation would obtain hearty compliance and instant obedience among the millions of liquor-loving fathers today? Multitudes drink today with or without invitations extended to do so. Ponder well the reaction of the ancient Rechabites, "We will drink no wine: for Jonadab the son of Rechab our father commanded us, saying, Ye shall drink no wine, neither ye nor your sons for ever . . . Thus have we obeyed the voice of Jonadab the son of Rechab our father in all that he hath charged us, to drink no wine all our days, we, our wives, our sons, nor our daughters . . . But we have dwelt in tents, and have obeyed, and done according to all that Jonadab our father commanded us" (Jer. 35:6, 8, 10). This obedient spirit among the Rechabites prompts God's full commendation of their action. This worthy example furnishes an opportunity to contrast the Rechabite spirit of reverence for their ancestor's wishes with that spirit of irreverence and disrespect so consistently characteristic of the Jews toward their heavenly Father's rules and regulations (Jer. 35:12-15). The chapter contains the promise that the obedient Rechabites would continue to exist (Jer. 35:19). It would be a mistake to conclude that Jonadab was an immediate ancestor of these temperate Rechabites. Jonadab is mentioned as being contemporary with Jehu, 884 B.C. (II Kings 10:15-23). The probable date for the events of Jeremiah is 591 B.C., or nearly three centuries later. Jonadab could not have known just how far-reaching would be his temperate teachings. His future descendants still remembered and revered his temperate request three centuries later. Temperate fathers themselves who thoroughly inculcate habits of total abstinence toward all alcoholic beverages among their children could well be establishing a course of conduct that will provide guidelines for generations yet unborn.

God Almighty never intended for the words *drinking* and *father* to be linked. When drawn together they always form an unholy alliance. When joined, as is frequently the case, the father's influence vanishes. Many times strong drink will make an unpredictable monster of a man. The wife knows a frightening fear and the children cringe in horror when Daddy comes home with unsteady step and that foul odor on his breath. As a thoughtful father you owe your children a life built upon sobriety and a set of teachings that will guard them against the perilous pitfalls of damnable drink. In formulating the various ingredients composing noble fatherhood let us remember the splendid examples established by Joshua and Jonadab. These men had far more in common than the mere fact that their names both began with a *J*. They thought, planned, and counseled for the best interests of their families. Have you been that mindful of your family's future? We need more fathers who will make great choices for their families. *Christ in the home* is the only concept guaranteeing such choices and a diligent practice of the same.

We need fathers who will emulate Zacharias, the father of John. Luke, the only evangelist who acquaints us with John's parents, wrote that Zacharias was a priest who along with his devout wife "were both righteous before God, walking in all the commandments and ordinances of the Lord blameless" (Luke 1:5-6). These high commendations could be laid at the feet of Zacharias before he became a father. Godly preparation for fatherhood is imperative. Children with righteous parentage have a rich heritage that defies appraisal. Men need to excel in the keeping of Biblical commandments if they would succeed as fathers. Men who lack righteousness may become parents in a biological sense but will never become parents in the spiritually acceptable sense. Jehovah chose a righteous father for John. Is this not His divine wish for your children? As the father of your children you are the only one on earth who can give them the blessing a righteous daddy. Is that what you are striving to be? Destinies of an eternal nature heavily weigh upon your attitude. Among fathers the tribe of righteous Zacharias needs a healthy increase. *Christ in the home* can make it so.

Joseph is another worthy example of fatherhood. This descendant of Judah and David had absolutely nothing whatsoever to do with the conception of the holy child Jesus, Mary's firstborn. In full harmony with prophetic utterances along this line the power of the highest overshadowed the young Galilean virgin who lived in Nazareth and permitted her to conceive and bring forth the Christ child into the world. Though Joseph was not the fleshly father of Jesus, he being strictly of the woman's seed (Gen. 3:15), nevertheless Jesus would grow to maturity in the home headed by Joseph. Joseph would be his foster father. What sort of man did the Almighty select to be head of the home where His only begotten Son would be a babe, a boy, and ultimately a young man? Matthew portrayed Joseph as a "just man" and one who had a deep sense of mercy and compassion (Matt. 1:19). When Joseph had serious misgivings about the propriety of completing his plans to marry his chosen, the angel's appearance dissolved all of his puzzling queries and Joseph acted in harmony with the angelic instructions. When the Babe of Bethlehem was in danger of Herod's cruel decree,

Joseph obediently followed heavenly revealed orders for a quick departure to Egyptian safety. He is just as quick to return in obedience to the angel's request when the danger period is past. Total obedience to heavenly commandments is a golden thread interestingly interwoven into every portrayal given of Joseph. He was also mindful of worshipful duties to Jehovah God. The beloved physician pictures the annual custom prevalent in Jesus' home of his parents going to Jerusalem for the Passover observance (Luke 2:41). Good Hebrew fathers such as Joseph did not stay home in religious indolence and allow the mothers of their children to do all the synagogue-attending on the Sabbath or the temple-appearing during the prescribed feasts each year. They took the lead in these matters. Jehovah chose a just man, an obedient servant, and a person of faithful and loyal worship habits to head the home in which His Son sojourned for some thirty years. Is this the kind of headship manifested in your home? Do your children have a father who is just, obedient to heavenly instructions, and a devout worshiper of the great *I AM?* Jehovah expected such service from Joseph. Will He be pleased with a fatherly service less than this from us? Just fathers, obedient fathers, and fathers who faithfully and lovingly worship God are the crying needs of today's youth in the home. *Christ in the home* provides this type of fine fatherhood.

We need men today who will attempt to fill the role of fatherhood as Thomas and Alexander Campbell respectively did to their children. Alexander Campbell wrote a book on the life of his illustrious father, Thomas Campbell. In the preface he paid high tribute to the great influence his father had had on his own life and on the lives of others. He wrote, "Such were the teachings which I received in my early life from the subject of the following memoirs; and whatever good, little or much, I may have achieved under God, I owe it all, and those benefited by it owe it all, to his paternal care and instruction, and especially to his example." The accomplishments of Alexander Campbell in behalf of restoring New Testament Christianity were many and varied for the first two-thirds of the nineteenth century. These were made possible because a faithful father and godly mother pointed his brilliant mind and indomitable energies toward the cause of Christ. In turn Alexander sought to be that kind of father toward his own children. Fourteen children were born to Campbell by Margaret Campbell, his first wife, and Selina Campbell, his second wife. These children were precious to this well-known preacher. He made ample provisions not only for their education but the education also of many other young people through the establishment of Buffalo Academy and later

Bethany College. Campbell never lost sight of the important need to educate a child's spirit. He was one of the busiest men of the nineteenth century. He was a preacher of the first rank, a writer, an author of remarkable ability, a champion debater on the polemic platform, a noted lecturer, and a highly successful farmer on the rolling hills of what is now the panhandle section of West Virginia. Campbell did not forget his duties as the spiritual head of a growing family. Campbell did not become so busy that he ignored the spiritual needs of his children. Neither should we. We need more fathers of that courageous caliber manifested by Thomas and Alexander Campbell of early Restoration fame. *Christ in the home* can motivate fathers toward all these glorious examples of worthy fatherhood which have been enumerated.

Men need to lift up the Bible in their homes. They need to extol Christ in their daily lives. They need to exalt Him as God's Son, their Saviour, and the potential Redeemer of all their children. When Christ and the Bible are lifted up within the home, God's Son and His holy word will lift up fatherhood to the royal role it should consistently assume.

QUESTIONS FOR DISCUSSION

1. Why, do you suppose, is there so much antagonism today toward anything that is negative in its approach? Is it safe to ignore God's negative warnings? Why, or why not?
2. Which Bible father pitched his tent toward Sodom? What influence did this choice have on his family? Discuss in detail. How does this same principle work in families today?
3. Discuss Eli and the sin of parental permissiveness. Discuss the permissiveness of many modern homes.
4. Of which sin was Achan guilty? Why do we not need his kind of example in the ranks of fathers today?
5. Tell what kind of father Jeroboam was to Nadab. How did his actions as the first king of the Northern Kingdom influence each of his eighteen successors?
6. Discuss the fathers in Nehemiah's day who reared children to speak Ashdodic language.
7. Discuss why we do not need fathers who curse, despise Christ and Christianity, drink, smoke, curse, and practice immorality. Can fathers participate in these evils without influencing their children? Tell why you answer as you do.
8. What kind of father was Enoch before his children?
9. Describe the fatherhood of Noah to his three sons.

10. Fully discuss Abraham as father. Memorize Genesis 18:19.
11. What great stand did just Joshua make in behalf of his family in Joshua 24:15? Why does this need strong duplication by modern men who head households?
12. Connect Jonadab, temperance, and the Rechabites.
13. Discuss Zacharias as father to John.
14. What type of father was Joseph?
15. Discuss Thomas and Alexander Campbell in their respective roles of fatherhood.

11

The Mother in the Home

An excellent gospel preacher once presented a sermon in which he paid deep respect to the wonderful mother and father who had reared him in the faith that is most holy. The preacher humbly recognized that his work was possible because of the two main factors: the goodness of God and the training he received from dedicated and God-fearing parents. In this chapter we shall examine the roles and responsibilities of the mother in the home.

SOME PROVOKING QUESTIONS

Are you a woman who has simply aided in the biological production of a child but has never taken seriously the God-given responsibilities that attend the total rearing of that little baby boy or darling daughter? Are you the kind of mother your children need? If you had a godly mother during your youth, are you striving to give your children the same treasured blessing? If you did not have a Christian mother during youth, are you seeking to bequeath a heritage to your children that was denied you? Can your children with youthful pride point you out as their lovely mother? Do they find the home over which you reign a haven of pleasure, a place of love, a security from an unkind world, and a place where the lessons of this present life and those for the great life beyond are devoutly taught and practiced? Is home a place where they can bring their friends and know that a welcome will be extended to

them? Do you radiate Christ in your daily behavior? Do your children hear you pray and read the Lord's Word? When it is time for
a church service what do they see you doing? Is the whole family
consistently present at worship services? Or is there the consistent
practice of ignoring these worship periods? Is there kindness upon
your lips, firmness in your parental requests for their behavior, and
a determination to do the right thing for both yourself and for
them? Do you follow John Dewey and his philosophy of permissiveness in parental practices or Jesus Christ and His recommendation
of strong and sturdy discipline in the rearing of your children?
When your children leave home and form marriages of their own
will they take with them correct concepts of motherhood which
have been formed by your valiant efforts to be the type of mother
God wanted you to be? In the course of normal circumstances
you will more than likely precede your children in meeting death.
What memories will flood the minds of your children when they
stand beside the open casket and observe your silent lips and cold
brow? Can they truthfully feel that you have been a good Christian
wife to their father and a devoted Christian mother to them?
Will the memory linger the rest of their life, "I had the finest
Christian mother in all the world"? Will they thank God that He
allowed you to be their mother? Or will severe truth constrain
them to say, while witnessing your lifeless form, "We loved our
mother but she was not a good wife to our daddy nor ever a
Christian mother to us. We never heard her pray. We never saw
the Bible in her hands. We never went to church as a family unit.
If we went at all, it was always Daddy, never Mother, that took us.
We never were encouraged by her to love God, revere Christ, and
be Christians. We loved her but if only she had been a godly
mother, how happy we would have been and how consoled our
hearts would now be." What memories will your children have of
you as their mother? What you are doing now as mother will form
the very material from which will come those later memories for
your children, memories that will be either pleasant or painful for
them.

PRELIMINARY CONSIDERATIONS

God's Book is replete with references to the far-reaching influences a mother has upon her precious offspring. Common experience also bears strong testimony to the truthfulness of the above
affirmation. Jehovah has decreed that the mother shall have a
primary influence in the molding of the child during its most forma-

tive period. Its mind is most pliable during this time of heavy motherly influence. The spirit of the child is most impressionable in this period. Accurate appraisals and correct concepts of a mother's power and influence are reflected in the following proverbs. "The hand that rocks the cradle rules the world." "An ounce of mother is worth a pound of clergy." Many years spent in the gospel ministry have convinced me that a devout mother can do far more with her preschool child in the way of spiritual training than any preacher can with a hardened teen-ager whose past has been totally void of spiritual influences.

Mother love is a synonym for deep, sacrificial affection which knows neither death nor limitations. With undying loyalty mother love has followed a wayward daughter into the mire of degradation and a son to the utter loneliness of a prison cell. Disobedience and rebellion from the young child and baseless ingratitude from a grown child may break a mother's heart but cannot crush her love for her child. A mother's love and a proper sense of child direction can inspire a son or daughter to fill a place of usefulness in God's cause and human society. Tremendous power resides in godly motherhood. Motherhood, to a large degree, holds the key for a better tomorrow. The church and society stand to be noticeably improved when motherhood functions properly in its God-ordained spheres.

MARRIAGE FIRST — MOTHERHOOD NEXT

Courtship, marriage, the physical relationship, and parenthood should be kept in that exact order. A reversal of this sane and sensible system is responsible for many of the mismated and poorly formed marriages hastily entered and speedily ended today. God intends for a young woman to be the wife of a man before the two of them engage in the physical act that can produce a child. "Marriage is honourable in all, and the bed undefiled: but whoremongers and adulterers God will judge" (Heb. 13:4). Paul wrote, "I will therefore that the younger women marry, bear children, guide the house, give none occasion to the adversary to speak reproachfully" (I Tim. 5:14). The Bible has always decreed that marriage is to precede the conception and birth of children. However, in the highly permissive age in which we live, boys and girls frequently turn the dating game into a situation where they live together as though they were husband and wife. They have reversed God's order. With hundreds of thousands annually the order is the physical relationship, conception of a child out of wedlock, and perhaps a hastily planned and rapidly executed marriage. No wonder such marriages frequently end before the child's first birthday is observed. The new morality is having quite a heyday among its promiscuous and permissive participants. Worshipers of the flesh have swallowed the situation ethics system hook, line, and sinker! However, this infamous and satanically contrived system will reap a harvest of miserable problems. A young woman who allows her body to be exploited by some eager young man is asking for more trouble than she ever dreamed was possible for one person to face. First Timothy 5:14 needs to be followed in our highly permissive, sex-charged generation. When the *Christ in the home* concept prevails courtship, marriage, the physical relationship, and the conception of children will be kept in their proper order.

FAITHFULNESS AS A WIFE:
A PREREQUISITE FOR MOTHERHOOD

Many people seem to think that parenthood can be separated from marriage. I believe God has joined the two together. Though there may be marriages with no subsequent parenthood for reasons beyond the couple's control, there should be no parenthood without marriage. The idea appears to be widespread in many circles today that a woman can be a good mother to her children while she is a faithless companion to the father of those children. You no doubt have heard it expressed like this, "She runs out on her husband, consorts with other men, and likes the gay times but she is a good mother to her children." I emphatically deny that the same person can be a faithless wife who promiscuously participates in immoral escapades and also be a good mother to her children. The two concepts are totally incompatible. The children will not be deceived long. Sin has a way of finding people out (Num. 32:23). Perhaps no sin is more difficult to conceal than adultery. It is doubtful that a child ever has a more traumatic experience than discovering that his mother confers her love on a man who is not her husband and not the child's father. There is more than one way for a child to lose a parent. This is one of the most grievous ways.

How can a woman function successfully in the role of marvelous motherhood if she is pursuing the way of a wicked and wanton wife? How can a woman be the kind of mother her children need if she ignores the following directives from Holy Writ? The wife is to be a "help meet" to her husband (Gen. 2:18). Can she be a true "help meet" and dispense freely her bodily charms to other men? She is to be a good discovery for her husband and the one who will aid him in obtaining heavenly favor (Prov. 18:22). Can she do this and be faithless as a wife? She is to be a prudent wife and her origin is from the Lord (Prov. 19:14). Will prudence allow for faithlessness in the role of marriage? She is to be the kind of wife whose "price is far above rubies. The heart of her husband doth safely trust in her, so that he shall have no need of spoil. She will do him good and not evil all the days of her life" (Prov. 31:10-12). Can she ignore this model and be what she should be as a wife? If she is not what she should be as a wife, how can she be what she should be as a mother? She is to be submissive to her husband (Eph. 5:22, 24). She is not to submit to the carnal desires of other men. Disobedience in this realm robs a woman of success in motherhood. She is to reverence or respect her husband (Eph. 5:33). This passage cannot be obeyed in the framework of adulterous affairs. She is to love her husband, her children, be discreet, chaste, a keeper or worker at home, good, obedient to her husband, and seek to keep God's word from being blasphemed (Titus 2:4-5). Can she be a good wife and mother combination and fail in these worthy endeavors? How can a woman love her husband and be untrue to him? How can she love her children and consort carnally with other men who display a fleshly interest in her? The truth of the matter is that she cannot. A worthless wife and a marvelous mother do not come wrapped up in the same human personality. A mother cannot be what she ought to be if she mistreats her husband, the father of her children. Fidelity to her husband is an imperative to every woman who desires to be successful in motherhood. *Christ in the home* remains the all-pervading solution to the challenge of being a faithful wife and a godly mother.

THE UNIQUE ROLE OF MOTHERHOOD

Jehovah has chosen the wife of the home as the instrument through whom a new soul enters the world. Wrapped up in those few pounds of new flesh is an immortal spirit that will live forever. If this child lives, he will in a few years take his place as a responsible individual in society. Will the world be better or worse because this child passes through? This child has both an earthly and eternal role to fill. He will need care to become strong physically. He needs training and discipline to help him ultimately to master a trade or profession. He will need education to help him to learn how to live happily in a world inhabited by more people than any previous generation has known. Correct training can develop the mental powers that a wise God has entrusted to him. The prudent mother will not only recognize her child's needs for preparation for living out his seventy-year-span upon this terrestrial globe but also she will earnestly and tirelessly direct him toward an inheritance in the celestial mansions made ready by a righteous Redeemer. Habits and the direction of a person's existence are formed during the first few years of a child's life. Normally these years are spent with his mother. The production of a better individual for society and a prospective heir of heaven has a direct connection to the mother's success or failure during these tremendously important formative years. How fearful is the task placed on the mother of children. Truly it is a unique role. Woman has no greater challenge than meeting responsibly the queenly role she has as wife and mother in the home. By patiently pursuing the *Christ in the home* philosophy she can experience satisfying success in this sphere.

MOTHERS: TRAINERS OF SOULS

The little boy or girl who follows mother's every footstep, tugs at her apron strings begging for parental attention to a passing interest, and breathes a steady stream of questions will very soon be a teenager. Jehovah will then hold that youthful person responsible for his or her deeds. Perhaps that boy will one day confess his faith in a risen Redeemer and come into covenant relationship with the Godhead because a mother was not too busy to point his impressionable mind toward Jesus. She may live to see him become a mature, dedicated, and dynamic servant of Jehovah God. How rich and rewarding it will be to know then that her training of his soul was so wonderfully worthwhile and is now bearing precious fruit. What joy it will be for her to stand approved in judgment and to observe him also on Jesus' right hand. The fruits of her labor will have reached a mighty climax at that point of time. Perhaps that little girl who today lovingly embraces her dolls and plays house in a miniature world of her own will one day purify her heart by faith, change her mind toward sin by repentance, sweeten her lips with the good confession, and change her relationship toward Christ because of her mother's tireless teaching. How rewarding it will be for a mother to see her daughter fill a similar role as worthy wife, marvelous mother, and consecrated Christian. For both mother and daughter to be heirs of the heavenly world is surely one of the supreme rewards of pursuing successful motherhood. Mothers, Jesus has committed a sacred trust into your hands. These little children have souls. Those souls need truth. Be diligent and faithful in training their souls for service here and their spirits for the heavenly hereafter. Failure here is filled with tragic consequences. *Christ in the home* is your greatest safeguard against failure.

CHANGING CONCEPTS OF MOTHERHOOD

Paul establishes the Biblical concept of motherhood in a number of plain passages. "That they may teach the young women to be sober, to love their husbands, to love their children, To be discreet, chaste, keepers at home, good, obedient to their own husbands, that the word of God be not blasphemed" (Titus 2:4-5). "I will therefore that the younger women marry, bear children, guide the house, give none occasion to the adversary to speak reproachfully" (I Tim. 5:14). "When I call to remembrance the unfeigned faith that is in thee, which dwelt first in thy grandmother Lois, and thy mother Eunice; and I am persuaded that in thee also" (II Tim. 1:5). "But continue thou in the things which thou has learned and hast been assured of, knowing of whom thou has learned them; And that from a child [babe- ASV] thou hast known the holy scriptures, which are able to make thee wise unto salvation through faith which is in Christ Jesus" (II Tim. 3:14-15). These and kindred passages portray the mother as a faithful wife, one who loves her children, displays a proper example before them, is respectful of the authority over her, exercises a queenly guidance over her children, and is a keeper or worker in the home. A good mother in Bible times believed that the teaching of God's word to her children was one of the supreme tasks of motherhood. She valued an unfeigned faith and sought to bequeath such to her impressionable offspring. Mothers in Bible times recognized that spiritual elements constituted the foundation of marriage and the rearing of children. It is shocking and sad that multitudes of mothers today haven't the faintest awareness of these important concepts.

The twentieth-century concept of motherhood calls for her part in the biological production but turns the rearing of the child over to another. I recognize that in some cases unusual circumstances demand that mothers work outside the home. I have nothing but admiration for these mothers for their lot is frequently hard with but little time for rest and relaxation. It is difficult to be the chief or only breadwinner and also be what the children need in a mother. However, there are many women who leave the home by day to engage in work and then fill their nights with a heavy schedule of entertainment and social activities. They choose to work and the

choice may be made over the protest of husbands who make com·
fortable livings. Mothers who are never home in daytime and
seldom home during the evening become strangers to their own
children.

The American way of life with its love for luxury calls for a
hefty regular income that may greatly exceed what one person may
ordinarily command in the way of wages or a salary. Hence in over
half of the homes of our nation the wife and mother has joined
the husband as a co-breadwinner. Nothing yet appears on the
horizon which promises any reversal of this expanding tendency.
In fact, everything seems to confirm the theory that the practice
will not only continue but will also increase. With both parents
gone children are frequently left to shift for themselves. Some
parents do make excellent provision for their children under such
circumstances. Others allow their children to see to their own needs
with little adult supervision. That arrangement is far from satisfactory. In the process seeds for future trouble are sown. No doubt
many boys and girls would have been kept out of an early life of
juvenile deliquency had they had a mother to supervise them instead of an hireling that served for the dollar and was quite careless about the child's real welfare. It is the unusual hired housekeeper who is as interested in the children as the mother who
brought them into the world. I believe that no one under heaven
will offer the same loyal and unselfish service toward my children
as the mother whose journey into the valley of the shadow of death
brought them into the world and upon whose heart their earthly
and eternal destinies lie so heavily.

Some concepts do not need changing. Being a mother in the
Biblical sense of the word is one of these. The *Christ in the home*
philosophy can help elevate motherhood to its intended glorious
position.

"GUIDE THE HOUSE," "KEEPER AT HOME"

She who would fill God's divinely prescribed role of great motherhood must be a willing worker in the sphere which God has outlined. In writing to Timothy, Paul urged "that the younger women
marry, bear children, *guide the house,* give none occasion to the
adversary to speak reproachfully" (I Tim. 5:14, emphasis added).
The divine order, as set forth here, should strike us significantly.
God's order is marriage first, bearing of children next, and ultimately
the successful guidance of the home in such fashion as to avoid
possible word of censure from hostile adversaries. Many modern

mothers may lodge no complaint against the injunctions of marriage and bearing of children. It is in the realm of guiding the house that many of them balk. This wise counsel from Paul is ignored and forgotten. Through Titus Paul challenged the older women to assume the sacred task of teaching young women "To be discreet, chaste, *keepers at home,* good, obedient to their own husbands, that the word of God be not blasphemed" (Titus 2:5, emphasis added). This apostolic prescription plainly gives God's guaranteed formula for successful motherhood. It has not been tried and found wanting; it just has not been tried at all by millions of today's mothers. When young women practice the very opposite of this passage by being indiscreet, unchaste, strangers to home life, and disobedient to their husbands, the seeds of bankrupt womanhood will produce the fully grown plants of meaningless wifehood and corrupt motherhood.

Mothers should major (not minor) in maintaining a home that radiates an atmosphere of spiritual activity, reflects purity and peace, and is a haven of holiness, a scene of serenity, and a school where all are taught to seek salvation. *Christ in the home* can make all this possible.

CHRISTIAN MOTHERHOOD

These two words have a natural affinity for each other. They have been approvingly linked from the beginning of the Christian movement. How tragic though when motherhood has to be termed *non-Christian.* I shudder to think of a non-Christian mother rearing children. Real mothers by all means must be zealous and dedicated Christians. That is not optional if they wish to do right with their offspring. Women should be Christians first of all due to their own great need for salvation. They should be Christians in the second place in order that they may be Christian mothers to their little boys and girls.

In the next full century a woman's descendants may be numbered in the scores or even the hundreds. Within five centuries the number may climb to the thousands or even hundreds of thousands. Look at the multitude of Israelites that came from Leah, Rachel, Bilhah, and Zilpah in the short centuries between Jacob and Moses. Whether or not a woman is a loyal child of God may determine the eternal destinies not only of her immediate offspring but may also strongly touch generations yet unborn. How can a young mother who has never confessed Christ be effective in pointing a young child's mind to Jesus? Can the non-Christian mother successfully instill Christian truths in her children when she has never been a Christian herself? A Christless mother cannot impart Christ to her children. Every child deserves a Christian mother. As the mother of your children you are the only person who can bequeath to them the precious heritage of Christian motherhood. If death were to cross your unsuspecting threshold today, would your children have a lingering memory of you as their *Christian* mother? Seeking to separate the word *Christian* from motherhood robs a mother of the most powerful weapon at her command. Let motherhood and Christianity be joined together and children are going to be richly blessed.

Mothers should be acutely aware of their daily habits. The robes of pure and undefiled religion are garments needed by each woman seeking to become the type of mother pleasing to Jehovah God. Our picture of ideal motherhood has no room for a mother who smokes, gambles, drinks, curses, appears in public displaying nearly all her body, is lax in her conduct with members of the opposite sex, and is more interested in climbing the social ladder than advancing up Jacob's ladder toward the heavenly home.

Christ in the home will help each mother to be a shining example to her offspring. Nothing is so powerful in parental influence as an example of sobriety, righteousness, and godliness. When mothers lift up Christ and the Bible in the home, Christ and His Holy Book will lift up motherhood in the home.

QUESTIONS FOR DISCUSSION

1. List and discuss the questions with which this chapter was begun.
2. Why does motherhood have such a far-reaching influence?
3. Discuss mother love and the sacrifices it will gladly make in behalf of children.
4. Discuss how motherhood holds the key for a better tomorrow for both the church and human society.
5. Why should marriage always precede expectant motherhood and the birth of a child? What happens when sin reverses this wise procedure?
6. What evil contribution has the new morality provided toward reversing God's order as stated in the previous question? Can the new morality adequately solve the problems it creates by its permissiveness? Why, or why not?
7. Why is faithfulness to the marriage vow a prerequisite for real

motherhood? What happens to a child when the discovery is made that his mother is an immoral woman?

8. Discuss the unique role of motherhood.
9. Describe mothers as trainers of souls.
10. Discuss some of the Biblical concepts of motherhood.
11. Describe the concepts of motherhood largely in vogue today. What consequences are we reaping from these drastic changes?
12. Discuss the woman as guide of the house and keeper at home.
13. Why should there be such a close affinity between the words *Christian* and *motherhood?* What happens when they are disconnected?

12

Portraits of Bible Mothers

As we have done in the case of husbands, wives, and fathers we wish to paint some portraits of Bible mothers. We shall note first the kind of mothers we do not need and then take a look at the kind we do need.

THE KIND OF MOTHERS NOT NEEDED

This aspect of our topic perhaps could best be introduced by the two following examples. Both stories tell of mothers who neglected their role. A small boy once sat by himself in a church building as the worship service began. Though there were others nearby the two most important people in his world, father and mother, were nowhere to be seen. His feeling of loneliness and insecurity could no longer be concealed. He burst into tears. There was no father or mother to comfort him for this child had been *sent* to church. The non-Christian father cared nothing about the boy's soul. The mother, though a professing Christian, was not a faithful member of the Lord's body. Most any excuse was sufficient to keep her away. The little fellow had never known what it was like to attend church as a family unit. When he went to church, he was sent there and many times it was without mother. How tragic!

Another child was once asked why he never attended Midweek Bible Study. The preschooler responded by saying, "Mother will not take me." Mothers, could this have been your child? Looking at the Wednesday night attendance figures of most congregations reveals that the number of little boys and girls who could say the same thing would be legion.

Such attitudes as the foregoing are sure invitations for spiritual trouble ahead. A ten- or twenty-year projection might well find both mothers wondering why their children did not grow up to be responsible Christians. It will not require a brilliant mind to supply them with the obvious answer. We do not need mothers who will be so derelict in their duties as to be obstacles in the pathway of their children's church-going habits. As a mother, does either of the foregoing stories apply to you? If so, are you making any attempts to correct the situation?

We do not need the type of motherhood such as is displayed in Jezebel. She is first mentioned in I Kings 16:31: "And it came to pass, as if it had been a light thing for him to walk in the sins of Jeroboam the son of Nebat, that he took to wife Jezebel the daughter of Ethbaal king of the Zidonians, and went and served Baal, and worshipped him." In her new role Jezebel was the epitome of feminine wickedness. It is doubtful if any daughter of Eve ever surpassed her unbending iniquity, total lack of conscience, and extreme cruelty to any person who crossed her. Her nearest competitor was her own daughter, Athaliah. Ezekiel, the great prophet of the Babylonian Exile, wrote centuries later a principle that fully applied to Jezebel and Athaliah. He said, "Behold, every one that useth proverbs shall use this proverb against thee, saying, As is the mother, so is her daughter" (Ezek. 16:44). Jezebel was a passionate promoter of Baalism, an open foe of Jehovah God, a hater of His holy law, a slayer of prophets, and a malicious murderer of good men such as Naboth. Such was the ink which painted the portrait of Athaliah's mother. As Princess Athaliah grew up she watched a mother in action who majored in mischief, wallowed in wantonness, and served sin with total abandonment and unabated energy. If Athaliah ever saw Jezebel perform that first noble deed, the Bible is totally silent in recording the deed. Her life was apparently as void of good as that of any person who ever lived on God's green footstool. Idolatry, iniquity, and indiscretion were the three big I's in Jezebel's life. From the information given there are some things that Athaliah surely never saw or heard her mother do and say. It is highly unlikely that she ever heard Jezebel pray to Jehovah God. It is highly unlikely she ever heard her mother praise Him in song. We seriously doubt that she ever witnessed her mother reading from the law of Moses or telling the wonderful stories of Enoch, Noah, Abraham, Isaac,

Joseph, Moses, Joshua, Samuel, David, and other great heroes of the Hebrew faith. Athaliah never heard her infamous mother speak a good word about the colorful Tishbite Elijah. Goodness, God, and generosity would have been foreign words upon the unholy lips of Jezebel. Trust and appreciation for the development of the Abrahamic promises meant nothing to Jezebel. For them she had nothing but total contempt. Had it been within her power she would have forever thwarted them. If she had had her way, these ancient promises would have been thwarted. Such is the kind of mother who bore and reared Athaliah. We are not shocked therefore to read of the kind of woman Athaliah became. She ultimately married Joram, the son of the good king, Jehoshaphat. Joram ruled eight years in Judah and his reign was extremely wicked. Part of his wickedness was attributed to the influence of Athaliah. "And he [Joram] walked in the way of the kings of Israel, as did the house of Ahab: for the daughter of Ahab was his wife: and he did evil in the sight of the Lord" (II Kings 8:18). Jezebel and Athaliah formed an unholy team. No more infamous mother-and-daughter team ever disgraced the human family. Satan possessed the hearts of them both and they aided his cause with fervency and ardor. We do not need mothers of this kind today.

We do not need mothers such as Athaliah became to her off-spring. When her husband, Joram, died son Ahaziah became king. With a wicked parental background we are not surprised to read of his extremely wicked reign. The Bible says that in the twelfth year of Joram Ahaziah began to reign (II Kings 8:25). "Two and twenty years old was Ahaziah when he began to reign; and he reigned one year in Jerusalem. And his mother's name was Athaliah, the daughter of Omri king of Israel. And he walked in the way of the house of Ahab, and did evil in the sight of the Lord, as did the house of Ahab: for he was the son in law of the house of Ahab" (II Kings 8:26-27). One of the most pathetic of all statements relative to his mother is found in II Chronicles 22:2-3. ". . . and he reigned one year in Jerusalem. His mother's name also was Athaliah the daughter of Omri. He also walked in the ways of the house of Ahab: *for his mother was his counsellor to do wickedly*" (emphasis added). What a terrible tragedy when motherhood degenerates into the role of counseling sin, treachery, and transgression. The men of any generation have enough temptations to commit wrongdoing without their own mothers encouraging hearty participation therein. We do not need mothers who will encourage their sons to do wickedly. The curses of an aroused heaven will forever rest upon such mothers. But the end of Athaliah's terrible life is not yet fully told. She not only outlived Joram, her husband, but also Ahaziah, her ruling son on the throne of Judah. When Ahaziah died Athaliah usurped the throne. Neither by legal nor blood right was she in line for this post of rulership. In her enraged craze for the powerful throne of Judah she sought to destroy all the royal seed. She killed even her own grandchildren. This must rank as one of the most despicable crimes of antiquity. If she had succeeded in her plans, she would have cut off the Abrahamic promise some nine centuries before its ultimate fulfillment. One of the grandchildren whom she sought to slay was a genealogical link in Abraham's and David's family line from whom the Messiah was to be born. God spared the child Joash who was a necessary link in the developing chain of the Abrahamic promise. Jezebel and Athaliah were fit neither for wives nor mothers. Their extreme cruelty and infamous wickedness touched the lives of many people. A wicked wife and malicious mother may carry husband, children, and a host of others to the fiery pits of a devil's hell. We do not need mothers like Athaliah's.

We do not need mothers such as Herodias was to Salome. Several centuries separate Herodias from Jezebel and Athaliah. However, she came from the same infamous mold as they did. She was their daughter in motive, attitude, and action. The Bible failed to record any good in the lives of either Jezebel and Athaliah. The same is obviously true of Herodias. By birth and two marriages she was part of the wicked and vicious Herodian family. She was the granddaughter of Herod the Great, daughter of Aristobulus, and a niece to both Philip and Herod Antipas. The latter two were also her husbands. The New Testament account of her takes place after she had left Philip, a private citizen of Rome, and had become adulterously involved with Herod Antipas. Both Herod and Herodias had living companions from whom they had been divorced. It was a clear-cut case of open and flagrant adultery. John the Baptist fearlessly and sternly confronted them with the unlawful nature of their unholy alliance. The message of this courageous proclaimer raised the bitter, unrelenting, and vindictive feelings of Herodias to a fervent pitch. Had it been possible she would have had John killed right on the spot. Unable at the moment to halt his uncompromising tongue, she vowed to silence him at her first opportunity. Herod's birthday observance offered a made-to-order occasion. Many of Herod's highest officials were present. No doubt the wine flowed freely and was consumed in large quantities. Herodias had a daughter who had mastered well the dance steps of the first century. She would be a welcome object for the lustful eyes of drinking men. According to the Jewish historian Josephus her name was Salome. At a moment when the best effects could be produced this dancing daughter pleasingly performed before the king and his unholy companions. The king's heart was lifted high and in an unguarded and irrational moment he foolishly promised the dancing daughter anything, even to the half of his kingdom. Salome, after consultation with her malicious mother, requested the head of John the Baptist on a platter. She apparently made known her desires with no more feeling of remorse than one would display at the swatting of a pesky insect. The king is stung with sorrow but lacks the spine to refuse the evil and unjustified request. Word is sent for the dastardly deed to be performed. An awareness of the heinous act they have just maneuvered is completely lacking in the hearts of both mother and daughter. They have conspired as partners in sin and crime. Together they have committed a most atrocious act.

Some observations of Herodias as a mother are now in order. She was living in adultery. A mother cannot live in an unlawful marriage framework and be a wholesome mother. She cannot be a purifying influence upon her impressionable offspring. It is impossible for a mother who has trampled underfoot God's marriage laws to impress the seriousness of permanent matrimony upon her daughter's heart. Herodias had neither love nor respect for God and His great preacher, John the Baptist. She despised the law that classed her a sinner. She became violently vindictive toward him who so courageously and uncompromisingly told her the truth about her highly public sin. Apparently Salome shared the mother's attitude toward the great forerunner of the Messiah. Mothers who today condemn God's law and despise God's preachers may very well expect a duplication of those attitudes in their children.

Herodias wanted Salome to dance. Salome danced with her mother's full endorsement. This dancing was possibly done in the most immoral of fleshly frameworks. By its very nature this is where dancing finds its greatest success. Satan knows where to peddle his chief wares and this is one of his effective weapons. Dancing is his child and bows meekly to his Satanic devices. Salome learned to dance as a youth. Later her dancing led a king to perform one of his most despicable crimes and caused one of the greatest men of all time to die. Dancing and destruction have far more in common than simply beginning with the same letter of the alphabet. The devil, dancing, and destruction form a trio of d's that has wrought great damage to humanity. Mothers today who encourage their daughters to dance may be paving the way for future destruction. The number of dancing feet on the road to hell is legion. Their number on the heavenly way is none for dancing feet, praying knees, and hearts of holiness are not found linked. Salome had no respect for human life. With no show of human compassion she unfeelingly requested the beheading of John. Jesus said of him, "Verily I say unto you, Among them that are born of women there hath not risen a greater than John the Baptist: notwithstanding he that is least in the kingdom of heaven is greater than he" (Matt. 11:11). From all recorded information Salome was a replica of her infamous mother.

Mothers, your children may one day represent you as Salome did Herodias. Will the examples you give them now and the teaching you are doing today represent you favorably or unfavorably? We do not need mother-daughter combinations like Herodias and Salome. It was because eternal truth was never enshrined in that home that such heinous actions occurred. An Antipas who revered the Almighty, a Herodias who loved holiness, and a Salome who desired the salvation of her youthful soul would have made all the difference in that home. There would have been no wife theft. There would have been no break-up of two homes. There would have been no dancing, no rash vow, and no execution of the courageous John. But alas, God was not directing the acts of Antipas. Holiness was a stranger to Herodias' heart. Salvation was foreign to the expressed wishes of the sensual Salome.

We do not need mothers today who practice idolatry. The mother of King Asa was a practitioner of idolatry. We read: "And Asa did that which was right in the eyes of the Lord, as did David his father. And he took away the sodomites out of the land, and removed all the idols that his fathers had made. And also Maachah his mother, even her he removed from being queen, because she had made an idol in a grove; and Asa destroyed [*cut off,* marginal reference] her idol, and burnt it by the brook Kidron" (I Kings 15:11-13). Asa was strong in his faith and determined in his convictions to serve God. He was courageous enough to resist the idolatry openly embraced and practiced by his mother. A weaker son could have been destroyed by his mother's idol. In this episode the credit goes to the son while the censure properly belongs at mother Maachah's feet. Many women today have their own pet idols. They may be bowing before the goddess of fashion. Possession of a beautiful body may consume their primary interest. Popularity's applause may have bypassed them in their own youth. Now they are determined that their children will not be bypassed. They will seek to woo and win the approval of popularity for their children at any cost to the child's present virtue or future chances of going home to heaven. Many mothers today possess a craze to have a good time. Pleasure is their chief concern. Very easily they can transmit this love of pleasure to their offspring. We do not need mothers who are "lovers of pleasures more than lovers of God" (II Tim. 3:4). It is tragic for children to be reared in a household where any object except God holds first place in parental hearts. Children may do as Asa did and resist the influence. However, many of them will not be modern Asas. They will not take mother's idol and destroy or cut it off as Asa did. When motherhood is allied to idolatry grievous consequences are in the making. We need mothers who will hate and despise every vestige of idolatry.

We do not need mothers who bring their Ashdodic influences to bear upon their offspring. Nehemiah observed just such a condition existing among his generation. "In those days also saw I Jews that had married wives of Ashdod, of Ammon, and of Moab: And their children spake half in the speech of Ashdod, and could not speak in the Jews' language, but according to the language of each people" (Neh. 13:23-24). Children will be influenced by the speech patterns of their mother. The children born to these mixed marriages had Jewish fathers who spoke the language of God's people. But their mothers were heathen. They spoke the language of Ashdod. The influence passed to their children. The children could not speak the pure language of the Jews. Many of their daily expressions were Ashdodic in nature and not Hebrew in origin. Every Christian man who marries a non-Christian wife should expect an exact duplication of this in the future lives of his children. Half of their expressions may be Christian in nature and the other half may be Ashdodic. The very prospect of this should keep Christians from marrying the modern daughters of Ashdod. We do not need mothers such as are pictured in the concluding verses of Nehemiah.

In conclusion, we do not need mothers who curse, lie, cheat, drink, gamble, become addicted to drugs, are unfaithful to their husbands, smoke, or seek to climb the ladder of social success at the expense of keeping the home and working in its confines. *Christ in the home* will not allow the practice of any of these vices.

THE KIND OF MOTHERS WE NEED

We have already looked at some mothers who were and are liabilities to the human race. With refreshing relief we now turn our attention to some great mothers, mothers who proved to be real assets to the cause of God and the ultimate upbuilding of human society. A study of these mothers will provide encouraging sparks to inspire modern women onward and upward in the great and rewarding role of being successful mothers.

Let us first consider the mother of Moses. Two interesting paragraphs open the second chapter of Exodus. "And there went a man of the house of Levi, and took to wife a daughter of Levi. And the woman conceived, and bare a son: and when she saw him that he was a goodly child, she hid him three months. And when she could no longer hide him, she took for him an ark of bulrushes, and daubed it with slime and with pitch, and put the child therein; and she laid it in the flags by the river's brink. And his sister stood afar off, to wit what would be done to him. And the daughter of Pharaoh came down to wash herself at the river; and her maidens walked along by the river's side; and when she saw the ark among the flags, she sent her maid to fetch it. And when she had opened it, she saw the child: and, behold, the babe wept. And she had compassion on him, and said, This is one of the Hebrews' children. Then said his sister to Pharaoh's daughter, Shall I go and call to thee a nurse of the Hebrew women, that she may nurse the child for thee? And Pharaoh's daughter said to her, Go. And the maid went and called the child's mother. And Pharaoh's daughter said unto her, Take this child away, and nurse it for me, and I will give thee wages. And the woman took the child, and nursed it. And the child grew, and she brought him unto Pharaoh's daughter, and he became her son. And she called his name Moses: and she said, Because I drew him out of the water" (Exod. 2:1-10). Additional insight into the character of Moses' parents is offered in Hebrews 11:23, "By faith Moses, when he was born, was hid three months of his parents, because they saw he was a proper child; and they were not afraid of the king's commandment."

Moses was born in the critical period of Hebrew history. The treacherous hand of the powerful Pharaoh was keeping close tabs on the rapidly growing nation of Israelite slaves. To stunt their tremendous multiplication an evil decree had been issued to kill all Hebrew baby boys at birth. Amram and Jochebed, Moses' parents, had too much fear of God in their hearts and too much love for that beautiful baby boy to obey Pharaoh's infamous law of male infanticide. For three months they concealed Moses' birth and presence from the Egyptian authorities. Then other arrangements had to be made. Even young children are familiar with the next events: Moses in the little waterproof ark, Miriam's watchful guardianship over him, and the Egyptian princess' discovery and instant affection for the Hebrew babe. In what seems to be a certain case of God's sure providence, it fell to the lot of Jochebed to nurse and take care of the little baby boy until the time came for him to become the adopted son of Pharaoh's daughter. Only eternity will reveal fully how powerful was the impact of this godly Hebrew mother upon her son in that short period. No doubt the seeds then sown reaped a fruitful harvest when Moses became deliverer, leader, and lawgiver of the downgraded and humiliated Israelites. When we read of Moses pleading before the powerful Pharaoh, leading the people across the Red Sea, receiving the law upon Sinai, bearing patiently the Herculean task of leading a rebellious nation during four decades of wandering in the wilderness, or acting as an intercessor to save the unfaithful Israelites from Jehovah's wrath, let us never forget his mother who gave Moses to the descendants of Jacob and early directed his little feet toward his great destiny in life. We need men such as Moses today. But it will take women of faith to produce and rear them. May the tribe of Jochebed increase.

Let us next consider Hannah, the mother of Samuel. Our first glimpse of her is as a barren wife. Though she has a devoted husband who is exceedingly kind to her, nothing will substitute for her intense desire to become a mother in Israel. The family is assembled at Shiloh, the center of Israelite worship for that generation. From the deep depths of her hungry heart she prays, "O Lord of hosts, if thou wilt indeed look on the affliction of thine handmaid, and remember me, and not forget thine handmaid, but wilt give unto thine handmaid a man child, then I will give him unto the Lord all the days of his life, and there shall no razor come upon his head" (I Sam. 1:11). Eli, the high priest, observes Hannah but mistakes her anguish of soul and manner of prayerful petition for the actions of an intoxicated woman. Hannah offers a satisfactory explanation of her actions to the interested priest. He sends her home with the gratifying assurance that the Lord would grant her request. Several months later Hannah became a mother. She named her boy Samuel because she had "asked him of the Lord" (I Sam. 1:20). The little Hebrew baby must have been a constant source of happiness and radiant rejoicing. Now that she is blessed with that long-desired and anxiously-awaited son would she conveniently forget the vow made in Shiloh? Indeed she would not! She lovingly and loyally cared for him until time for his weaning and then presented him to the Lord. She faithfully fulfilled that vow and lovingly loaned him to Jehovah God all his days. What a wise investment she made in the Lord's cause.

Hannah possessed some prime ingredients necessary for true motherhood. She *wanted* to be a mother. How tragic when a child is born to a reluctant mother. Real motherhood demands far more than simply the biological power to reproduce. Samuel was an answer to devout prayer. Hannah was a woman of *prayer*. Devout prayer and true motherhood have a natural affinity for each other. Mothers who seldom or never pray lose one of the great weapons at their disposal. It is doubtful that the song, "If I Could Hear My Mother Pray Again" was written by the child of a parent who never prayed. Hannah *loaned* her son to the Lord. What a strong contrast to modern mothers who are rearing children without God and Christ. Hannah was paving a right way for little Samuel's feet to tread. From that example he never wavered. The future course of his manhood was decided and determined by a woman who worshiped and a parent who prayed for a son who would be a real man of God. What a man he became! When Samuel finished his earthly pilgrimage he had added a beautiful dimension to the definition of manhood. Hannah's loan of him to God really enabled her to gain him in a higher and nobler sense. There is only one real way to gain permanently a son and that is to loan him to the Lord. When mothers fail to rear sons and daughters in the fear and admonition of the Lord, they are running the sure risk of losing them forever. The word *lose* is used here with eternal consequences in mind. We can only "keep" our children by "giving" them to the Lord.

Samuel became a mighty man that God used to save an entire nation from spiritual apostasy. However, in heaping credit upon Samuel for his heroic accomplishments let us not forget the devout mother who bore him and loaned him to God and the Lord above who graciously permitted Samuel to become this mighty instrument in furthering heaven's cause on earth. The world desperately needs multitudes of modern mothers who will prayerfully rear children for God's glory and humanity's happiness. Our weary and wicked world greatly needs men who possess the sterling stature of a Samuel. The church and the world will have more men like Samuel when we have more Hannahs for mothers. The *Christ in the home* concept can help to multiply these marvelous mothers.

We need mothers today who will earnestly emulate the worthy woman described in Proverbs 31:10-31. This is the finest portrait of womanhood in the annals of sacred and secular literature. As a wife she is faithful and loyal. As guide of the house she is kind, firm, industrious, and fruitful. She loves her family and works diligently for the cultivation of their spiritual and physical profit. In Proverbs 31:25-27 the scribe writes, "Strength and honour are her clothing; and she shall rejoice in time to come. She openeth her mouth with wisdom; and in her tongue is the law of kindness. She looketh well to the ways of her household, and eateth not the bread of idleness." The ingredients for majestic motherhood — strength, honor, happiness, wisdom, kindness, foresight, and industry — all meet and merge in her personality. I especially like the verse which details her courageous concern for giving her household a total education. She looks well and wisely "to the ways of her household" (Prov. 31:27). Her children need to walk the way of mental development. She therefore seeks the acquisition of knowledge and wisdom for their expanding and impressionable minds. Members of her family need to walk the way of physical development. As a loving and faithful mother she desires for each of them growth in stature. A strong physical constitution is a tremendous aid for a life of industry, toil, and fruitful activity. Her children do not live in a world of isolation. They live in a world of human beings. Therefore she is interested in leading them to walk the way of social development. She strongly desires that they master the necessary art of getting along with others. The worthy woman recognizes that her children owe a primary place in their lives to their Creator. She desires that they walk the way of spiritual and moral development. The fruits of her worthwhile activities are seen in the following verse, "Her children arise up, and call her blessed; her husband also, and he praiseth her. Many daughters have done virtuously, but thou excellest them all. Favour is deceitful, and beauty is vain: but a woman that feareth the Lord, she shall be praised. Give her of the fruit of her hands; and let her own works praise her in the gates" (Prov. 31:28-31). How very desperately do we need a modern increase of this woman's tribe. *Christ in the home* can help make such mothers a reality today.

We need mothers today who are wise. Too many homes have foolish wives and mothers. Proverbs 14:1 states, "Every wise woman buildeth her house: but the foolish plucketh it down with her hands." Wisdom builds; foolishness destroys. The wise woman spends her life and energies in building a good home. She directs her part of the home by means of wise words and prudent practices. Any woman can wreck a home. It takes a wise woman to build a happy home. Her daily prayer is to be blessed with the wisdom that comes from above. She will desire to use her knowledge effectively. Homes desperately need wise wives and prudent mothers. *Christ in the home* can help make them so.

The critical times in which we live demand mothers who will earnestly seek to emulate the worthy Elisabeth. The fulness of

time was now at hand. God's plan for human redemption called
for the birth of two baby boys. One of these boys would fulfill
Isaiah's prediction of the voice crying in the Judean wilderness
(Isa. 40:3-8). The voice was destined to pave the way for the
Lord's coming. As the harbinger or forerunner of the Lord' anointed
he would be "the prophet of the Highest" as he turned a rebellious
and perverse nation into an acceptable framework for the coming
Messiah. The second boy was to be the Word who would make an
advent into our world and be made flesh. From His exalted position
as the Word in the Sacred Three, this one was to be born of a
woman and would ultimately die as a ransom for humanity's transgressions. No devout believer will deny or treat with irreverent
lightness the momentous responsibility resting respectively upon the
shoulders of the child John and the Babe of Bethlehem at the times
of their births. Two mothers must now be chosen who will serve
as God's instruments. Women in whose hearts noble and inspiring
qualities rest will bear the son John and the holy child Jesus. We
shall study both of these mothers. Elisabeth will be first in our consideration because she conceived before Mary received the visit from
the angel.

Elisabeth was a descendant of the Aaronic family. Her husband,
Zacharias, was one of the priesthood, belonging to the priestly
course of Abia. Both of these Levites were "righteous before God,
walking in all the commandments and ordinances of the Lord blameless" (Luke 1:6). Parenthood had thus far been denied them due
to no fault of their own. The first chapter of Luke allows us to form
the impression that this goodly couple had desperately wanted a
child and that many prayers for a child had been directed to the
heavenly throne. Gabriel said, "Fear not Zacharias: for thy prayer
is heard; and thy wife Elisabeth shall bear thee a son, and thou
shalt call his name John" (Luke 1:13). Jehovah is about to answer
their prayer. Failure to become a mother in Israel was considered
a real reproach and was a deep disappointment to Elisabeth. When
she learned that she was soon to become a mother she said, "Thus
hath the Lord dealt with me in the days wherein he looked on me,
to take away my reproach among men" (Luke 1:25). The Lord
approved the righteous and blameless ways which characterized this
aged Israelite couple. They became Jehovah's choice to bear John.
According to the angelic announcement, joy and happiness would
permeate their hearts when their eyes first beheld the promised son
and rejoicing would be felt in numerous other hearts at his birth.
Three months before John's birth Mary paid a visit to Elisabeth.
Their meeting on this interesting occasion prompted Elisabeth to

speak a beautiful tribute to the youthful virgin and to address an even higher and holier tribute to the fruit of Mary's womb. Elisabeth, so far as I can determine, became the first Israelite woman to refer to Jesus as "my Lord" (Luke 1:43). This she did nine months before His birth. The time for John's birth arrives and Elisabeth brings forth a son. This unique child would herald the approach of God's own Son. Elisabeth and her neighbors rejoiced at his birth. When her friends strongly insisted on naming the eight-day-child in honor of Zacharias, Elisabeth refused and plainly declared the child be named John. This was in strict obedience to the angelic announcement made nine months earlier.

Elisabeth was righteous before God long before she became a mother. How wonderful for a child to have a righteous mother at the moment of birth. She was obedient to all God's commandments and ordinances. Women who possess this disposition of heart can rear God-fearing children today. The unborn Jesus was her Lord. How vital for a mother to be able to call Jesus Lord. If she cannot do this, she is lacking in one of the greatest requisites for prudent parenthood. John grew into a mighty man of God. I think it is highly significant that Jehovah chose for John's mother a woman whose heart and life were righteous. Elisabeth provides an inspiring example for every Christian mother. *Christ in the home* can make possible our having more mothers who follow the example of Elisabeth.

We need women today who will seek to emulate the mother of our blessed Lord. Of course no one can emulate her in the virgin birth for this was a unique occurrence. Note the attitudes and practices which made Mary a great and worthy mother.

Many people have sought to make Mary a person worthy of receiving divine honors. References to Mary as "Mother of God," "Queen of Heaven," her "Perpetual Virginity," her "Immaculate Conception," and the more recently ordained dogma of her "Bodily Assumption" into heaven have been skillfully woven into the Roman Catholic web of religious fancy. Not one shred of Biblical evidence can be adduced in support of such sinful appellations. Early church history also does not support such titles. However, in counteracting the absurd doctrines taught about Mary perhaps many have swung to the other extreme and have failed to honor her as a faithful instrument of God. She richly deserves all the honors that were rightly hers as the mother of the human part of the divine Logos. Modern mothers can learn from her and aspire toward holier heights in parenthood.

Before the first human couple made their sad exit from Eden's garden Eve was informed by Jehovah God that the seed of the woman would bruise the head of the serpent (Gen. 3:15). This was the first promise of a Redeemer for fallen humanity and it also foretold how His thrilling advent into the now cursed earth would occur. Isaiah lived and prophesied more than seven centuries before the birth of Bethlehem's Babe. God's Spirit through the messianic prophet promised that "a virgin shall conceive, and bear a son, and shall call his name Immanuel" (Isa. 7:14). Perhaps the hope of bringing the Messiah into the world was present in every generation of pious Hebrew maidens from Adam to Joseph. The fulness of time had now arrived (Gal. 4:4). The Word would now make His long-awaited advent to a weary world. Jehovah God surveyed the scene and chose a young virgin in Nazareth of Galilee to become the mother of Jesus. She belonged to the house of David, was engaged to Joseph, and was a cousin to Elisabeth. The Lord dispatched Gabriel to a despised town of southern Galilee with the annunciation to Mary.

The angelic message began with a tribute to the high favor about to be conferred upon the Galilean virgin. The Lord would be with her and she would enjoy from henceforth a blessed place among women (Luke 1:28). Gabriel gave a detailed account of what this son would be and the great work He would achieve (Luke 1:31-33). The maiden from Nazareth meekly inquired how all this could occur since she had never known a man. Gabriel offered a satisfactory explanation to her perplexed mind. Mary then pictured herself as the handmaiden (the feminine form of a literal slave or bondservant) of the Lord and was content to wait for the fulfillment of the angel's announcement. Soon she took a journey to the home of Elisabeth. The two cousins now had much more in common than a fleshly kinship. The visit lasted for three months. Following Elisabeth's Spirit-prompted message in Luke 1:41-45 Mary voiced her own song of deep thanksgiving. In this beautiful song she pictured her soul as magnifying the Lord and her spirit as finding its deepest joy in God her Saviour. Deep humility marks each word of this lovely lyric. The joyful visit with Elisabeth was soon completed and Mary returned home. Before the time for Jesus' birth, circumstances prompted Mary and Joseph to be in Bethlehem of Judaea. This is where prophecy indicated He would be born (Mic. 5:2). The birth of the glorious child in the manger surroundings, the shepherds' visit, the predictions made by Simeon and Anna during the temple presentation, the appearance of and worship accorded Him by wise men from the East, the hasty departure into Egypt, the temple incident when He was twelve, and the earth-shaking events of His personal ministry must have constantly challenged the pondering mind of Mary. Finally, she viewed Him on Golgotha's hill. As predicted thirty-three years earlier by Simeon, surely the sword had now pierced her own soul (Luke 2:35). The loving John took her to his home. The last glimpse we have of Mary is with her other children and the disciples of Jesus shortly before Pentecost (Acts 1:14). She is exactly where we would expect to find her, with the disciples of her now risen and ascended Lord.

God knew all women of that eventful era. That He chose Mary above all other women to bring His Son into the world is highly suggestive of the superb qualities of true motherhood lying in potential form in Mary's heart. Jehovah used motherhood to allow His Son an entrance into the world; He still depends upon motherhood for a continuation of His Son's cause on earth.

We need more mothers who will emulate Mary as a mother. She knew from firsthand experience what it was really like to have Christ in the home.

We need a multitude of mothers who will emulate the example set by Lois and Eunice, the grandmother and mother of Timothy respectively. It seems evident that Paul came into contact with the youthful Timothy while Paul was on his first missionary journey (Acts 13, 14). This is ascertained by the fact that Timothy was already a budding disciple of considerable influence when Paul saw Timothy during the early stages of the second journey (Acts 16:1-2). In I Timothy 1:2 Paul styles him "my own son in the faith." In II Timothy 1:2 Paul writes, "To Timothy, my dearly beloved son . . ." These passages seem to indicate that Paul converted Timothy and the first missionary journey strongly appears to be the time when this conversion of far-reaching importance occurred. Paul made contact again with this young man as Paul and Silas were yet in the beginning stages of the second missionary tour. In this goodly Lycaonian youth Paul observed the potential for dynamic discipleship. Timothy had already built up an enviable reputation among Christian brethren both at Lystra and Iconium (Acts 16:2). Paul persuaded the young man to join his company and from that day till Paul breathed his last breath Timothy served him in unparalleled fashion.

However, in Timothy's past lay the invaluable influences of a godly grandmother and a marvelous mother. From these two pious souls Timothy had received a rich heritage of fervent faith, holy hope, and pious practice. Paul once wrote the following to his beloved son in the gospel, "And that from a child [babe, ASV] thou hast known the holy scriptures, which are able to make thee wise unto salvation through faith which is in Christ Jesus" (II Tim. 3:15). Who had taken the time to impart a knowledge of the sacred scriptures to young Timothy? Noble motherhood performed this great spiritual service for the growing Timothy when his mind was so pliable and his youthful spirit so impressionable. Paul remarked, "When I call to remembrance the unfeigned faith that is in thee, which dwelt first in thy grandmother Lois, and thy mother Eunice; and I am persuaded that in thee also" (II Tim. 1:5). Lois first possessed a sincere faith in Jehovah and a reverent regard for His law. Eunice walked in her mother's footsteps. Timothy thus had a double set of well-directed steps to imitate and grand success marked his determination to walk therein. How exceedingly wonderful when a child has a good mother to emulate. If Lois had not been devoted to Jehovah God, perhaps Eunice would never have developed an unfeigned faith. Had there been no spirituality in Eunice, the world possibly would never have heard of the young man from central Asia Minor who became Paul's most trusted colaborer. The church and our sin-infested world desperately need more women who possess the unfeigned faith of Lois and Eunice and will diligently direct their precious children to the Bible from babyhood. Again, the *Christ in the home* concept can provide such women.

We need the kind of mothers such as the late John D. Cox had. This outstanding minister of the gospel once wrote an article in which he paid high honors to his godly mother. This goodly mother taught her sons to abstain from the use of any and all alcoholic beverages. She reared seven sons who faithfully pursued the pathway of total sobriety. Great power resides in right teaching. She taught her boys to be honest. Oh, how we need honesty taught from childhood on. Honesty has too few practitioners in a day when the law of the jungle dominates most human circles. This mother urged her sons to treat young women as they would have their own sister to be treated. Sister Cox became a wise counselor for good in the lives of her sons. What a strong contrast to Athaliah who counseled her son to live wickedly. In urging moral purity to dominate every date Mrs. Cox stands in marked contrast to a parent that encouraged his son to go "as far as the girl would permit" on a date. Sober sons, honest sons, and morally clean sons can be produced by Christian parents who teach well and live excellently before their children. It was truly the *Christ in the home* philosophy that prompted this kind of teaching in the Cox household.

We need mothers who are regular attenders at all church services. Several years ago a boy was in service. He was far from home. Some of the boys had planned a night of sin, revelry, and debauchery. They invited him to go. He was tempted and agreed to accompany them. Then he remembered that it was Wednesday. Back home his mother would be at Bible Study. When they had their prayers she would be remembering her son in service. This was too much. He could not spend a night in sin while his mother prayed for him in a church service. He told the young men that he would not be going after all. What would have happened if this boy had had a mother that ignored Wednesday Bible Study as many mothers do? What if she had been of the disposition that prayer is prayer and I can pray just as well for my boy at home as at a scheduled church assembly? The matter could have ended in a night of tragedy for that young man. He might have gotten into moral trouble that would have wrecked his whole future. If your boy had been in this young man's shoes, would he have had this memory of you, his mother, as a lever to lift himself out of a sinful escapade that was in the planning stages and very soon would be satanically executed? I Corinthians 10:13 came to my mind after hearing this story. Who can tell but what this was the Lord's way for this young man to escape? We need mothers such as this boy had.

When motherhood lifts up the Bible, the Bible will lift up motherhood.

QUESTIONS FOR DISCUSSION

1. Why do we not need mothers like Jezebel?
2. Why do we not need mothers like Athaliah?
3. Tell the story of Herodias and tell why mothers of her type are not needed.
4. Discuss some of the observations made relative to Herodias. Discuss the mother of today who defies God's law in marriage and brings up her daughters to walk the ways of worldliness.
5. Why do we not need mothers today who practice idolatry? Discuss the mother of Asa and what he did about her and the idol she worshiped.
6. Why do we not need mothers who speak the language of Ashdod? What effect will they have on their offspring?
7. Relate the story of Jochebed the mother of Moses.
8. Tell the story of Hannah the mother of Samuel. What necessary ingredients did she have for noble motherhood?
9. Discuss in detail the picture of the worthy woman given in Proverbs 31.

10. Discuss Proverbs 14:1. What is the difference between a wise woman and a foolish woman in building a home?
11. Discuss in detail Elisabeth, the mother of John the Baptist.
12. Relate the story of Mary, the mother of Jesus. What lessons can mothers learn from her?
13. Describe the motherhood of Lois and Eunice.
14. Describe the kind of mother the late John D. Cox had. What lessons did she seek early in life to impress upon her sons?
15. Tell about the boy who was tempted to spend a night in sin but chose later to say no when he thought of his prayerful mother at Midweek Bible Study.

13

The Child in the Home

The first recorded command which appears in the Bible and is directed toward newly formed humanity has reference to children. Genesis 1:26 tells of Jehovah's intentions of making man in the image and likeness of the great Godhead. Genesis 1:27 reveals the accomplishment of this amazing feat. Male and female form the whole of created humanity. Genesis 1:28 gives man his great duty of populating a world which was made to be inhabited by humanity. Isaiah 45:18 tells us that God "created it not in vain," but "he formed it to be inhabited. . . ." Adam and Eve are told, "Be fruitful, and multiply, and replenish the earth, and subdue it . . ." (Gen. 1:28). This includes the conception, birth, and rearing of children. That the home is the proper and only approved institution for these tasks receives Biblical support from Genesis through Revelation. Children are frequently conceived and born when there is no marriage relationship between the father and mother but such circumstances are a violation of heaven's will and a staggering blow to the future welfare of decent society. The sin does not lie with the child though the child frequently bears an undeserved stigma of reproach. The fault lies between the two consenting people who conceived the child.

No home can be at its best nor enjoy its greatest happiness without children. I can speak with some experience here. My wife and I were married over four years before the birth of our first child in 1956. We agree that even though the first few years were happy ones indeed that the addition of a daughter in 1956 and a son in

1960 have given a dimension of radiant happiness and rewarding pleasure never experienced while our marriage was childless. We do not regret the four years without children because these supplied us with the opportunity of becoming adjusted to marriage and perhaps the achievement of a little more maturity than we possessed in our early twenties.

Children who are not reared to respect God and honor their parents can be a source of untold sufferings and heavy heartache. A father once spoke from bitter experience, "When children are little they are upon your feet; when older they are upon your heart." Some of the saddest people I have counseled have been parents whose children forsook the Lord and His church. Wayward children can put weary parents into a premature grave. I once listened to a man tell the story of his son who turned from the Lord and embraced infidelity. The man bore a great burden. He expressed the hope that when the son hit the bottom of unbelief that he would come back to the strong belief of his youth. The father died with the son still alienated from God's family. A broken heart is one of the most tragic occurrences in the life of a human being. Real parental love will never cease caring for a wayward child. Due to the nature of parental love the heart can be broken so easily when the child deserts the family and turns his wayward feet in the direction of the far-off country of sin, dissipation, and waste (see Luke 15:11-32).

WHAT PARENTS OWE THEIR CHILDREN

I choose to speak of this aspect of the parent-child relationship first for two reasons. (1) The parents realize what they owe a child before he realizes what he owes his parents. Right-thinking parents are aware of their obligations from birth onward. However, the child is not born with an awareness of his obligations toward his parents. It will be sometime later, after much thorough training that he will recognize those obligations. (2) The degree to which parents fulfill their obligations to their child will have a decided effect in how well he later fulfills his obligations.

The child should be recognized for his great value. From a purely evolutionary viewpoint the child is merely a biological product of the union of two consenting adults. God is not involved. A soul is not at stake. No eternal destiny is acknowledged. The little package of flesh is that and nothing more. What a sharp contrast to the concept of childhood shared by believers in God. The Bible teaches that every child is the offspring of God. To the Athenian philosophers on Mars' Hill, Paul spoke this vital truth: "For in him we live, and move, and have our being; as certain also of your own poets have said, For we are also his offspring. Forasmuch then as we are the offspring of God, we ought not to think that the Godhead is like unto gold, or silver, or stone, graven by art and man's device" (Acts 17: 28-29). There is a big difference between the theory of godless evolution and that of Biblical creation just as there is between the idea of a child being the offspring of God and a product of chance, the child of no design and no destiny.

The Bible also points to the great value of children and the blessings they bring to the home: "Lo, children are an heritage of the Lord: and the fruit of the womb is his reward. As arrows are in the hand of a mighty man; so are children of the youth. Happy is the man that hath his quiver full of them: they shall not be ashamed, but they shall speak with the enemies in the gate" (Ps. 127:3-5). Solomon observed that "Children's children are the crown of old men; and the glory of children are their fathers" (Prov. 17:6). Happy are the older men and women who have grandchildren on whom to lavish their tender affections. These youngsters bring an indescribable ray of sunshine into the sunset years of senior citizens. I have a friend who longs for the day when his married son and daughter-in-law will have their first child and his first grandchild. Occasionally he will inquire of his friends, "How does a fellow go about *adopting a grandchild?*" No words can give an apt description of the tremendous value of a child in the home.

Every child deserves to be wanted. Ideally, this should be true at the moment of conception and also at the hour of birth. Sometimes it is not true at the moment of conception. Wise parents, however, will make the necessary adjustment during the months of pregnancy and the child will be given a wonderful welcome into the family. Tragic is entirely too weak a term to describe the birth of an unwanted child. The child will soon sense this and unhappiness will be his lot even at a young age. Think of some inspiring stories in the Bible where children were wanted before conception, at the time of conception, and when the eagerly anticipated day of birth arrived. Isaac was wanted by Abraham and Sarah long before his conception. Romans contains this statement, "Who against hope believed in hope, that he might become the father of many nations; according to that which was spoken, So shall thy seed be. And being not weak in faith, he considered not his own body now dead, when he was about an hundred years old, neither yet the deadness of Sarah's womb: He staggered not at the promise of God through unbelief; but was strong in faith, giving glory to God; And being fully persuaded that, what he had promised, he was able also to perform" (4:18-21). Deep joy permeated the patriarchal household when "the Lord visited Sarah as he had said, and the Lord did unto Sarah as he had spoken. For Sarah conceived, and bare Abraham a son in his old age, at the set time of which God had spoken to him. And Abraham called the name of his son that was born unto him, whom Sarah bare to him, Isaac" (Gen. 21:1-3). Hannah wanted a son many years before she was granted motherhood. The Bible says of Hannah in I Samuel 1:11, "And she vowed a vow, and said, O Lord of hosts, if thou wilt indeed look on the affliction of thine handmaid, and remember me, and not forget thine handmaid, but wilt give unto thine handmaid a man child, then I will give him unto the Lord all the days of his life, and there shall no razor come upon his head." When this desire became a joyful reality she called her firstborn son "Samuel, saying, Because I have asked him of the Lord" (I Sam. 1:20). Samuel was conceived as a result of a prayerful petition. He was born amidst real gratitude for his coming to brighten and bless the lives of Elkanah and Hannah. John the Baptist was an object of prayer in the childless marriage of Zacharias and Elisabeth (Luke 1:13). When Elisabeth learned that she was going to be a mother she viewed it as the lifting of a bitter reproach which she had long endured (Luke 1:25). Great rejoicing accompanied the birth of John. Gabriel had earlier predicted that "many shall rejoice at his birth" (Luke 1:14). In Luke 1:57-58 we read, "Now Elisabeth's full time came that she should be delivered; and she brought forth a son. And her neighbors and her cousins heard how the Lord had shewed great mercy upon her; and they rejoiced with her." Eight days after John's birth the silent tongue of Zacharias was again permitted to speak (Luke 1:64). Luke 1:68-79 contains the prophecy of what Jesus and John would do. All of these children were wanted at conception and deep rejoicing accompanied their entrances into the world.

Every child deserves to be loved and respected. Older women in the church are commanded to "teach the young women to be sober, to love their husbands, to love their children, To be discreet, chaste, keepers at home, good, obedient to their own husbands, that the word of God be not blasphemed" (Titus 2:4-5). When parents fail to love their children the word of God is blasphemed. The arrival of perilous times would witness an absence of "natural affection" (II Tim. 3:3). This is the very type of love which should exist between parents and children. It is the height of human tragedy when parents bring little children into the world and then abandon them.

You may have heard of the little fellow from one of the orphan homes who wrote a pathetic petition to his mother. He served as the little penman who expressed the deeply felt hunger of all these little children for the mother who had abandoned them. The yearning love they had for her is woven into the fabric of his letter to her. There is the hope expressed that the mother will go to church and do right. Mention is made of their little pet. The little fellow had broken a tooth but no mother was there to comfort and sooth away the freely flowing tears. He conveys a message that one of the brothers wishes he could see his mother just one more time and that "he will love you for ages." Another sister sends a greeting "to her loved mother." The little fellow expresses his own love. He pleads for a reciprocation of that love from his mother. He longs for the day when the mother will be with them again and show her love for them. Tears will moisten your eyes when you read such expressions as "Mother, I still love you. I wish more than anything that you could be with us. When is the day going to come? I hope it won't be long until you show us that you love us. . . . Please write back to me, Mama. . . . We all love you so much, Mama. Please try to love us." The letter was returned to the sender!

Once in a Bible class the teacher was talking about love for Jesus and love being present in the home. A little fellow spoke up and said he did not know whether or not his mother loved him. Indeed he had grounds for his doubt because the mother had abandoned the family. A little later there was a divorce. It is a tragic day in a child's life when he has reason to doubt his mother's love for him. It will leave a scar on his emotional makeup that may never disappear. Every child deserves to have a father and mother who love and respect him.

A well-known juvenile judge once told the story of a family who came into his court room. Previously the man had left home and sought work in a distant city. The wife soon sent him word that he would have to come home and make arrangements for their four children. She said she could no longer be bothered with them! The distraught husband, rebellious wife, and the four darling children came into the chambers of his court. The husband pleaded with the wife. He promised to forgive her indiscretions. Let's keep the home together for the sake of our children was the essence of his pathetic plea. With an air of total disregard she told him that she wanted no part of him or their children. Paul's expression, "without natural affection," was an apt description of her calloused soul. Truly "The heart is deceitful above all things, and desperately wicked: who can know it?" (Jer. 17:9).

A child deserves to be trained and disciplined for life and eternity. Heaven smiled upon Abraham because of the training and discipline he would give his family (Gen. 18:19). The Lord was happy with Joshua's determination that his entire family would follow Jehovah God (Josh. 24:15). Solomon said, "Train up a child in the way he should go: and when he is old, he will not depart from it" (Prov. 22:6). "He that spareth his rod hateth his son: but he that loveth him chasteneth him betimes" (Prov. 13:24). Paul taught, "And, ye fathers, provoke not your children to wrath: but bring them up in the nurture and admonition of the Lord" (Eph. 6:4). Children need that type of discipline. They will not be well-adjusted adults without discipline. Many children grow to maturity and never know the rod of correction or the utterance of a single NO directed toward their wishes. Total permissiveness is the framework in which they grow up. A father once said he had never corrected his daughter as she grew up. A mother once confessed she had given her son everything he asked for in youth and never said no to him. Such parents do their children great wrong.

I have noted in many of the letters young people write to Ann Landers and other columnists that they are crying for parentally established boundaries. In essence they are saying, "If only our parents would give us some firm NOs, tell us where we may not go, with whom we may not associate, and establish a time for us to be home at night." Many parents could care less what their children do, where they go, with whom they associate, and what time they check in at night. It is the height of folly to rear children in such a permissive atmosphere. It is highly unfair to the children. They are left to make decisions that are above and beyond them. God gave children a set of parents in order to help them cope with just such decisions. It is highly unfair to parents also for in later years they will reap the fruits of their permissiveness. They may witness grown children who are as oblivious to them in old age as they were to their offspring a few years back. Then their children craved parental concern and family interest. Now the tables are reversed. The parents crave the affection of their children and it is now denied them. Galatians 6:7-8 works in family situations also.

Children deserve parents who will take time for them. They are children for only a short time and their years speed by so quickly. Parents and children should work together. They should attend church together and worship together in home devotions. They should play together. They should picnic together. They should take vacations as a family. They should be able to communicate with each other. Real love will not allow a permanent breakdown in communications.

A few years ago I was getting ready to leave for a gospel meeting. So many last-minute things had to be attended to in order that the local work might go on in my absence. Several things also needed to be taken care of at home. A long drive lay ahead for that Saturday afternoon and evening. My son was playing in the yard. He was having trouble with one of his toys. He asked for help. My first reaction was to say, "Son, I have so much to do and so little time in which to get it done. Can't that wait? Can't you fix it yourself?" Fortunately these thoughts were not translated into actual words. I took time to help him with the problem. When I finished he said, "Daddy, I don't know what I would do without you." The remainder of my tasks were performed with increased speed and I was grateful that I had taken a few moments to help a little fellow with a problem. This is an incident which time may erase from his memory but his words are not likely to be erased from my book of family memories. Our children deserve to be given time and attention.

As parents let us make a happy home for our children. Let us make it a place where they can bring their youthful friends without any worry that parental foolishness will embarrass them and their friends. Let us rear our children to love God and mankind. Let us give them the education that will fit them for today's complex world. Let us train their spirits to be fit for a heavenly paradise. Let us turn the home into a school of Bible study and a place of prayer. In summary, let us learn what God would have parents be and do and then major in both of these important areas. Lifting up the Bible in the home can help us achieve success in the realm of parent-child relationships. *Christ in the home* still says it best.

WHAT CHILDREN OWE THEIR PARENTS

How well parents do their work will be a decisive factor in determining the future attitudes and actions of children toward fathers and mothers. Parental failure can expect to reap rebellion from untaught and undisciplined children in later years. Parental success has every right to expect love, honor, respect, and filial regard from children.

The child in the home should be obedient and respectful to his parents. Good reasons can be given to support this divine injunction. Young people cannot successfully imitate Jesus unless they are obedient and respectful to parental authority. As Jesus stood on the threshold of His teen-age years the Bible clearly shows His attitude toward Joseph and Mary. "And he went down with them, and came to Nazareth, and was subject unto them: but his

mother kept all these sayings in her heart" (Luke 2:51). Betwixt
twelve and thirty "Jesus increased in wisdom and stature, and in
favour with God and man" (Luke 2:52). If the Son of God could not
afford to dispense with obedience to His parents during His youth,
then no young person today can afford to either. Had Jesus ignored
His parents He would have left Himself open for sure censure from
later enemies. If Jesus had despised parental authority in His youth,
He could not have made such advancement in gaining God's approval and man's favor. The approval of God and the favor of good
men have never rested upon rebellious youth and they never will.

The children of the family must be obedient to parental authority
because that is a commandment. It is a right commandment. It is a
commandment with a dual promise. Read what Paul has to say
along this line: "Children, obey your parents in the Lord: for this is
right. Honour thy father and mother; which is the first commandment with promise; That it may be well with thee, and thou mayest
live long on the earth" (Eph. 6:1-3). It has always been right for
children to obey their parents as long as those parents do not require something wrong. It has always been wrong for children to
disobey their parents. It always will be. God *never* has had a law
which read, "Parents, obey your children in the Lord: for this is
right. Honour thy son and daughter; which is the first commandment with promise; That it may be well with thee, and thou mayest
live long on the earth." Yet, this is the very procedure that is followed in many modern homes today. Many parents appear to be
afraid of their children. They wish to avoid at any cost stirring up
the anger of little Junior or little Suzie. Someone has remarked that
everyone in our nation seems afraid to say no except the young
people and they are saying it loudly and clearly and altogether too
frequently. What has happened to parental backbone? Not long
ago someone was telling me about the child-rearing practices of a
certain couple. They had a little boy who really ruled the household.
When this couple was at a church service frequently little Junior
would play after the service was over. When the couple was ready
to leave one of them would look up the little ruler and check to see
if he were ready to go home yet. Most often he would not be. The
one who did the checking would come to the other and say, "I
guess we will have to stay longer. He has not had his play out yet!"
Such practices must keep a constant smile upon the sinister face of
Satan. After all, he is the author of such child-rearing techniques!
Ephesians 6:1-3 has been totally reversed in such situations.
Frightening indeed is the thought of what such a child will ultimately become.

Grown children owe their aged parents honor, love, respect, care, and financial aid if needed. The extension of honor to those who begat us does not end when the child leaves the home of his childhood to form one of his own. The divinely revealed obligation to love and respect parents is a lifetime requirement. Aged parents deserve to receive some time from their children. I have heard stories of children away from home who never call, never write, and seldom visit. I have known of grown children who live within easy driving range of their parents but who never have them over for a meal or come by for a meal in the home of the parents. Frequently when such children bury their parents their tears are profuse and the weeping is long. The show of postmortem love and kindness will not make up for a clear lack of it prior to death. As a child whose aged parents yet live, call your parents right now and have them over for a meal this very week. Accept the very next invitation your aged mother extends to sit again under her table. Disregard the overly worked excuses of being too busy or having so many pressing commitments with business associates or your own peer group. One of these days you will not have to make such excuses to your lonely parents for they will then be occupying their spots in the silent city of the sleeping dead. If you are away from home, call them now or write them a long letter. Brighten their hearts while their ears can still hear your voice or their fading eyesight can still read your letters. Expressions of love, care, and concern will be too late when expressed by the open casket or the flower covered grave. The opportunity to express love and concern will have then passed forever in this life.

The Bible makes it mandatory for grown sons and daughters to render financial aid when their aged parents need it. Some children rationalize that Daddy and Mother should have put more back for the sunset years. Because they did not, then the child's duty to them is dissolved! Has it never occurred to these calloused children that their parents could scarcely put back anything because they were determined to feed properly, clothe adequately, and unselfishly provide the finest education for their children? By the time a large family was properly cared for in all these important areas the health of hard-working parents was broken. These parents may never have made anything but a living. The small pension and Social Security may not be equal to the basic needs they have for housing, food, clothing, and medical care in the inflationary times in which we live. Loving children will not let them suffer. They will willingly provide for their aged parents who are in need. Let us note what the Bible teaches on this very point. The Pharisees in Christ's era on earth possessed a very strong abhorrence toward the idea of parental support. With satanic ingenuity they had worked out a neat little system which enabled them to dodge this God-imposed obligation. Jesus exposed their wicked formula for ignoring parents in need. "Full well ye reject the commandment of God, that ye may keep your own tradition. For Moses, said, Honour thy father and thy mother; and, Whoso curseth father or mother, let him die the death: But ye say, If a man shall say to his father or mother, It is Corban, that is to say, a gift, by whatsoever thou mightest be profited by me; he shall be free. And ye suffer him no more to do aught for his father or his mother; Making the word of God of none effect through your tradition, which ye have delivered: and many such like things do ye" (Mark 7:9-13). This is how their cleverly conceived system worked. A man had aged parents in need. He had property the worth of which could be used to alleviate their needy condition. He strongly desired to evade this responsibility. He was permitted to pronounce the word *Corban* over the property. The term, according to the sinful system contrived in their malicious minds, meant the property was now devoted to Jehovah God. Hence, not any of its value or income could be employed for parental care. It also appears that the Pharisee likewise felt no obligation to use it for God either! Really the property was to be used selfishly. Jesus said the practice of such a system was a rejection of God's law. The Pharisees made the word of God of none effect. About the only difference between these practitioners of parental disregard in the first century and those who duplicate the practice today is the current absence of the pronounced word *Corban.*

Paul wrote, "But if any widow have children or nephews, let them learn first to shew piety at home, and to requite their parents: for that is good and acceptable before God . . . But if any provide not for his own, and specially for those of his own house, he hath denied the faith, and is worse than an infidel" (I Tim. 5:4, 8). Taking care of aged parents or grandparents (nephews is rendered as grandchildren in I Timothy 5:4, ASV) is of great importance. It is a demonstration of piety or kindness in action. Helping parents is an act which God finds acceptable. It is a form of requiting or paying back our lovely parents for all they have done for us. Unrequited love is one of the most despicable sights the human eye ever witnesses. A refusal to aid parents in need is equivalent to a denial of the faith. The holy faith cannot be maintained by those who mercilessly and maliciously trample under foot the parents that reared them. Such persons are beneath infidels. Even unbelievers many times take care of their own aged parents and grandparents.

Obedience and honor belong to our parents while we are under them in the home. Honor and respect should be our attitude toward them when we are grown and they are aged. God's law of honoring parents is in force as long as they live. Even when they have left earthly scenes we should honor their memory. *Christ in the home* will prompt right attitudes and actions toward our parents.

Every child in the home owes his parents something. Parents deserve more loving loyalty and more active allegiance than do your peers at school or on the playground. Your parents, not your peers, brought you into this world. Your parents, not your peers, cared for you when you were helpless as an infant. Your parents, not your peers, provide the food for your bodily nourishment, the shelter that is above your head, the medical needs when you are sick, and the education you presently receive. Which of your peers would work forty hours or more each week and spend most of it upon you, your brothers and sisters? Your parents do. Which of your peers at school or college would spend an entire paycheck to buy you the clothes you need to begin a new year of school work? Your parents have gladly done it time and time again. The only reciprocation they expect is your success as a Christian, happiness in your chosen line of work, achievement of a satisfying marriage and home life, and the extension of love, respect, and honor to them. Be diligent in returning such to them for they have made a great investment in you. Which of your peers would sit up night after night by your bed when you are seriously sick and nurse you back to health? Friendships among peers blossom and flourish much more easily in fair weather than in foul weather. God never commanded you to obey your peers but He did tell you to honor and obey your parents. You owe your parents a debt. Do not neglect its continued payment.

WHAT YOUNG PEOPLE OWE THE HOME

It is my desire to make this point somewhat broader than the previous section. A young person may live in a home where there is more than just the parent relationship to consider. He may have other brothers or sisters. An aged grandparent may live in that home. There will be guests in that home from time to time. It is highly unhealthy for children and totally destructive to happy homes for boys and girls to imagine themselves to be the total center of importance. Children are important. Toward that concept I offer no word of denial. But I do deny that the child is the only one with rights or needs worthy of consideration. Hence children need to develop good habits and avoid bad ones as they grow toward maturity.

Friendliness is an absolute must. Solomon said, "A man that hath friends must shew himself friendly: and there is a friend that sticketh closer than a brother" (Prov. 18:24). Children should learn to be friendly in the home. Friendliness should be in evidence when guests are in the home. Sometimes when I visit in homes I am fortunate to get even a passing nod or a reluctant grunt from some of the young people. When real friendliness is practiced in the home it will become easier to practice friendliness outside the home also.

Cultivate the twin characteristics of helpfulness and cooperation. There is no finer training ground for this than the home. Do your part to make home life happy. Your mother has a day of constant work before her from the time she arises until she retires. Learn to pick up your own clothes. Keep your room tidy and clean. Do your chores cheerfully. Do not expect to be idle or indolent while others do the tasks assigned to you. Be helpful; do not be a hinderer. Be cooperative; do not be lazy and indifferent to your assigned work.

Be dependable. The adult world is looking for young people who have this good characteristic. Your chances for obtaining a part-time job are much greater if dependability is one of your virtues. Cultivate this golden virtue from early childhood on. Do not make promises unless you fully intend to keep them. The Bible says, "Be not rash with thy mouth, and let not thine heart be hasty to utter any thing before God: for God is in heaven, and thou upon earth: therefore let thy words be few. For a dream cometh through the multitude of business; and a fool's voice is known by multitude of words. When thou vowest a vow unto God, defer not to pay it; for he hath no pleasure in fools: pay that which thou hast vowed. Better is it that thou shouldest not vow, than that thou shouldest vow and not pay" (Eccles. 5:2-5). Be a keeper of promises and confidence in your dependability will grow among your acquaintances. Some young people do not enjoy the confidence of their parents while others enjoy an unlimited degree of such confidence. Your actions will place you in either the unenviable former group or the enviable latter class of youth. Aim for the latter. Do not let your parents down; they brought you up. Do not turn your back upon God; He is the maker of your body, the sustainer of your life, and the Father of your immortal spirit. Be dependable.

In the home and out of the home young people should practice purity of thought, word, and deed. Purity must be inward as well as outward. External purity alone is hollow and lacks permanent value. One of the beatitudes states, "Blessed are the pure in heart: for they shall see God" (Matt. 5:8). In Philippians 4:8 Paul supplies the fine counsel: "Finally, brethren, whatsoever things are true, whatsoever things are honest, whatsoever things are just, whatsoever things are pure, whatsoever things are lovely, whatsoever things are of good report; if there be any virtue, and if there be any praise, think on these things." Paul wrote the youthful Timothy, "Let no man despise thy youth; but be thou an example of the believers, in word, in conversation, in charity, in spirit, in faith, in purity" (I Tim. 4:12). First Timothy 5:1-2 explains how this young gospel preacher was to conduct himself among the various ages of both sexes. "Rebuke not an elder, but entreat him as a father; and the younger men as brethren; The elder women as mothers; the younger as sisters, with all purity." There are no three finer words addressed to youth than these "keep thyself pure" (I Tim. 5:22). Concerning the kind of speech we allow to pass from our lips the Bible speaks directly, "Let no corrupt communication proceed out of your mouth, but that which is good to the use of edifying, that it may minister grace unto the hearers" (Eph. 4:29). "Let your speech be alway with grace, seasoned with salt, that ye may know how ye ought to answer every man" (Col. 4:6). Jesus teaches that our words will be a decisive factor in determining our salvation or damnation come that final day of reckoning (Matt. 12:36-37). The child owes the home a youthful life earnestly devoted to purity. Zealously pursuing purity will enable you to avoid profanity. Bad books will be strictly off limits. Because it is an impure habit and quite dangerous to bodily health, you will not take up smoking. Drinking, gambling, drugs, and such things have no place in the lives of practitioners of purity.

Another obligation you owe yourself and the home which produced you is diligent preparation to make your own way in today's world. For the accomplishment of this worthwhile endeavor get all the education you can. Never forget though that making a life is more important than learning how to make a living. Do not get these two concepts out of perspective. You have already gone too far in your educational pursuits if you have relegated God to a position lower than Number One in your heart. It is better not to know so much as to know so much which is not true.

If you come from a Christian home, you owe that home the great joy that can come from your obedience to the gospel of Jesus Christ. If you come from a non-Christian home, you should obey the gospel as soon as you are accountable and know what the Lord would have you do. You may be the very means of leading your whole family to the saving Christ. This you owe to God first, yourself next, and then to those who will profit from your example. The next chapter will deal with this in much greater detail. *Christ in the home* is a concept young people must accept. It will aid them in the diligent performance of their God-given responsibilities.

When children lift up the Bible in the home, the Bible will lift up childhood in the home. There is no exception to this rule.

QUESTIONS FOR DISCUSSION

1. Discuss Genesis 1:26-28. What is the only honorable way in which a child can be brought into the world? Discuss the sin of bringing children into the world in any other fashion.
2. Can a home be at its best and enjoy its greatest happiness without children? Why do you answer as you do?
3. Discuss the suffering and heartache that untrained and wayward children can bring into the lives of parents. Evaluate the statement, "When little they [children] are on your feet; when older they are on your heart."
4. What two reasons were given for discussing parental obligations to children first?
5. Discuss the great value of children.
6. Why does a child deserve to be wanted? Discuss some of the differences between a child wanted at birth and one unwanted. Give some Bible examples of children who were fervently desired by their parents prior to birth.
7. Why does every child deserve to be loved and respected? What does the Bible say relative to this point?
8. List some examples where parental love is absent in the hearts of children.
9. Why does a child deserve to be trained and disciplined for life and eternity? List some appropriate Scripture references.
10. Why do parents need to take time for their children?
11. Why do our children deserve a home of happiness?
12. List several reasons why children should be obedient and respectful to their parents.
13. What do grown children owe their aged parents? Discuss the responsibility to give financial aid when they are in need.
14. Why do young people owe much more to their parents than to their peer groups?
15. List some of the things young people owe the home.
16. What will happen if young people are derelict in discharging their debts to the home?

14

Remembering God in Youth

The wise Solomon long ago offered some very practical and timely counsel for modern youth: "Remember now thy Creator in the days of thy youth, while the evil days come not, nor the years draw nigh, when thou shalt say, I have no pleasure in them . . ." (Eccles. 12:1). Great battles are currently being fought to capture the allegiance of young people. Numerous voices plead for their attention. Many pressures are daily exerted to seek their conformity to the ways of a wicked world. Young people who are wise will heed the voice of the Bible. Those who are foolish will ignore the accumulated wisdom of the ages and will speed ahead toward the perilous pitfalls of sure destruction. How desperately do young people need to take a long look at the injunction of the wise Solomon.

WHY REMEMBER GOD IN YOUTH?

Ecclesiastes 12:1 contains a commandment. It is an inspired injunction. To ignore it is to break one of Jehovah's commands. It is just as much a commandment for young people as God's command that Noah build an ark, that Abraham leave Ur of Chaldees for Canaan, that Moses deliver oppressed Israel from Egyptian tyranny, that Jonah preach to Nineveh, that the Galilean disciples follow Jesus, or that the rich ruler sell all his earthly goods and follow the Master. (Gen. 6:14-22; 12:1-3; Exod. 3:1-10; Jonah 1:2; 3:2; Mark 1:16-20; Matt. 19:16-22.) If any would object that this is an Old

Testament precept and has no binding power today, I would present a twofold answer. (1) Obedience to God in youth is not limited to just one covenant. It has been demanded in every dispensation. (2) Paul offers the same basic principle in his writings. "Let no man despise thy youth; but be thou an example of the believers, in word, in conversation, in charity, in spirit, in faith, in purity" (I Tim. 4:12). Those who obey I Timothy 4:12 will also be obedient to the commandment in Ecclesiastes 12:1.

Some passages of Scripture can be obeyed in any period of life. Others cannot. One cannot obey Ephesians 6:4 until he becomes a parent. Ephesians 6:4 does not apply to a boy who is five or ten years removed from parenthood. Ephesians 6:4 will never apply to the man who remains unmarried all his life. Ecclesiastes 12:1 can be obeyed only when one is young. The precept in Ecclesiastes 12:1 is addressed exclusively to youth and cannot be obeyed when one is facing the sunset years of his rapidly vanishing life on earth. Then other passages apply.

Young people need to remember God early because this may well be the only period of life they will have. No one has the guarantee that he will reach the proverbial threescore and ten years before the pale horse and his rider death crosses his threshold (Ps. 90:10; Rev. 6:8). The old must die before long. The young do die. And often they die instantly in an accident. The Hebrew writer said, "And as it is appointed unto men once to die, but after this the judgment" (Heb. 9:27). Young people are not excluded or immunized from meeting this appointment. They are very much included. James says our life "is even a vapour, that appeareth for a little time, and then vanisheth away" (James 4:14). The life of a young person is also likened to a vapor. It too can vanish with stunning rapidity. Youth may be the only time you will ever have to remember God. How very tragic if you had planned to remember Him only when you are older.

God should be remembered in youth because He deserves our loyalty. No one can point to one beneficial thing Satan has ever done for young people or older ones. Selfish Satan is interested in the eternal damnation of all youth. He will ruin you bodily, mentally, socially, and spiritually. He dangles the pleasures of sin before you but fails to tell you that all sinful pleasures are temporary in duration. He also will not show you the deep regrets that surely follow sinful indulgence. He carefully conceals that his ways of so-called pleasure lead straight to eternal hell.

On the other hand, Jehovah is your maker. He gave you being. All good and perfect gifts flow from His hand of continued generosity. Jehovah and His Son Jesus Christ desire your salvation. They want you to wear the crown of life eternal in the new Jerusalem. They want you to be happy throughout eternity. The devil seeks your eternal damnation. Jehovah God, not sly Satan, deserves your youthful loyalty.

You should remember God in youth because your friends need to see that Jesus really lives in your life. You may well be the only Bible they are currently reading. You may be the only Bible they will *ever* read. Paul said to the Corinthians, "Ye are our epistle written in our hearts, known and read of all men . . ." (II Cor. 3:2). Just as first-century citizens in the mighty metropolis of corrupt Corinth were reading the lives of these Grecian saints, so also your contemporaries are reading your lives. How does the gospel read according to you? Paul urged Timothy and Titus to live circumspect lives before others. To Timothy he wrote, "Let no man despise thy youth; but be thou an example of the believers, in word, in conversation, in charity, in spirit, in faith, in purity" (1 Tim. 4:12). To Titus he wrote, "Young men likewise exhort to be sober minded. In all things shewing thyself a pattern of good works: in doctrine showing uncorruptness, gravity, sincerity, Sound speech, that cannot be condemned; that he that is of the contrary part may be ashamed, having no evil thing to say of you" (Titus 2:6-8). The beloved John strongly commended the noble youth of his day "because ye are strong, and the word of God abideth in you, and ye have overcome the wicked one" (I John 2:14). Youth can win people to the Lord that older people might possibly never reach at all.

God should be remembered in youth because He has remembered you in youth. Not for a single moment of your life has the Almighty forgotten you. Even when your thoughts may have been hostile and antagonistic toward Him, He has been kind and gracious to you. As a matter of mere reciprocation you should remember Him in youth. He does not wait until you are old to confer blessings upon you; you should not wait until you are old before you remember Him obediently and reverently.

Jehovah should be remembered in youth because you, too, have kingdom responsibilities now. God expects you to become a citizen of His heavenly kingdom on earth (the church) when you are old enough to distinguish between right and wrong and when you know what His stipulations are for salvation. The Great Commission of Matthew 28:18-20, Mark 16:15-16, and Luke 24:46-49 applies to young people as well as to older people. Jehovah wants you to obey it in the days of your youth and to carry its saving message to the lost of our present generation. "Ye are the salt of the earth" and

"Ye are the light of the world" include young Christians as well as older dedicated disciples (Matt. 5:13-14). Christian youth can help in the needed preservation of faltering society. You can give a much-needed flavor to the corruptible times in which we live. By living a good, clean, and wholesome life for Jesus you can make others thirsty for the radiant happiness they sense in you. As a Christian, the light of your Christian pilgrimage can help illuminate a world where darkness is the general rule.

Those are some of the many weighty reasons why you should remember God in youth. I challenge you to produce one good reason why you should not remember Him in youth. *Christ in the home* will prompt you to remember your Creator in the days of your youth.

WHY DO SOME NOT REMEMBER HIM?

It is absolutely essential that youth be taught about Jehovah before they are in position to remember Him. But, alas, many young people grow to maturity in a completely irreligious home environment. Their parents are not church-goers. They never see Daddy read the Bible and never hear Mother read them a Bible story or pray with them and for them before they retire for the night. These young people do not have fathers like Enoch. He walked with God all the days of his life (Gen. 5:21-24). Unfortunately they do not have fathers like Abraham who by precept and pattern commanded his children to seek Jehovah and live under His providential protection (Gen. 18:19). Their fathers have never taken a strong stand to follow the Lord as did Joshua (Josh. 24:15). These youngsters do not have godly mothers such as Jochebed, Hannah, Elisabeth, Mary, Lois, and Eunice who planted the feet of their little children firmly on the pathway of righteousness. Multitudes of young people do not remember or reverence God in early life because they are totally unacquainted with the character of Him who is holy and inhabits eternity.

Many young people ignore God in youth because they persistently prefer the wild and reckless ways of sin to a life that wholeheartedly follows the Master. In the words of Paul, they are "lovers of pleasures more than lovers of God . . ." (II Tim. 3:4). Unlike Moses they choose to enjoy the seasonal pleasures of sin rather than suffer afflictions with Jehovah's people (Heb. 11:25). In slavish imitation of the younger son in that "pearl of the parables" they sensually seek that far-off country of sin and vice which glows with far greater prospects of earthly pleasure than does loyal service in the Father's work (Luke 15:11-32). The bright lights of what they dream is ahead blind them to the hog pen of shame and degradation which is the certain consequence just beyond. The early chapters in their book of youthful indulgences are written with zestful energy and a carefree attitude. However, the finale of their self-composed book of sin will bring the sure pages of real remorse and deep-seated regrets. Hell itself brings the final curtain down on the life lived without God.

A preacher friend and I once did personal work with a carefree young man. Though we studied thoroughly with him and sought with all the persuasive power at our command to win him for the Lord, he demurred. We both concurred on the way home that love for sin tugged at his youthful heartstrings with far greater power than did God's love. Recently I talked with this same young man. Now he is married and thinking in terms of starting a family. Is he yet a Christian? No. Satan still holds the deed to his soul. Young people, the longer you serve sin, the deeper Satan's hold on your heart will become. You can break the satanic clutch of his power over you much easier in youth than in later life.

Closely akin to the foregoing is another hindrance of young people remembering God in their early years. They feel that becoming a Christian will end all their popularity. Youthful reader, Jehovah God did not place you here to court, woo, and win the crown of earthly popularity. This crown has never been worth its cost. Many a young person has sold himself to do evil with Satan who offers temporary and short-lived popularity as the *only* enticing bait of recompense. People who dissolve their friendship with you because you became a Christian are better as *past* friends and no longer as *present* friends anyway. It is far better to lose the friendship of people like this and gain the friendship of Christ and real Christians. Friendship with the world has always led to enmity toward God (James 4:4). Remembering God in youth will help you to become popular with the righteous element of society. These friends will not forsake you when the need for real friendship arises. Friendships formed while living in a framework of unrighteousness and impurity are as short-lived as the morning mist before the rising sun. They will disappear when tested. Remember God in youth and you will have Him always on your side. You will also find a precious popularity with other kindred spirits who likewise seek to obey Ecclesiastes 12:1 in the early years of their earthly pilgrimage.

Some young people have accepted the idea that youth is a period for sowing wild oats and that youth is not a time for gospel obedience and Christian dedication. Satan has planted this idea in our world and many parents and young people have swallowed it hook, line, and sinker. This idea is one of the most fatal philosophies of all devilish propaganda.

Fathers have been known to pass this philosophy on to their sons. All young men must have their fling. They must "do their own thing," to use a devilish expression currently in vogue. They must taste of life in all of its enticing forms. A young man once confessed in my presence that his father actually encouraged him to practice fornication while dating! Modern mothers frequently do everything in their power to corrupt the morals of their daughters. They teach them to dance, to drink, to dress immodestly in order to catch the attention of lustful men, and to be popular regardless of moral or spiritual costs. Many parents make a god out of popularity, the number-one idol in the lives of their children. These godless parents apparently possess the absurd notion that young people will not be held responsible for the sowing of their wild oats, that somehow this period of their life makes them immune from all consequences. How very foolish it is for parents to encourage the sowing of wild oats while praying that there will be a crop failure. But this is one crop which knows no failures. Paul makes that crystal clear when he said we unequivocally reap what we sow. We need not think we can mock God in these matters (Gal. 6:7-8). This observation comes from the wise scribe of Ecclesiastes, "Rejoice, O young man, in thy youth; and let thy heart cheer thee in the days of thy youth, and walk in the ways of thine heart, and in the sight of thine eyes: but know thou, that for all these things God will bring thee into judgment" (Eccles. 11:9). Childhood and youth amount to nothing but vanity when lived with the "wild oats" philosophy. What if these young people who are coached to sow wild oats in youth decide to major in this type of life? Many do, you know. What then? What if they do not get it out of their system while young and continue this type of life as long as they live? Then what? What if they die while sowing wild oats? What then? A young person can die while under the damning influence of liquor. Then what? Young people can die while returning from a date which has been carried on in the framework of immoral escapades. Then what? Young people who are following this evil philosophy of life should listen again to this statement: "The crop of wild oats has *never* known a crop failure." Regardless of what you might think, you will not become the first exception to this rule. This rule has *no* exceptions. It never has. It never will.

Consider what happened when Joseph of the Old Testament had an opportunity to sow his wild oats. The opportunity was placed enticingly before him in Genesis 39 but the voice of conscience and reason prevailed. He said a clear and decisive NO and the ring of that NO has been heard for centuries. Do you suppose that Joseph ever regretted that no he gave to a fleshly woman's sinful proposition? I think not. A yes to that aggressive proposal and we might have never again heard of Joseph. His brilliant potential could have ended right there.

Many young people do not remember *now* their Creator because they are duped into accepting the fatal delusion that time is definitely on their side and salvation thus becomes a matter of *then* instead of *now* with them. Such young people do not believe that Jesus might come during their youth or that death really might be an imminent occurrence. They think that there will be plenty of time for God and religion in later life. They believe the period of youth is a time for irresponsible fun and careless frivolity. Old age will be soon enough to consider with care the needs of one's soul. The old devilish deluder knows that if he can keep youth and God separated now, he stands a good chance of effecting a permanent separation. Not many older people are converted. No one knows this better than Satan himself. That is a sufficient reason why youth should remember God NOW.

"Boast not thyself of tomorrow; for thou knowest not what a day may bring forth" (Prov. 27:1). This passage is applicable to young people as well as to older readers. A young man may boast of what he will do tomorrow but the last syllable of that boast may be uttered while he is experiencing his final heartbeat. What makes a rebellious youth of today think that this heart will be tender and open to gospel penetration tomorrow? Such a youth displays a woeful ignorance of the nature of sin. Continuation in sinful living tends to harden the heart, callous the conscience, and stultify the senses to the soul's obvious need for salvation. A person can reject God and salvation so many times that his tender conscience becomes seared and nothing will touch the mainsprings of his will.

The basic text for this section of our study says, "Remember *now* thy Creator in the days of thy youth . . ." (Eccles. 12:1, italics added). This power-packed passage cautions against procrastination. *Now* is the time to remember Jehovah God. Planning to remember Him later is sheer folly for you have no assurance that there will be a later time. Even if there is, you should want to be a Christian all the days of your accountable life.

In Mark 13:32 Jesus says of His second coming, "But of that day and that hour knoweth no man, no, not the angels which are in heaven, neither the Son, but the Father." What if Jesus were to come before you, as an accountable youth, began to remember Him? Then what? Suppose you plan to obey the gospel just as soon as you make your exit from the teen-age years? What if God's Son comes on your eighteenth birthday? Then what? What if a completely unexpected accident were to remove you while you are yet in your unsaved teen-age years? Then what? Have you considered that Jesus will come during the lifetime of some young people? Not everyone will be old at His second coming. Some will be your current age when He comes. Suppose you plan to become a Christian next year. What if He comes this year? The uncertainty of His second coming provides an important reason for youth to remember God now — not tomorrow.

The Bible is written to young people as well as to older people. Listen to Paul: "(For he saith, I have heard thee in a time accepted, and in the day of salvation have I succoured thee: behold, *now* is the accepted time; behold, *now* is the day of salvation)" (II Cor. 6:2, italics added). The writer of the Hebrew epistle said, "Wherefore (as the Holy Ghost saith, *To day* if ye will hear his voice, Harden not your hearts, as in the provocation, in the day of temptation in the wilderness . . ." (Heb. 3:7-8, italics added).

Saul is first mentioned in the New Testament as a young man (Acts 7:58). At this time Saul of Tarsus honestly thought he was remembering God in his youth. However, he was following the wrong religion. When he heard the truth he was urged to obey it immediately. Ananias said to the youthful Saul, "And *now* why tarriest thou? arise, and be baptized, and wash away thy sins, calling on the name of the Lord" (Acts 22:16, italics added). This youthful Hebrew arose and immediately accepted Christianity (Gal. 3:27; Rom. 6:3-4).

Young people, Satan says, "Wait!" Jehovah says, "Today!" Whose call will you answer? Your decision will affect your eternal destiny.

HOW CAN YOUTH REMEMBER GOD?

Children must learn about God before youth can remember Him. There is an immense amount of knowledge which children can absorb about the Bible. When portions of the Bible are learned during childhood, this knowledge will later become workable wisdom. Remember that Timothy had known Scripture from babyhood onward. Later his knowledge of Scripture made him "wise unto salvation through faith which is in Christ Jesus" (II Tim. 3:15). Biblical knowledge gleaned in childhood can ripen into seasoned wisdom for one's later youth and all his years of maturity. I can think of no finer way for children to remember God than to learn of Him early and thus form wholesome and reverent attitudes toward spiritual realities during youth. The greatest thing the church can do for children is to aid the home in teaching young children God's Word. Instead of clamoring for the church to offer recreational activities for our youth, let us emphasize what the church can do for our children; that is, teach and impress God's Word on their pliable hearts and instill it in their formative minds.

Youth can remember God by becoming Christians when they are old enough. Children often raise the question as to when they are old enough to do this. No set age can be given. Variation occurs in this area. Allow me to offer one or two observations, however. A child who will not listen to a sermon and refuses to behave in a Bible class, in my judgment, is not yet ready to be a Christian. A preacher friend told me of a little child who was baptized in a meeting and while the worship service was still being conducted created quite a disturbance by misbehaving. Young people who are thinking about baptism must make sure they are old enough to accept the responsibility of Christian work and worship suitable for their age before they take the initial step of discipleship. If you sleep through every sermon on your mother's lap or cannot reverently behave in Bible class, then some growing up needs to be done before church membership is seriously undertaken. I strongly disagree with the practice that as soon as little boys and girls are able to read they should immediately obey the gospel. There is a great deal of difference between recognition of elementary words in a simple reader and understanding the demands of gospel obedience. Children learn to read now about the age of five or six. In some cases they read even earlier. This is getting too close to infant membership to be comfortable. I earnestly desire the conversion of all young people to Jesus Christ but not before they are keenly aware of the seriousness of Christian discipleship. Those who are old enough and possess sufficient maturity to take Christianity seriously should obey the gospel immediately. It is dangerous to put it off one moment after arriving at the age of accountability.

Youth can remember God by being an example of vibrant Christianity. Dedicated youth can make tremendous strides in the richly rewarding realms of personal godliness and individual righteousness. Apparently Timothy was converted by Paul on Paul's first missionary journey. At the early beginning of Paul's second journey Luke was able to write that the youthful lad from Central Asia Minor "was well reported of by the brethren that were at Lystra and Iconium" (Acts 16:2). God needs young people today with sterling reputations. It is true that character and reputation differ. Character is what we really are (what God knows us to be) while reputation is what others consider us to be. Both are important. Neither should be minimized. Character is needed to stand approved before God. Reputations are essential because they constitute the capital stock with which we do business for the Lord. Young people cannot influence others for Christ unless they establish themselves as reputable youngsters. Unless people have confidence in your uprightness of life and sincerity of purpose, they will not heed your teaching or profit by your example.

The youthful Timothy received this good advice from Paul: "Let no man despise thy youth; but be thou an example of the believers, in word, in conversation, in charity, in spirit, in faith, in purity" (I Tim. 4:12). Young people who sincerely seek to follow this advice will remember Jehovah in the finest possible manner. There is nothing which speaks with such eloquent power as a living demonstration of daily Christianity. Again Paul wrote this young dedicated disciple, "neither be partaker of other men's sins: keep thyself pure" (I Tim. 5:22). Complete purity demands a threefold application. Purity of heart constitutes the firm foundation upon which the other two rest (Matt. 5:8). Purity of speech is second. Pure speech reflects a pure heart. Jesus declared that "out of the abundance of the heart the mouth speaketh" (Matt. 12:34). Purity of deeds comes third and crowns the other two with a fruitful performance. God needs young people who possess genuine purity to serve in His great cause. Titus was told to exhort young men "to be sober minded" (Titus 2:6). Young people can remember God by overcoming the wicked one (I John 2:13). The apostle of love strongly commended certain young men of his day "because ye are strong, and the word of God abideth in you, and ye have overcome the wicked one" (I John 2:14). Youth can greatly bless the home of which they are a vital part by giving diligent consideration to these passages of Scripture.

Youth can remember God by faithful worship. Each young person who really wishes to remember Jehovah God should devote some time each day for Bible study and prayer. Your minds are fresh, vigorous, and deeply impressionable. Fill your mind with the golden nuggets of eternal truth. With the psalmist be able to say, "Thy word have I hid in mine heart, that I might not sin against thee" (Ps. 119:11). Of all objects you might desire, God and His word constitute the most important addition ever made to the human heart. Of all bodily possessions your heart is the greatest receptacle available for the dwelling of God's word. The end result is that you learn to live well and to abstain from sin. When you fill your heart with Biblical truth, you are remembering God. Through prayer every day you live you may address the majestic one who inhabits eternity (Isa. 57:15). Live constantly in the atmosphere of prayer and you will find Him instantly available when you need Him in a time of crisis (I Thess. 5:17; Col. 4:2; I Tim. 2:8). Many young people do not know how to pray in times of sorrow because they have never sought the heavenly throne of grace in times of joy and happiness.

Public worship likewise has a claim upon you. Decide early in life that every worship service is vitally important and resolve that you will be there if at all possible. As Christian young people you will surely desire to emulate the noble example of regular worship diligently begun and faithfully practiced by the earliest saints in God's church. Luke wrote, "And they continued stedfastly in the apostles' doctrine and fellowship, and in breaking of bread, and in prayers" (Acts 2:42). In all probability the "they" of this verse included some young people. If we are right in this assumption, then the first young people to obey the gospel were faithful in their worship attendance. It will be recalled that the early Christians frequently met daily (Acts 2:46; 5:42; 16:5; 19:9-10). Young people, let it never be said of you that you are the ones who miss most of the public worship periods conducted by the church. By properly maintaining regular attendance you can be a means of encouraging others who are older to attend with greater regularity. We have known some fine young people who have helped convert their parents to a more faithful pattern of regular church attendance. The writer to the Hebrews said not to forsake "the assembling of ourselves together, as the manner of some is; but exhorting one another: and so much the more, as ye see the day approaching" (Heb. 10:25).

Young people can remember God by working for the conversion of others. Of course, you need to know the truth yourself before you can attempt to teach it to others. You also need to be living a faithful Christian life in order that you may back up your personal work with a living demonstration of what Christianity has done for you. Knowledge of truth, a daily walk with the Master, and a great concern for lost souls can lead you to become an early soul-winner for Jesus. There is no joy comparable to that of leading a lost soul to Christ. That will thrill your soul, lift your heart, and draw you closer to the Lord Jesus.

Young people, saving yourself and teaching truth to others are the two finest ways you can remember Jehovah in the early years of your life. Diligence in these two earnest endeavors cannot fail to help your home to be what God would have it to be. The *Christ in the home* concept will inspire greater work to be done in bringing Christ and Christianity into non-Christian families.

REWARDS OF OBEYING JEHOVAH IN YOUTH

Obeying the injunction to remember God in one's youth leads to a happier life. Millions of youth are currently seeking happiness and satisfaction in illicit sex, strong drink, drug addition, and other satanic devices. Each of these sins has a payday and Jehovah's wages for sin are horror, anguish, pain, and eternal damnation. Lasting happiness is not found in the lust of the eye, the lust of the flesh, and the pride or vainglory of life (I John 2:15-17). A young man was once asked if he was still experiencing a kick from his sins. His reply was, "I am now getting a kickback." Genuine happiness now and in the future is found in obedience to God even while one is in his youth.

Making Ecclesiastes 12:1 a part of your youthful life is the best possible preparation for successful adulthood. Tomorrow's adult is today's youth. Your youth is the foundation upon which your adult years will rest. You are building not only for today but tomorrow as well. Take heed and be wisely cautious what manner of materials you put into your foundation. Do not allow the old deluder to deceive you into thinking that sinful indulgence today will have no paydays of pain and scars of sin tomorrow. The way of any transgressor is hard and this is even more true of youthful transgressors, for you have more years, as a general rule, to bear the scars of misspent youth (Prov. 13:15). The scars of even forgiven sins can haunt you for a lifetime. I have heard older people confess that sins committed fifty or more years ago still bothered them even though Christ long ago removed their guilt. A father once told his son to drive a nail into the barn door for every wrong he committed. He was told to leave it there until he had made the wrong right. The son followed that practice for a considerable length of time. Many nails were driven into the door. When the wrong was corrected the nail was removed. One day the son showed his father the door and complained that after the nails were removed the holes remained. The father reminded him that wrongs always leave scars. A David can be forgiven the sin of adultery but the scars and consequences will not be erased in this life. A Saul can bitterly persecute the church but even full forgiveness will not erase the tragedy of a stoned Stephen or the bleeding bodies of dedicated disciples in Jerusalem (Acts 22:19-20; 26:9-11; I Cor. 15:9; I Tim. 1:13-15; Phil. 3:6). Prodigal sons may return from the foreign land of sin but there will always be elder brethren who will not forget the sordid chapters in their book of sin (Luke 15:11-32).

Obeying God in youth will make for happier days when one faces the sunset years of his life. There will be fewer regrets to plague the failing mind if one has lived a life of sobriety, righteousness, and godliness as a youthful soldier for Christ (Titus 2:11-12).

Christ could come while you are young. You could die while young. Thousands, younger than you are right now, have met the king of terrors when he was least expected. If you are presently remembering God in youth, His second coming or your premature death will not find you in a state of unpreparedness.

Obeying Jehovah in youth will make the home happier. Many Christian parents today never experience a moment free of real concern because they have accountable sons and daughters who are non-Christians. Within the uneasy hearts of those parents there is the gnawing fear of where these sons and daughters would go if Jesus were to return today or early death were to snatch them out of the land of the living. As a young person you may be the only person in the household who keeps your family from being a truly complete Christian family. As a Christian youth you could add immeasurably to the radiant joy of your good family. Presently, there may be no Christians in your family. Irreligion may have been the only general rule you have ever known. Were you to become a Christian today, within a few months you might be able to change the religious destiny of an entire family. By becoming a Christian in youth you add a meaningful chapter to your present home and also cast a favorable vote for one day having a Christian home of your own. Ponder this for a moment. Suppose you obey the gospel this year as a young man. Totally unknown to you there is a young girl in another place who likewise sweetens her lips with the good confession the same year as do you. She, too, becomes a Christian. Your path and that of hers do not cross for some few years. Each of you grows in grace. Each of you makes your respective set of Christian parents very happy because of your fervent faith and diligent determination to succeed in remembering Jehovah God in youth. Ultimately you both meet. Not long after the first introduction the dating period between you begins. Soon there is the birth of real love in both hearts. Your courtship reaches the serious step of a marriage proposal and an immediate acceptance on her part. After the engagement period comes a beautiful marriage. Now the formation of another home is in the making. You both have had helpful experience in the Christian homes of your respective parents. You both came from families where *Christ in the home* was an all-pervading concept. Now you will seek to build a home where Jesus and His Word will dominate all the facets of your marital and family ties. Your home is off to a much better beginning because you both have remembered God in youth. Young people, it pays in a thousand ways to remember God during youth.

There is no real good reason why you should not remember Him in your youth. There are many weighty reasons why you should remember Him in this period of your impressionable and pliable life. My prayer is that every young person who reads this chapter will seek immediately to follow Ecclesiastes 12:1 in his life.

CONCLUSION

I would encourage you to read your Bible every day. I would encourage you to pray to your heavenly Father on a regular basis. Attend regularly all the public services of the church. Take your religion seriously. Become a soul winner for Jesus. There may be people in your family who are not Christians. Be an Andrew and bring a brother to Jesus (John 1:40-42). Let the great heroes of faith inspire you. For purity follow Joseph (Gen. 39). For courage look to the youthful David (I Sam. 17). For youthful determination and dedication look to Josiah (II Chron. 34). In matters of temperance and an avowed intent to remain loyal to Jehovah at all costs Daniel is a worthy example (Dan. 1:8). In character development Timothy is one of the greatest of all examples for your daily emulation (Acts 16:1-2; Phil. 2:20-22; I Tim. 4:12). In all things Jesus is the truly great example. Be like the Greeks in John 12:20-22 and desire to "see Jesus." The Bible provides you with His portrait. Be diligent in pursuing His footsteps (I Peter 2:21).

When children lift up Christ and the Bible in the home, they are truly remembering Jehovah God in youth. Then the Godhead and the Bible will lift up childhood in the home.

QUESTIONS FOR DISCUSSION

1. Memorize Ecclesiastes 12:1.
2. List the reasons given why Jehovah should be remembered in youth. Can you add additional ones? If so, what would they be?
3. Memorize I Timothy 4:12. Compare this verse with Ecclesiastes 12:1.
4. Can you name one *reason* why young people should not remember God in the early part of their lives? If so, what would it be?
5. Why do some young people fail to remember God in youth?

6. List and discuss texts which suggest that today or now is the proper time for youth to remember God.
7. List some ways in which youth can remember Jehovah.
8. List some of the rewards of obeying Jehovah in youth.
9. List some of the young people from the Bible you should imitate as you remember God in youth.

15

The In-law in the Home

Marriage and the formation of a home produce a number of new and varied relationships. Marriage immediately turns a man into a husband and a woman into a wife. The coming of a child sometime later turns the husband into a father and the wife into a mother. Entrance into marriage means that a closer tie is formed with the family of the marital mate. Unless the parents of the mate are dead, there is an entrance into the relationship of son-in-law and daughter-in-law. These parents in turn become a father-in-law and a mother-in-law to the one who has married their child. If the mate has brothers or sisters, there will be the formation of brother-in-law and/or sister-in-law also. Every couple should be aware of the ramifications of these new relationships. It is not true that one marries only the mate and has no subsequent relationships with his or her family. We marry into a family and there will certainly be relationships with each in-law.

Forming harmonious relationships with each in-law will enhance any marriage. Any husband who is worth anything is going to desire that his wife have an affectionate interest in his good family. Any wife who has love for her family is going to desire that her husband develop a love for and an abiding interest in her parents, brothers, and sisters. Where there is formed an early resentment toward the in-law relationships, there can soon develop a serious rupture in the marriage tie itself. Human nature being what it is, it is rather naive to ignore such considerations and demands.

Many homes will begin, continue, and ultimately conclude at the death of husband and wife without any in-law ever living under the same roof. But even in cases like this there will be temporary visits back and forth among the families. It is wise for each mate to welcome these in-law visits and to develop a genuine interest in visiting the homes of the in-laws. Though there may be extenuating circumstances in some instances it seems such a tragedy when a parent is not welcomed into the home of his own child. It seems such a tragedy when parents never bid a sincere welcome to the one who married their son or daughter. Something is seriously wrong somewhere. The *Christ in the home* concept is not at work in such circumstances.

In other homes it may be necessary for an in-law to live there on a more or less permanent basis. This arrangement calls for many adjustments and they should be made within a Christian framework. Biblical principles must operate here as in all facets of home life. There is a right way to approach every known re-responsibility. Finding that right way and diligently pursuing it should be of uppermost concern to every child of God.

There are some Biblical pointers for establishing a general framework in which these in-law situations can be worked out satisfactorily for the glory of God and the profit of the family. The Golden Rule of Matthew 7:12 should have an application in all areas of human relationships. "Therefore all things whatsoever ye would that men should do to you, do ye even so to them: for this is the law and the prophets." In addition let us consider several other passages. "Let love be without dissimulation. Abhor that which is evil; cleave to that which is good. Be kindly affectioned one to another with brotherly love; in honour preferring one another" (Rom. 12:9-10). "Distributing to the necessity of saints; given to hospitality" (Rom. 12:13). "Watch ye, stand fast in the faith, quit you like men, be strong. Let all your things be done with charity" (I Cor. 16:13-14). "As we have therefore opportunity, let us do good unto all men, especially unto them who are of the household of faith" (Gal. 6:10). "Let all bitterness, and wrath, and anger, and clamour, and evil speaking, be put away from you, with all malice: And be ye kind one to another, tenderhearted, forgiving one another, even as God for Christ's sake hath forgiven you" (Eph. 4:31-32). "Let nothing be done through strife or vainglory; but in lowliness of mind let each esteem other better than themselves. Look not every man on his own things, but every man also on the things of others" (Phil. 2:3). "Put on therefore, as the elect of God, holy and beloved, bowels of mercies, kindness, humbleness

of mind, meekness, longsuffering; Forbearing one another, and forgiving one another, if any man have a quarrel against any: even
as Christ forgave you, so also do ye. And above all these things
put on chairty, which is the bond of perfectness. And let the
peace of God rule in your hearts, to the which also ye are called in
one body; and be ye thankful" (Col. 3:12-15). "Finally, be ye all
of one mind, having compassion one of another, love as brethren,
be pitiful, be courteous: Not rendering evil for evil, or railing for
railing: but contrariwise blessing; knowing that ye are thereunto
called, that ye should inherit a blessing. For he that will love life,
and see good days, let him refrain his tongue from evil, and his
lips that they speak no guile: Let him eschew evil, and do good;
let him seek peace, and ensue it. For the eyes of the Lord are over
the righteous, and his ears are open unto their prayers: but the
face of the Lord is against [upon, marginal reference] them that
do evil" (I Peter 3:8-12). "But to do good and to communicate
forget not: for with such sacrifices God is well pleased" (Heb. 13:
16). "Follow peace with all men, and holiness, without which no
man shall see the Lord" (Heb. 12:14). "If it be possible, as much
as lieth in you, live peaceably with all men" (Rom. 12:18). To be
sure, these Scriptural principles have a much wider application than
merely home relationships but they certainly include home relationships.

THE YOUNG IN-LAW IN THE HOME

I begin with the observation that it is *far, far* better for a young
couple to have their own living quarters than to move in with the
girl's parents or the boy's parents. It is better to have a one- or
two-room apartment than to live in the spacious quarters of in-
laws those first few critical months after marriage is entered. Many
adjustments will be required and a couple can make them more
harmoniously if in-laws are not a part of the same family framework.

Many couples never think seriously about where they will live or
how they will meet family expenses. They just automatically assume that either set of parents will take care of such matters.

If the decision is made to move into the home of one of the
parents, some guidelines should be followed. First of all, this arrangement should be satisfactory to and approved by all concerned. Next, the young girl who moves in with her in-laws should
recognize that the home is still theirs and not hers. She should
not expect to become the guide of this household. That would be

usurping the place of her mother-in-law. She should not expect to change a household routine that has become second nature for that mother. She should come in as a helper and learner. She should not expect that mother to wait on her. She should do her part in the preparation of meals, the cleaning of the house, and by all means keep her clothing and that of her husband's clean and pressed. She is no longer a girl at home but now a wife. As she does more and learns more, the right-thinking mother-in-law will give her more and more household responsibilities. By doing the right thing she can earn the undying love and abiding respect of her in-laws. She will be wise if she allows her in-laws to take care of any younger brothers-in-law and sisters-in-law without directions or comments from her. If her counsel is sought, she should give it. She should not give unsolicited advice. It is not desired and would be unwelcome. The young girl who temporarily enters the household of in-laws should determine to be a blessing and a help to that family. She will gain nothing by entering such an arrangement with a haughty attitude, an uncontrollable temper, and a spoiled disposition. In fact, she stands to lose in every direction if she takes these dispositions with her. And, let it be emphasized that such living arrangements should be temporary. The couple should begin to lay plans immediately to furnish their own living quarters away from both families.

When a boy moves in with his new in-laws he should likewise recognize that it is still their home to rule and guide not his. It would be most improper and presumptuous for him to assume the throne of decision-maker and legislator for that household. That family functioned as a home unit before his arrival and will continue to direct its own destiny after his departure. This young man should do his part of the work. If he is gainfully employed, he should provide an agreed upon amount weekly or monthly toward the living expenses of the household. Even if he is in school, a part-time job could enable him to help with some of the expenses. When it comes time to cut the grass, trim the shrubbery, plant the garden, or paint the trimwork around the house he should contribute his working energies. He should enter this temporary living arrangement with a determination to live in harmony with each member of the family. This is no place for a person who is spoiled and expects others to wait upon him.

How should mother-in-law and father-in-law act in such situations? They should have an agreement with the younger couple that this two-family arrangement is strictly temporary and that a move to their own private quarters is better for all concerned.

Until this happens they should do all they can to give the young couple a good start in their newly entered marriage. If facilities permit, they should be given the most private area the family house will allow. They should expect the young couple to do their part in meeting the added expenses of the household and in the performance of the work. However, they should not expect more than what is proper and fair. As many decisions as can be made by the young couple alone should be freely allowed. Though human nature prompts parents to side with their own offspring in a disagreement, this should be strictly avoided. The young couple should begin to assume more and more of the new responsibilities that are theirs. This is a time for them to finish maturing. Prudently plan for them to lean less on your help and more and more on their own efforts. If the son-in-law is in college and his earning powers are limited, help them a little more if possible and let them live in an apartment of their own. If the young wife is employed, let them meet all or nearly all of their living expenses. Encourage them to make their own way if that is at all possible, and it will be in most cases. You will help them best by letting them help themselves.

While the young couple is living with the in-laws there should be a time set aside each day when the Bible is read, songs are sung, and a prayer is sent to the heavenly throne of grace. These family devotions can do much to erase friction and create harmony in the hearts of all. It is difficult to retire at night with wrong feelings if a period of worship has brought the activities of the day to a close. If both families accept the *Christ in the home* concept, then harmony, happiness, and joy can reign during this temporary arrangement.

THE OLDER IN-LAW IN THE HOME

Many older people are able to keep their homes throughout their senior years. They never face the decision of moving into the homes of their children. In most cases they are happier to keep their own homes where they can have quiet and peace. This way they can retire when they get ready, arise when they feel like it, take a rest in the middle of the day, and make their own decisions without regard to how it will affect those much younger in years and with far greater energy. When the older-in-law lives with a son or daughter who has a growing family, those decisions cannot always be made so freely or simply.

Circumstances will not always permit each senior citizen to retain his or her home throughout life. A financial pinch may make that impossible. A loss of bodily or mental health may make it inadvisable for the older person to stay alone. The choice of a new living arrangement must be made. It may be the wish of the aged person to go to a nice home for older people. That decision may be necessary because a daughter or daughter-in-law may be in failing health herself. She may not be physically capable of caring for that aged person. Many older people have received far better care in a nursing home where their medical needs are met by especially trained personnel than they would ever have received in the home of a loving son or daughter.

The decision may be made for an aged father or mother to move into the home of a son and daughter-in-law or the home of a daughter and son-in-law. Such a move calls for adjustments among all members of the family. These adjustments should be made with Christian principles prevailing. It is never right to do wrong. It is never right to be mean, ugly, and despiteful. These are some considerations when such a move is made.

The aged person should recognize that he or she is now living in the home of another. The son is not to have his place as head of his family usurped. The daughter-in-law is not to have her place as guide of her family usurped. The aged person should come with the determination of fitting in just as harmoniously and smoothly as is humanly possible. It is not realistic for him or her to think that grandchildren will cease to be and act like children just because a grandparent is now living in the household. It is neither realistic nor fair for the older person because of his presence to expect that their children will stop entertaining friends of their own age and other relatives. It is not realistic to think that their children can stop making a living and keeping a family going just so *all* available moments can be spent ministering to the older person's wishes. The older person who is still in fair health should continue to be active in helping around the house and yard. This will be of great benefit to both the older person and the younger people of the household also. Those who have spent active lives will be happier if they remain as active as health permits. It seems only fair and reasonable that the older person, if financially able, will assume his part of the living expenses. He should not expect to bank all his pension and/or Social Security check while his children are providing for his living expenses. The family may be struggling to meet house payments, educational needs, food, clothing, and medical bills. Biblical principles would suggest that the older person meet his share of the living expenses. If the older person has several children and only one child and his family are willing to care for him during his sunset years, it seems only right and fair that this be remembered in a special way in the making of that person's final will. There are too many children today who are perfectly willing for one brother or sister to care completely for an ailing father or an invalid mother many years without one bit of help except an occasional visit but who expect the parent to treat all the children alike in the will.

The older person who has grown old gracefully can bring a rich chapter of meaningful relationships with him as he moves into the family of one of his children. He can enrich the life of his child, in-law, and grandchildren by being exactly what an older Christian should be. My paternal grandfather lived in our home when I was young. My Christian mother could not have been any better to her own parents than she was to him. Pa-Pa, as we affectionately called him, brought a great blessing to our home. That older mother can bring a measure of great warmth as she fits right in with her daughter-in-law. If both of them are Christians, they can live together in holy harmony. That mother will never seek to come between her son and his wife. She will recognize that there was a time when she was the first and most important woman in her sons's life. Now his wife is first. There will be no feeling of jealousy or envy about this. She will recognize that it must be this way. The older father who moves in with a daughter and son-in-law will recognize the same principle and gladly abide by it. Though there was a time in years gone by when he was first in her life as father, now her husband must be first. A recognition of this Biblically approved principle can aid greatly in the smooth transition of an older parent moving into the household.

How should the older parent be treated when this move has been made? Naturally, Biblical principles should again be followed. A genuine welcome should be extended. The aged parent should be warmly received and made to feel that this is now his or her home. It should be the determination of every member of the family to make sure that nothing is ever said or done which will make the older person feel he is in the way or an unwelcome intruder in the home. If there is genuine love and real regard, this matter will largely take care of itself. The needs of the older person should be met cheerfully. Kindness is a must. This will even allow and demand family firmness when the older person does things against his best welfare and ignores things which may be imperative for his or her good.

Christ in the home is the answer to these circumstances too. If every family member will be truly guided and governed by the precious principles of the Prince of Peace, the home with an aged parent present can be happy, holy, and harmonious. Where the principles of Jesus are ignored there will be no happiness, no holiness, and no harmony regardless of who does or does not reside in the home.

IN-LAWS MENTIONED IN THE BIBLE

Throughout these chapters I have sought to place each home relationship in a Biblical framework. The Bible has something to say about in-laws also. We shall note two in-laws who did not measure up to Biblical standards and two in-laws that will serve as excellent examples to follow.

LABAN: FATHER-IN-LAW TO JACOB

Jacob was related to Laban before he became son-in-law to the inhabitant of Padan-aram. We learn from Genesis 24:29 and 28:2 that Rebekah had a brother by the name of Laban. Jacob was Rebekah's son and this made Laban his uncle. Jacob, in Genesis 28:1-2, is forbidden by his aged father Isaac to take a wife from among the Canaanites. Instead he is to arise and "go to Padan-aram, to the house of Bethuel thy mother's father; and take thee a wife from thence of the daughters of Laban thy mother's brother." Jacob obeys his father's instructions and begins the long journey to the northeast. In Genesis 29 he comes to the place and meets the beautiful and well-favored Rachel. The first meeting of Jacob and Laban seems to portray a future of cordial and harmonious relationships. "And Jacob told Rachel that he was her father's brother, and that he was Rebekah's son: and she ran and told her father. And it came to pass, when Laban heard the tidings of Jacob his sister's son, that he ran to meet him, and embraced him, and kissed him, and brought him to his house. And he told Laban all these things. And Laban said to him, Surely thou art my bone and my flesh. And he abode with him the space of a month" (Gen. 29:12-14). At the end of that month "Laban said unto Jacob, Because thou art my brother, shouldest thou therefore serve me for nought? tell me, what shall thy wages be?" (Gen. 29:15). Such a move on Laban's part seemed to indicate that he desired to do right by Jacob. Jacob turned toward the beautiful Rachel. He said, "I will serve thee seven years for Rachel thy younger daughter" (Gen. 29:18). Laban's response was instantly favorable. He said, "It is better that I give her to thee, than that I should give her to another man: abide with me" (Gen. 29:19). For her lovely hand in marriage Jacob worked seven years "and they seemed unto him but a few days, for the love he had to her" (Gen. 29:20). When the years were fulfilled Jacob asked for her hand in marriage. At this point the cunning deception of Laban comes to light. Instead of fulfilling his agreement, Laban deceived Jacob and gave him Leah rather than Rachel. Jacob immediately confronted the deceptive Laban with these words, "What is this thou hast done unto me? did not I serve with thee for Rachel? wherefore then hast thou beguiled me?" (Gen. 29:25). Laban's weak response was, "It must not be so done in our country, to give the younger before the firstborn" (Gen. 29:26). Every implication is that this must have been a practice among those people for many years. Surely the practice, if uinversally held among people of Padan-aram, did not begin within these last seven years, for Jacob would without doubt have been aware of that new development. Being a stranger and sojourner in that land Jacob was not knowledgeable of all their ancient customs. If that was their custom, why did not Laban seven years earlier say something like this in his initial agreement with Jacob, "It is not the custom of my people to allow the younger child to marry before the older child does. If at the end of the seven years, Leah, the older, has been given in marriage, then you may have Rachel's hand. If both are still unmarried at the time the seven years are concluded, you will be obligated to take Leah first. The older has to precede the younger in marriage." Had such a conversation occurred seven years earlier Jacob would have known what to expect. He placed full confidence in Laban and worked diligently during the seven years. Love was the expected reward and a labor of love is the most powerful of all inducements for a job well done. Laban repaid that confidence and those years of sacrificial toil with deliberate deception. Laban told him to fulfill Leah's week and then he could have Rachel for wife (Gen. 29:27-28). Rachel was given to him as wife but for her Jacob had to serve an additional seven years (Gen. 29:29-30). Jacob became son-in-law to Laban within the framework of dishonesty and deception. That has never been a proper foundation for good in-law relations. It is true that Jacob had deceived his aged father Isaac about the blessing reserved for the firstborn (Gen. 27). However, he had done the honorable thing with Laban. Laban was clearly in the wrong here. Fathers and mothers cannot deal dishonorably with a prospective son-in-law or daughter-in-law and expect to have a beautiful beginning for the in-law relationship. Christian principles should prevail here as well as in all other home relationships.

Laban was to show the true colors of his sly deceptiveness and cunning nature in subsequent dealings with his son-in-law. Every indication of Genesis 30 leads us to form the conclusion that Laban grew rich as a result of Jacob's presence. Laban recognized from past experience "that the Lord hath blessed me for thy sake" (Gen. 30:27). When Jacob spoke of leaving for his own country Laban begged him to tarry. Jacob reminded him of the past service he had rendered him with the accompanying results, "Thou knowest how I have served thee, and how thy cattle was with me. For it was little which thou hadst before I came, and it is now increased unto a multitude; and the Lord hath blessed thee since my coming; and now when shall I provide for mine own house also?" (Gen. 30: 29-30). Laban proposed a gift to Jacob (Gen. 30:31). Jacob refused to be on the receiving end of a gift. He made a proposal whereby he would again feed and care for Laban's flocks (Gen. 30:31-43). This proposal resulted in Jacob's rise to power and riches. As a result Jacob heard his brothers-in-law bring a serious accusation against him, "Jacob hath taken away all that was our father's; and of that which was our father's hath he gotten all this glory" (Gen. 31:1). Jacob noted a change of Laban's countenance toward him (Gen. 31:2). Jehovah God instructed Jacob to return to Canaan and He would be with him (Gen. 31:3). Jacob called Rachel and Leah to him and spoke these words, "I see your father's countenance, that it is not toward me as before; but the God of my father hath been with me. And ye know that with all my power I have served your father. And your father had deceived me, and changed my wages ten times; but God suffered him not to hurt me" (Gen. 31:5-7). Rachel and Leah respond by saying, "Is there yet any portion or inheritance for us in our father's house? Are we not counted of him strangers? for he hath sold us, and hath quite devoured also our money. For all the riches which God hath taken from our father, that is ours, and our children's: now then, whatsoever God hath said unto thee, do" (Gen. 31:14-16).

Then Jacob and his family fled. Laban learned of it and followed in hot pursuit. In Genesis 31:24 Jehovah God warned the sly Laban in a dream, "Take heed that thou speak not to Jacob either good or bad." Laban overtook them and chided Jacob that he had left in secrecy. Jacob told him why they had left in that manner. Laban accused Jacob and his family of stealing his gods. Unknown to Jacob Rachel had really taken them. Jacob told Laban to seek out the gods but Laban did not find them due to Rachel's sly manner of concealing them (Gen. 31:32-35). Incidently, this occasion furnishes us with an example of the power of idolatrous parents. Laban was an idolater and the influence passed to his offspring. Rachel stole them and deceptively concealed them from the searching eye of her father. Jacob knew nothing about these actions.

Jacob's reaction to all of this is set forth in the following paragraph, "And Jacob was wroth, and chode with Laban: and Jacob answered and said to Laban, What is my trespass? what is my sin, that thou hast so hotly pursued after me? Whereas thou hast searched all my stuff, what hast thou found of all thy household stuff? set it here before my brethren and thy brethren, that they may judge betwixt us both. This twenty years have I been with thee; thy ewes and thy she goats have not cast their young, and the rams of thy flock have I not eaten. That which was torn of beasts I brought not unto thee; I bare the loss of it; of my hand didst thou require it, whether stolen by day, or stolen by night. Thus I was; in the day the drought consumed me, and the frost by night; and my sleep departed from mine eyes. Thus have I been twenty years in thy house; I served thee fourteen years for thy two daughters, and six years for thy cattle: and thou hast changed my wages ten times. Except the God of my father, the God of Abraham, and the fear of Isaac, had been with me, surely thou hadst sent me away now empty. God hath seen mine affliction and the labour of my hands, and rebuked thee yesternight" (Gen. 31:36-42). This entire episode does not leave Laban in a favorable light either as a father to his own children, Leah and Rachel, or a father-in-law to Jacob. It is to his credit that he suggested the making of a covenant between Jacob and himself before their final separation. This is done in the remainder of Genesis 31. The chapter closes with the kisses bestowed and the blessings conferred upon his sons and daughters. Laban departs for his own home. Laban was not honorable in his role as a father-in-law. He serves as an example of what a father-in-law should not be. No father-in-law can mistreat his son-in-law without mistreating also his own daughter and grandchildren.

SAUL: THE FATHER-IN-LAW TO DAVID

Another sad in-law in Scripture is King Saul. While Saul reigned as the first king over the Israelites and the youthful David kept watch over his father's sheep on the Judean hills near Bethlehem, there seemed little likelihood that the paths of the two would ever cross. But meet and merge they did indeed. David's ability as a gifted musician and his unparalleled youthful courage against the Philistine giant Goliath were the two elements that drew these widely differing personalities together. First Samuel 16:14-23 relates how that David's presence was sought out in order that he might play for the moody, intensely troubled, and deeply depressed monarch. The major thing that brought David to the attention of Saul and created national esteem for him was his courageous acceptance of Goliath's challenge. David met the giant in battle in the name of the Lord God and came away with one of the greatest military victories ever witnessed. This great victory caught the admiration of an entire nation. Saul was temporarily pleased. However, when greater praise began to be showered upon David than he was receiving as king himself, Saul showed the devilish side of his personality. The more Israel loved David as its newest and most courageous hero, the deeper became Saul's contempt and hatred for Jesse's son. It was through a proposal for David to become his son-in-law that Saul hoped to remove David permanently from the Israelite scene. He would silence the praising tongues of singing Hebrew maidens by taking the life of the object of their affection. Saul longed to see David dead. He preferred to have a dead prospective son-in-law than a live one. "And Saul said to David, Behold my elder daughter Merab, her will I give thee to wife: only be thou valiant for me, and fight the Lord's battles. For Saul said, Let not mine hand be upon him, but let the hand of the Philistines be upon him. And David said unto Saul, Who am I? and what is my life, or my father's family in Israel, that I should be son in law to the king?" (1 Sam. 18:17-18). Saul had only deep hatred for the powerful and persistent Philistines but he would have rejoiced if they could have been victorious over the youthful Hebrew hero that held an entire nation's esteem and affection. He strongly desired to see Jesse's son die upon the battlefield. He used the in-law proposal to further his pernicious plans. Murder lay upon the king's heart; deep humility permeated the heart of David at the thought of becoming son-in-law to the king. When the time came for Merab to be given to David she was given to another instead (I Sam. 18:19). Keeping his word was not one of Saul's noted virtues.

Saul learned that another daughter, Michal, was in love with David. This pleased the evil ruler very much (I Sam. 18:20). "And Saul said, I will give him her, that she may be a snare to him, and that the hand of the Philistines may be against him. Wherefore Saul said to David, Thou shalt this day be my son in law in the one of the twain" (I Sam. 18:21). Through his servants Saul conveyed word to David that no dowry was desired for Michal's hand in marriage but physical evidence that David had slain one hundred Philistines would make happy the king's heart. By hypocritical words Saul desired David to think that the proposal was based upon the concept of being "avenged of the king's enemies" (I Sam. 18:

25). His real intentions were "to make David fall by the hand of the Philistines" (I Sam. 18:25). The devout David did not suspect a thing. He thought the kind monarch was acting nobly and honorably. In fact "it pleased David well to be the king's son in law: and the days were not expired" (I Sam. 18:26). With immediate dispatch David went against the Philistine foes and slew two hundred instead of the one hundred. This time Saul gave him a daughter for wife (I Sam. 18:27). This marriage not only made David the husband of Michal but also the son-in-law to the king and a brother-in-law to the lovable Jonathan, already a dear friend of David's. The deeply envious king became more determined to destroy David as time went on. The Bible says that "Saul became David's enemy continually" (I Sam. 18:29). Saul tried to work through Jonathan to destroy David (I Sam. 19:1). He sought to catch David in his own home and while asleep but Michal helped David escape. Saul strongly chided Michal because she had aided in David's escape (I Sam. 19:17). Saul sought to slay David with his own hand in moments of deep desperation (I Sam. 18:10-11; 19:10). Saul even sought to slay Jonathan on one occasion because of his loyal friendship toward David (I Sam. 10:30-34). Much of the latter part of I Samuel has Saul hunting his son-in-law as though he were an incorrigible criminal and a dangerous outlaw. Through it all David acts honorably toward the king, his vicious and vindictive father-in-law. Needless to say we do not need fathers-in-law like Saul was toward young David. Following Biblical principles in the in-law relationship will not permit such circumstances to occur.

NAOMI: THE MOTHER-IN-LAW TO RUTH

All Bible believers have been deeply thrilled to read and reflect on the lovely story of Ruth told in the book that bears her name. Much of the beauty of this story revolves around the in-law relationship between the older Naomi and the younger Ruth. How their paths crossed is an interesting story for in that day it was highly unlikely for a Hebrew woman and a maid of Moab to be drawn together. This is how it happened. Elimelech, Naomi, and their two sons, Mahlon and Chilion, left their native land of Bethlehem because of a famine and went toward the east to sojourn in the land of Moab. While there Elimelech died. The two sons married women of Moab. Mahlon married Ruth and Chilion took Orpah for his wife. They sojourned there for about ten years. The hand of death had already taken the husband of Naomi. That was a tragic loss for her. But death's hand had not yet been stayed as far as her immediate family was concerned. The "king of terrors" crossed her threshold a second and third time and took both sons. She had come to Moab as a wife and now she was a widow. She had come to Moab as a mother and now she was childless. Preparations are soon made for her return to her native land since the famine was now past. Naomi urged her daughters-in-law to return to their families. She bequeathed heaven's kind benedictions upon them since they had dealt kindly with her and her now deceased sons. She fervently hoped that future happiness might be theirs (Ruth 1:9). Their reaction toward her proposal speaks volumes about the type of relationship that had existed between the two of them and the older Naomi. They said, "Surely we will return with thee unto thy people" (Ruth 1:10). Their relationship with her was the very opposite of the frequently held in-law relationship today. Naomi continued her plea that they remain in Moab. There were no future sons in her life that could one day claim their hands in marriage by the leviratical system practiced under the law of Moses (Deut. 25:5). Even if Naomi had a husband and sons soon to be born, she knew the women would not be content to wait until those sons arrived at marriageable age. Orpah lifted up her voice and wept and left the bereaved mother-in-law with a kiss. But Ruth was not about to leave. The Bible says that "Ruth clave unto her" (Ruth 1:14). Naomi responded by saying, "Behold, thy sister in law is gone back unto her people, and unto her gods: return thou after thy sister in law" (Ruth 1:15). Ruth's response reveals a depth and beauty of courageous character. "Entreat me not to leave thee, or to return from following after thee, for whither thou goest, I will go; and where thou lodgest, I will lodge: thy people shall be my people, and thy God my God: Where thou diest, will I die, and there will I be buried: the Lord do so to me, and more also, if aught but death part thee and me" (Ruth 1:16-17). It can be safely asserted that Ruth never learned such majestic principles of honor, steadfastness, and real love from Chemosh, the Moabite idol, or even her heathen family, for idolatry and heathenism are totally incapable of inculcating such holy principles. She must have learned much of Jehovah's law and its spirit from this goodly Hebrew family into which she had married and of which she fully intended to remain an integral part. The subsequent part of the story tells us that this was not an unrequited love on Ruth's part but fully reciprocated by Naomi. The youthful and resourceful Ruth was a diligent helper to Naomi upon their return to Bethlehem. She went and gleaned in the fields of Boaz. With the skill of a wise woman Naomi guides the Moabitess into a marriage with Boaz. This was the finest gift she could give her daughter-in-law, a godly husband to take the place of the deceased Mahlon. The story ends beautifully as a son is born to Boaz and Ruth. Naomi became a nurse to this baby boy (Ruth 4:16). This little boy would one day have a child of his own. That child would be Jesse. Then Jesse would have several sons the most famous of which was King David. Of even greater importance though is recognition of the fact that each of these formed a genealogical link in that wise providential chain from which the Messiah would humanly spring (See Matthew 1).

Naomi was the right kind of mother-in-law. Ruth was the right kind of daughter-in-law. Each thought of the other's welfare before that of her own. Each desired to do the right thing and be the right kind of person. This always makes for a right relationship. We need more mothers-in-law who will imitate Naomi. We need more daughters-in-law who will emulate the great example set by the lovely Ruth. *Christ in the home* is still God's finest recipe for all home and family relationships.

THE MOTHER-IN-LAW OF SIMON PETER

The mother-in-law of Simon Peter is mentioned only in the gospel records of Matthew, Mark, and Luke. The Bible does not supply us with her name nor that of her daughter who became wife to Simon Peter. Note what the three inspired scribes have to say relative to the mother-in-law of Simon Peter. Matthew says, "And when Jesus was come into Peter's house, he saw his wife's mother laid, and sick of a fever. And he touched her hand, and the fever left her: and she arose, and ministered unto them" (Matt. 8:14-15). Mark relates the same incident, "And forthwith, when they were come out of the synagogue, they entered into the house of Simon and Andrew, with James and John. But Simon's wife's mother lay sick of a fever, and anon they tell him of her. And he came and took her by the hand, and lifted her up; and immediately the fever left her, and she ministered unto them" (Mark 1:29-31). The beloved physician treats the case in these words and adds a medical observation, "And he arose out of the synagogue, and entered into Simon's house. And Simon's wife's mother was taken with a *great* fever; and they besought him for her. And he stood over her, and rebuked the fever; and it left her: and immediately she arose and ministered unto them" (Luke 4:38-39 italics added).

Though the foregoing accounts are rather brief, a few implications are plainly presented. The family was greatly concerned for the seriously ill relative. Doctor Luke describes her illness as being that of a great fever. Galen, a great man of medicine who lived a few years later than did Luke, described fevers as little and great. She had the more serious type of the two fevers. The woman at this time was in Simon's home. Whether she was a permanent resident in that home or was there temporarily while she was ill, we do not know. After the recovery she immediately began to serve those present. This might suggest her permanent residency in the home but no dogmatic affirmation could be made. Concern, love, and real interest sum up the attitudes apparently manifested toward this ill member. It seems they had the right set of attitudes toward her. They besought the Lord for her. When we beseech the Lord for an in-law we reflect our intense interest in the loved one and our belief that the Lord will hear our petitions. The Lord heard their plea and immediately responded to it with an instant cure. All three of the inspired writers relate how she arose and began to minister or serve those in Simon's house. The implication seems very strong that she was just doing what she had been doing prior to the coming of this fever. If this assumption is valid, then we can well understand why she was greatly respected and deeply loved. She was a useful and fruitful person. She was not an in-law that expected to be waited upon but diligently sought to do her part. Health permitting, any normal in-law is going to want to pull his or her share of the family load. This is an accepted part of any wholesome in-law relationship.

MODERN EXAMPLES

I go into many homes each year as a preacher of the gospel. I do this in both local and meeting work. I have frequently visited in homes where the in-law arrangement is a part of the family framework. Sometimes it is the young in-law where a son or daughter has recently married and the two are living temporarily with parents. This means an in-law arrangement for one of the marriage mates. At other times it is perhaps a widow or widower living with a son or daughter. I know that a guest in a home for a short visit or even during a week's gospel meeting cannot always evaluate correctly the real way a family acts. However, when one has visited a family with an in-law arrangement several times in many years, there is some basis for making fairly accurate appraisals. I think now of a lovely home where I have stayed. It is a home that extends royal hospitality to guests. Many have enjoyed its goodness and friendliness. Preachers especailly have been blessed by staying there. This home comes as close to being a home away from home as any I know. For many years this home has known the in-law arrangement. This son and his good wife cared for his aged father as long as he lived. They were good as gold to him. They loved him and he loved them. Since the aged father's death they have lovingly cared for the aged mother. She is a gracious charming Christian. They are devout in their Christianity. They believe in following principles of Biblical righteousness. We have yet to hear that first word of complaint between the mother-in-law and the daughter-in-law. They love each other. They do their respective tasks in the spirit of holiness and harmony. They work together as a marvelous team. She does not interfere with their lives. They respect her age and extend to her the privacy she deserves and needs. I have been deeply impressed with their excellent in-law arrangement. Christ lives there and that makes all the difference in the world.

Many years ago I came to know, love, and deeply respect a Christian family in a certain community where I preached and later went back for gospel meeting work. Often I was a guest in their humble home. The family consisted of husband, wife, two children, and the man's invalid mother. Again all were Christians. That invalid mother was cared for with love, interest, and deep concern by every member of the family. If she ever felt unloved and unwanted, I never detected such in my frequent visits. When she died the family asked me to conduct her funeral. At the funeral service the son said, "I have no regrets about the way we cared for her during her last years on earth." They had given her the best care they could. His wife had treated her mother-in-law just as if she had been her own mother. I cannot help but feel that heaven will reward such sincere service with warm approval at the resurrection of the just.

Christ in the home is the answer here even as it is in every other home relationship. When in-laws lift up Christ and His Book in the home, Christ and His Book will lift up the in-law relationship in the home.

QUESTIONS FOR DISCUSSION

1. Discuss some of the new relations produced by entrance into marriage and later the coming of a family.
2. Why is it wise to form harmonious relations with each in-law?
3. What principles should guide and govern the visits made by in-laws to the home of their children and vice versa?

4. List the passages which should serve as a general guideline when in-laws live in the same home.
5. Discuss thoroughly the young daughter-in-law and son-in-law in the home of one set of the parents.
6. How should the parents treat the in-law that has come to live with them just after marriage?
7. Why should every home, whether it has in-laws or not, have daily family devotions?
8. Discuss thoroughly the older in-law in the home.
9. Discuss thoroughly Laban as a father-in-law to Jacob.
10. Describe thoroughly Saul as a father-in-law to David.
11. Use David as an example of one who returned good for evil.
12. Relate the story of how the paths of a Hebrew woman, Naomi, and a maiden from Moab, Ruth, met and merged.
13. What three sad tragedies did Naomi experience while in Moab?
14. As she made preparations to return to Bethlehem what counsel did Naomi give her two daughters-in-law? How did each react to her suggestion?
15. Memorize Ruth 1:16-17. Where do you think Ruth learned such majestic principles?
16. How did Naomi and Ruth form an excellent team?
17. Why do you think Naomi and Ruth got along so well?
18. Read all the Bible accounts relating to the mother-in-law of Simon Peter.
19. How did the family evidently feel toward this seriously ill relative?
20. What did the mother-in-law who was now restored to full health begin to do immediately? What might this suggest about her past habits?
21. Relate some examples you know where there has been a happy relationship in a home with an in-law arrangement.

16

"What Have They Seen in Thine House?"

Students who know the Old Testament will recognize the question that heads this chapter as being a Biblical query. It has its setting during the days of the prophet Isaiah and Hezekiah the king of Judah. They lived in eighth-century Judah. Therefore this question has some twenty-seven centuries of hoary age resting on it. It was asked by God's prophet and directed to a king who had just hosted a delegation of dignitaries from a far-off land. The writer of II Kings 20 tells the story. So does Isaiah in the thirty-ninth chapter:

"At that time Merodachbaladan, the son of Baladan, king of Babylon, sent letters and a present to Hezekiah: for he had heard that he had been sick, and was recovered. And Hezekiah was glad of them, and shewed them the house of his precious things, the silver, and the gold, and the spices, and the precious ointment, and all the house of his armour, and all that was found in his treasures: there was nothing in his house, nor in all his dominion, that Hezekiah shewed them not. Then came Isaiah the prophet unto king Hezekiah, and said unto him, What said these men? and from whence came they unto thee? And Hezekiah said, They are come from a far country unto me, even from Babylon. Then said he, *What have they seen in thine house?* and Hezekiah answered, All that is in mine house have they seen: there is nothing among my treasures that I have not shewed them. Then said Isaiah to Hezekiah, Hear the word of the Lord of hosts: Behold, the days come, that all that is in thine house, and that which thy fathers have laid up in store until this day, shall be carried to Babylon: nothing shall be left, saith the Lord. And of thy sons that shall issue from thee, which thou shalt beget, shall they take away; and they shall be eunuchs in the palace of the king of Babylon. Then said Hezekiah to Isaiah, Good is the word of the Lord which thou hast spoken. He said moreover, For there shall be peace and truth in my days" (Isa. 39:1-8, italics added).

Second Chronicles 32:31 relates another interesting observation. "Howbeit in the business of the ambassadors of the princes of Babylon, who sent unto him to inquire of the wonder that was done in the land, God left him, to try him, that he might know all that was in his heart." Pride was one of the besetting sins that gnawed at the heart of this Hebrew monarch (II Chron. 32:24-26).

Sinful pride and heavenly wisdom are not found together in the same human heart. A man full of pride, which is really self-centeredness, is not apt to do the wise thing. It appears that Hezekiah's heart may have been lifted up with pride because these distinguished dignitaries from a foreign monarch were sent to him with a letter and a present. Quite foolishly he showed them all that was in his house. Isaiah showed him the folly of such a disclosure and predicted that the Babylonians would come against Hezekiah's descendants to plunder their wealth and take them into captivity. Hezekiah was not compelled to show these visitors all that was in his house. He did so upon a voluntary basis. If there is evil in our homes, we cannot always conceal it from the vision of our guests. If there is good, it likewise cannot be hidden. People who visit our homes will often see what our homes are really like. The all-seeing eye of heaven is aware of every proceeding of the home in which we live. That eye surveys all that is good and right. From its all-encompassing vision no evil is hidden. "What have they seen in thine house?" Let's look at some Biblical homes and apply lessons from these homes to our own homes.

NOAH, "WHAT HAVE THEY SEEN IN THINE HOUSE?"

Many commendable things can be stated to the credit of this ancient builder of the ark. He was a preacher of righteousness (II Peter 2:5). He was a man of deep faith (Heb. 11:7). The writer of the Pentateuch presents a threefold tribute to Noah's nature in Genesis 6:9. He "was a just man and perfect in his generations, and Noah walked with God." He was a man who believed in obeying God completely (Gen. 6:22). He and his wife were highly successful in rearing their sons for God's glory in a world universally wicked. Yet after the flood there is a sad incident which happens in Noah's home. One of the closing paragraphs in Genesis 9 relates how "Noah began to be an husbandman, and he planted a vineyard: And he drank of the wine, and was drunken . . ." (Gen. 9:20-21). Then followed the shameful act which involved Ham.

The entrance of strong drink into a home has always brought with it the strongest of curses and the most damnable of consequences. There is practically no sin but what alcohol forms an active affinity therewith. It brought a tragic chapter into Noah's home. It will do the same for any home that bids it welcome today. If someone were to open your refrigerator seeking a drink of cold water. would he find strong drink there also? If someone were to enter your house by the place where you keep empty bottles, would he find a number of beer bottles side-by-side with empty soft drink bottles? How would you explain and justify their being there? In reality it does not make nearly as much difference that a human guest discovers strong drink in a professing Christian's home as it does for the Lord to observe it there. Remember, you cannot hide the presence of strong drink in your home from the Lord's all-seeing eye. What kind of attitude toward strong drink will your children have if its presence in the home is just as common as meat, bread, and vegetables? Will they not accept the fact that beer, wine, and whiskey belong? What if they learn to drink while at home? That is precisely where many young people take their first drink. What if in ten years one of your children is a hopeless alcoholic? It has happened to millions of Americans within this generation. Have they seen strong drink in your house? If so, what is your justification? Does not wisdom tell you to pour down the drain all the devilish liquid currently in your possession and raise the wall of strict prohibition against the entrance of any more of the fiery spirits? Do not say that you cannot keep your friends from bringing in the damnable stuff. Who runs your house, you, or your friends? A professing Christian woman once told me that she and her husband were quite powerless in keeping their friends from bringing in their strong drink. Not for one moment do I buy this argument. We had headed a home far longer than she and her husband, and had entertained far more guests than had they. Not one drop of the fiery liquid has ever crossed the threshold of our home. She and her husband needed a new set of friends! A number of years ago I baptized a young Catholic lady who has made a very strong Christian. Not long ago I conducted a gospel meeting in her area. She told me that her father, whom she had not seen for many years, recently called her and wanted to come for a visit. She knew of his strong drinking habits. She told him that he would be welcome but she would not allow him to drink or bring liquor into her home while he was visiting there. Evidently he thought more of his drinking than he did of her family for he chose not to come under those stipulations. Do you not admire a person with such deep convictions? What a strong contrast to the weak spine of the other family who said they could not keep it out!

Let it be said to the credit of Noah that the account of his earthly pilgrimage contained only one recorded confrontation with strong drink. We never read about his getting drunk a second time. Many who fool with the satanic liquid today return to it time and time again. *Christ in the home* and liquor in the household are just about as incompatible as two concepts can be. Where the one is the other will be conspicuously absent. It is not Christ and liquor in the home but Christ *or* liquor. Choose this day whom you will serve.

JACOB, "WHAT HAVE THEY SEEN IN THINE HOUSE?"

Polygamy is our first answer. There never has been a home big enough and broad enough for two or more wives to be married to the same man. That is precisely why heavenly wisdom and common sense have always suggested the propriety of monogamy or one man for one woman and one woman for one man. Neither polygamy (one man with more than one wife) or polyandry (one woman with more than one husband) has a workable basis. In Genesis 29 we read of Jacob's marriages to Leah and Rachel. The succeeding chapter tells of each of these wives supplying Jacob with a handmaid. This made a total of four wives. These four women bore Jacob thirteen children: twelve sons and one daughter. Leah bore him six sons and a daughter and each of the other three bore him two sons each. When Leah was able to bear Jacob one son right after the other and Rachel remained barren, this produced envy in the heart of Rachel toward Leah and resentment toward Jacob (Gen. 30:1). Rachel's resentment made Jacob angry and there were strained relations between Jacob and his favorite wife (Gen. 30:2). There was a dishonest vying between Rachel and Leah for Jacob's sexual affections (Gen. 30:14-16). In subsequent years deeply destructive attitudes developed between the sons of Leah, Bilhah, and Zilpah, and the firstborn son of Rachel,

Joseph. Women who are married to the same man never have been able to get along. Neither can their offspring know the type of harmony experienced by those who have the same father and mother. The laws of our land keep a man from being married to more than one woman at the same time but the lax divorce system allows a person a number of mates within a lifetime, provided he has just one at a time. When a man has many wives within a lifetime the frequent divorces and the offspring of children by many mothers never will produce a happy and wholesome relationship within the home framework.

Partiality is our next answer. It has always seemed strange to me that Jacob failed to learn a very obvious lesson from his own home with Isaac and Rebekah. He had grown to maturity in a home that actively and openly demonstrated partiality. Isaac showed preference for Esau. Rebekah made no bones about preferring Jacob as her favorite (Gen. 25:28). This partiality led to some sad and grievous experiences in Jacob's boyhood home. Yet in the formation of his own home and the rearing of his own family Jacob repeated the same mistake. "Now Israel [Jacob] loved Joseph more than all his children, because he was the son of his old age: and he made him a coat of many colours. And when his brethren saw that their father loved him more than all his brethren, they hated him, and could not speak peaceably unto him" (Gen. 37: 3-4). The hatred, contempt, and hostility grew to such proportions that the envious sons finally sold Joseph and deceived their aged father into thinking that he had been devoured by a wild beast. That coat of many colors which they so greatly despised was used as the very device to carry out their malicious and cunning crime (Gen. 37:31-33).

The showing of partiality in families today is still in evidence in some homes and it always seriously ruptures happy and harmonious homes. Partiality is not fair to the child receiving the preferred treatment. It robs him of a healthy adjustment in growing to maturity. He may be led to feel that everyone in his future should continue to give him preferred treatment and pet him as his parents have done. Partiality is not fair to the ones who are left out. Resentment is built up toward the preferred brother or sister and toward the parent or parents guilty of showing partiality. This resentment may grow into hatred and that hatred may turn toward wrath and malice. Violence of a serious nature may be the end result. The showing of partiality may be the main factor in keeping every child in the home from growing into well-adjusted adults.

Idolatry is our third answer of what was seen in Jacob's home.

Jacob was a devout worshiper of the one true and living God himself but members of his family were not always as true to God as they should have been. The presence of idols was sometimes a snare in their lives. In Genesis 31 we read of Jacob's hasty departure from Laban. Unknown to Jacob Rachel had stolen the gods of her father Laban. She kept them cleverly concealed when Laban made search for them in the tents belonging to Leah and Rachel (Gen. 31:30-35). Genesis 35 gives another insight into the power that idols had in Jacob's family. "And God said unto Jacob, Arise, go up to Bethel, and dwell there: and make there an altar unto God, that appeared unto thee when thou fleddest from the face of Esau thy brother. Then Jacob said unto his household, and to all that were with him, Put away the strange gods that are among you, and be clean, and change your garments: And let us arise, and go up to Bethel; and I will make there an altar unto God, who answered me in the day of my distress, and was with me in the way which I went. And they gave unto Jacob all the strange gods which were in their hand, and all their earrings which were in their ears; and Jacob hid them under the oak which was by Shechem" (Gen. 35:1-4). In the earlier instance of Rachel's theft of her father's gods Jacob was in the dark. In this instance he was in the know. Jacob was now under instructions from the true and living Jehovah to journey to Bethel. There he was to erect an altar. Jacob had some vivid memories of Bethel from his stay there many years before (Gen. 28:10-22). In fact he had given the name Bethel to this favored spot (Gen. 28:19). Having supplied its very name he knew that the word meant "The house of God." How inappropriate it must have appeared to the "prince of God" (Gen. 32:28) to be headed toward "the house of God" when his own household was full of strange gods. How utterly contradictory it must have appeared to be on his way toward the erection of God's altar when his family was extending adoration to strange gods.

Fathers who wish to build an altar of private worship in the homes they head and lead their families to the "house of God" must annihilate the popular idols adored within their households. It may require a curbing of television as the most popular god in the home. Television can become an idol to any family that allows an indiscrimate use of it or allows it to consume time which should be spent doing the Lord's work. Truly, it has become the one-eyed idol in millions of homes today. When television was quite young I knew a man who would not leave home for the prayer meeting service on Wednesday night until he saw his favorite television show which ended at 7:30. Services began at 7:30 but he preferred to miss the first ten or fifteen minutes of Bible Study rather than miss the conclusion of his show. The eradication of idols from the home will include the ouster of any bad books, dirty magazines, and sensual records. In many homes it will include the strict prohibition of what may be worn publicly by the family members. Women and young girls who wear but little in public are lending their support to one of the most popular and dangerous practices of our time — the adoration of the female figure by fleshly minded men of our day. It becomes more and more difficult for men who desire to live the Christian life to keep their minds free of evil and impure thoughts.

Let it be said in summary that anyone or any object which comes first in a family's love or an individual's affections is an idol. We need more men like Jacob who will declare war on all the strange gods in their families and will call for their hasty extermination. Have they seen idolatry in our homes today?

DAVID, "WHAT HAVE THEY SEEN IN THINE HOUSE?"

Seven words describe the sordid story of the saddest chapter in David's life which so adversely affected his relationship with God, his family, the entire nation, and prompted onlookers from surrounding nations to scoff. Those seven words were: idleness, lust, adultery, deception, murder, guilt, and consequences. That catalogue of David's crimes had its inception in a moment of idleness (II Sam. 11:1). The next step was a look of lust on beautiful Bathsheba as she indiscreetly bathed herself where she could be seen by the king's eye (II Sam. 11:2). Step number three was the committal of crime, the act of adultery. This act of adultery occurred in the king's house. Adultery usually calls for close concealment and many times calls for the practice of deliberate deception. It did in David's case. Murder has often been the concluding chapter in many of the books written by the practitioners of uncontrollable passion. David, the offender, slew Uriah, the offended. The prophet Nathan confronted David and told him of the Lord's reaction to David's sins.

The scarlet crimes of fornication and adultery can be committed in homes today. A young girl who is frequently left at home with no parental oversight may turn the family home into a convenient center of fornication between her boy friend and herself. A woman whose husband is frequently away may turn the very house he is buying into a center of promiscuous behavior. A man may find himself alone while the wife is gone a few days or away for a day of work. He may turn her castle into an area of adultery with a female visitor. According to the statistics of a leading woman's magazine some years back, millions of American couples practice mate-swapping on a regular basis. Homes thus become places where mutual adultery is freely practiced with full endorsement by all participating persons. Other homes are filled with salacious stories, naughty novels, and pornographic pictures which encourage such immoral escapades as fornication and adultery. Needless to say, the *Christ in the home* concept will not tolerate any adulterous activities. Have they seen the elements of immorality in our homes? Remember, no action of any home has ever escaped the all-seeing eye of Jehovah God. The darkness of a Palestinian night in Jerusalem and the privacy of a king's palace did not conceal adultery from the eye on high that surveys all.

HEROD ANTIPAS,
"WHAT HAVE THEY SEEN IN THINE HOUSE?"

The stolen wife of his brother Philip would be our answer. Though married himself, Herod Antipas went to Rome on empire business and visited with his brother Philip, a private citizen in the imperial city. This hospitality was repaid with Herod taking Herodias, Philip's wife, back to Palestine with him. To form this adulterous union Herod had to renege on his first wife. Herodias had to do the same to her husband, Philip. The fearless John the Baptist told Herod, "It is not lawful for thee to have thy brother's wife" (Mark 6:18).

The acquisition of an illegal wife proved to be highly disastrous to this Herodian monarch. Through her maliciousness and a shameless Salome who delighted to dance and please lustful men, Herodias turned Antipas into the reluctant executioner of John the Baptist. The day Antipas brought Herodias home with him was perhaps the most foolish day of his life. Taking another's wife, the issuance of a rash vow, the presence of a dancing damsel, and a spineless backbone led to unhappy chapters in the life of Herod Antipas.

In many homes today there are men who for all practical purposes have stolen other men's wives. From time to time they may make vows just as rash as was Herod's. These men may be married to women who are as devilish as was Herodias. They may hate and display stinging contempt for every vestige of decency and morality. They may be rearing their daughters to dance and display their curvacious charms for the roaming eyes of lusty men. They may be as lacking in conscience as were the mother-and-daughter team of Herodias and Salome. No righteous mind will deny for a moment that ingredients such as the foregoing will destroy a home. Are there situations in our homes closely akin to those we have observed in the home of Herod Antipas? "What have they seen in thine house?" What has Jehovah God seen in our homes?

A LOOK INTO THE HOME OF LUKE 15

The beloved physician relates the parables of the lost sheep, the lost coin, and the two lost sons in this chapter. Note a few things relative to the man who had two sons. This "pearl of the parables," as it has been frequently designated, tells of the loving father, the younger son, and the older son. The younger son was terribly dissatisfied with his good home. The far off country of sin was tugging at the heartstrings of his restless personality. He requested his share of the family estate. The father made no attempt to keep him at home against his will. Homes cannot be run like jails. They are made up of people who choose voluntarily to live in a family framework. Soon the boy was physically where his heart had been for some months already. In the far off country of sin he "wasted his substance with riotous living" (Luke 15:13). Possibly there was no sin but what he fully experienced. He was now doing what he thought would bring meaning and relevancy to a life that had been filled with boredom and drudgery back at the family home. The bright lights of vice and the boisterous laughter of the pleasure seekers blinded his eyes to the hog pen of shame just beyond and his ears to the pleadings of an uprooted conscience. Soon the money was gone. So were his fair weather friends who no doubt were seeking another naive heir of some estate who would lavishly spend the family inheritance upon them. Formerly he had known the hunger to have his youthful fling; now he knew hunger of body and poverty of spirit. In this awful condition he came to himself. He was not really himself while in sin and vice. No sinner ever is. He resolved to return home and confess the enormity of his sins. This he did. This resolution is translated into reality. The loving father no doubt had looked each day for the return of his son. The home was so sad with his absence. The empty place at the family dining area was a constant reminder that one was away in sin. Finally the familiar form of the long lost son greeted the father's searching eyes. He ran to meet, greet, and receive him. The returning prodigal was not even permitted to finish his confession. He had intended to return as a servant. Instead he was received back as a son. A note of cheerfulness and joy permeated the entire household.

The parable would have ended upon a happy note indeed if Jesus had closed the story with Luke 15:24. But there is the portrait painted of the elder brother also. He is the self-righteous one. No brotherly love fills his soul. No spirit of forgiveness tugs at his proud heartstrings. Not once does he refer to the returned boy as brother. The father pleads but the soured saint remains adamant. The story closes with the elder brother still outside the home. In this remarkable parable we see the loving father, the restless rebel who longs for the carefree life but later returns as the penitent prodigal, and the elder brother who remains unbrotherly, self-righteous, ungrateful, and fully soured by the whole affair. In many homes today there is a prodigal in the making or a prodigal of the past who has finally learned that sin does not pay except with the most grievous of consequences. There is the elder brother who fails to venture but is just as lost while at home. There is the loving parent who stands constantly ready to receive the returning prodigal or plead with the unbrotherly conduct of the firstborn. "What have they seen in thine house?" What has God seen in our homes?

MARY, "WHAT HAVE THEY SEEN IN THINE HOUSE?"

There are many Marys portrayed in the New Testament. Something beautifully commendable is said about each one. In this section we look at Mary of Nazareth. She was married to Joseph but it is not of her faithful husband that we now speak. Mark 6:3 and Matthew 13:55-56 inform us that Mary had James, Joses, Simon, Judas, and an undetermined number of daughters in her home, but of these other children we do not now speak. Among these brethren there was unbelief toward a greater one in the household, but of this brand of infidelity toward the unique older brother we do not now write (John 7:5). We do speak of the Heavenly Guest that lived in Mary's house. For many golden years Mary literally had Christ in her home. She watched Him as he grew in wisdom, stature, favor with God and favor with man (Luke 2:52). What a blessing it must have been to be associated with deity in human flesh. How much He must have meant to her parental heart. What great truths she must have pondered in her heart as she thought of the way He had come into the world, the shepherds' visit, the presentation in the temple and the utterances of Simeon and Anna, the wise men's gifts, adoration and worship, the quick flight into Egypt to escape Herod's evil decree, the events that surrounded the trip to Jerusalem when He was twelve, and His marvelous and majestic advancement in everything that was right and admirable. How she must have missed Him when He journeyed to Jordan and there meekly and obediently submitted to the baptism administered by John. How she must have tried to understand all the great things which characterized His ministry. She was His mother and yet He was before her. She was His mother and yet He had made her. Never was there a parallel situation between a mother and her son. How much of her Son's deity she understood as He lived upon earth we may never know. But Mary knew about the *Christ in the home* concept in a very unique way. Mary, "what have they seen in thine house?" The Christ was the all-pervading answer.

EUNICE, "WHAT HAVE THEY SEEN IN THINE HOUSE?"

An unfeigned faith would have been one of the firstfruits witnessed by the eye of a guest in this home located in the central regions of ancient Asia Minor. This type of sincere faith was first witnessed in the life of Eunice's mother, Lois. In the only Bible verse in which Timothy's mother and grandmother are called by name Paul talks of three generations who possessed an unfeigned faith. Paul wrote, "When I call to remembrance the unfeigned faith that is in thee, which dwelt first in thy grandmother Lois, and thy mother Eunice; and I am persuaded that in thee also" (II Tim. 1:5). Eunice was greatly blessed because she had witnessed this unfeigned faith in the heart and life of her godly mother. Her own life was greatly blessed with the rich possession of this same type of faith in Jehovah God. She was superbly successful in bequeathing such a legacy to her own son Timothy. Sometime following her marriage to an unnamed Greek (Acts 16:1) there was another object in her home that would have caught the eye of every guest. This was a little baby boy whose name was ultimately destined for great spiritual fame as it would frequently adorn many pages of Holy Writ. Two books of the New Testament would ultimately be written to this youthful Timothy.

When Timothy was born Eunice must have faced many problems. She did not have a Hebrew husband to join her in rearing a son for God's glory. He was a Greek. The Bible is silent about whether or not her Greek husband ever became a proselyte of the Hebrew religion or a practitioner of Christianity. It seems safe to assume that Timothy's religious counseling rested only upon the shoulders of Lois and Eunice. But they were equal to the task that heaven had given them. The implication is strong that they determined very early that Timothy was going to be Hebrew and not Greek in outlook. He was going to be taught about the Jehovah of Mount Sinai and not about Jupiter or Zeus of Greek mythology. Paul said, "But continue thou in the things which thou hast learned and hast been assured of, knowing of whom thou hast learned them; And that from a child [babe-ASV] thou hast known the holy scriptures, which are able to make thee wise unto salvation through faith which is in Christ Jesus" (II Tim. 3:14-15). Eunice would have none of the modern parental philosophy which suggests that a child should be left alone as far as the planting of religious inclinations is concerned and when he is old enough he will decide his own religious route to tread and the direction of his own destiny. She recognized the fact that if Jehovah did not capture his impressionable mind and pliable heart, the sinister forces of Greek infidelity and Roman idolatry would. How well she succeeded in her endeavors is seen in tributes later given to Timothy by Luke and Paul. The beloved physician wrote that Timothy, shortly after his conversion, "was well reported of by the brethren that were at Lystra and Iconium" (Acts 16:2). Paul said, "But I trust in the Lord Jesus to send Timotheus shortly unto you, that I also may be of good comfort, when I know your state. For I have no man likeminded, who will naturally care for your state. For all seek their own, not the things which are Jesus Christ's. But ye know the proof of him, that, as a son with the father, he hath served with me in the gospel. Him therefore I hope to send presently, so soon as I shall see how it will go with me" (Phil. 2:19-23). It should not be forgotten that these tributes were written under the guidance of the Holy Spirit. We know that these were accurate appraisals of Timothy's righteous character and sterling worth not only in the sight of great and godly giants in the faith such as Paul and Luke but also of holy heaven above.

In the home of Eunice we have seen an unfeigned faith, a little baby boy trained diligently for the Lord, and a home that had high regard for the power of Scripture. Would to God every guest in every religious home today could observe similar characteristics. Too many homes today are derelict in the very things which claimed the major energies of Eunice and Lois.

WHAT HAVE THEY SEEN IN OUR HOMES?

Most homes have guests from time to time. What type of impressions do these guests carry away with them? Have they seen a home that is a place of purity or an environment of evil? Have they seen husbands and wives who are Christians and seeking to make a happy and harmonious marriage work in these days of loosely knitted marital ties? Have they seen men and women who are Christian fathers and mothers to their children? Have they seen sons and daughters who are seeking to grow in the same areas that claimed the Lord's undivided attention betwixt twelve and thirty (Luke 2:52)? Did they see home as a place where Jesus and His word were uppermost in the hearts of every family member? Did they see a home where earthly usefulness and heavenly hope were being cultivated and encouraged at each opportunity? A family may behave itself unusually well during the visits of guests. The guest may get a pretty accurate glimpse of what that home life is like or he may not. However, the all-seeing eye of our Heavenly Father is keenly aware of all proceedings in the home. From his all-knowing vision nothing is concealed (Heb. 4:13). In making some concluding observations for this chapter I shall keep in mind what the human eyes of guests and the all-seeing eye witness in our homes.

Have they seen love or hatred, concern or indifference, gratitude or ingratitude, unselfishness or selfishness in the home relationships? Among the family members there will be either love or hatred. An absence of love automatically means the presence of hatred. Is there genuine concern for each other's needs or does the ugly air of indifference breed contempt for other members of the household? Where concern is lacking there will be an abundance of indifference. Are expressions of gratitude for favors bestowed frequently witnessed within the home? Gratitude and ingratitude are mutually exclusive. Where the one is the other will be conspicuously absent. Does each member think others exist only to meet his every whim and fancy? Is the foundation of personal relationships among family members composed of selfishness or unselfishness? Is each one primarily concerned with how other family members can make him happy or with how he can work for their happiness in the home?

Have they seen cleanliness or uncleanliness, a tidy home or an unkept household, industry or indolence, organization or disorganization within the home? "Cleanliness is next to godliness" is not a Scriptural quotation but it is an important ingredient for a happy home. I have visited in homes that were clean and others not fit for human habitation. Without exception homes of the latter type were facing serious problems. I have visited with families who had but little of this world's goods but what they had was clean and tidy. Unclean homes with unclean inhabitants do not make for sensible living, wholesome relationships, and happy homes. Soap, water, and industry can still perform wonders for any house and those that live therein. We do not believe the *Christ in the home* concept will allow for constant filth. Tidiness can do wonders in helping achieve happy homes. An unkept home is repulsive to any person who takes pride in cleanliness. To the husband it is an invitation for him to spend time elsewhere and maybe in a place where he will be tempted to do wrong. To a child it will be an invitation to come home only as a last resort. Some women who are so lazy as never to be a worker or keeper of a decent home wonder why husbands wander and children vanish as soon as time and opportunity permit. Industry and not indolence is a prime ingredient for building happy marriages and lasting homes. We cannot imagine a family framework that would be promoted by the ugly vice of indolence and laziness. Some people are more prone toward organization than are others but this is a virtue that can be cultivated to some extent. A family that lives in a disorganized family frame work will never know the orderliness that comes with a well-planned family unit. Building happy and harmonious homes takes hard work and wise planning.

What have they seen in the way of recreation or entertainment? What type of reading material is allowed in our home? Is the chief type of reading material built upon the base things or erected upon the excellencies of the Bible and written works true to it? Are there *True Confessions* in the home or the confessions of truth as found in the Bible and sound reading material? Are the magazines majestic or malicious? Are the pictures pure or pornographic? Are the novels noble or naughty? Are the stories sensual and salacious or saintly and safe? What about the television programs we watch? Certain movies are rated as R and X. Families who intend to please God literally need to Restrict and "Xclude" those shows designed to appeal to our lower and baser elements. Would people see alcoholic beverages in your home if they were to walk in at an unexpected hour? Does gambling go on at your house? What kind of stories are exchanged by you and your guests from time to time? Would people hear profanity if they were at your house when something went wrong? Would they witness the long face of pouting, the quick flare of a temper tantrum, or uncontrollable bursts of anger when something fails to please you? What type of behavior is characteristic of you and your friends when there are visits in your home? Are there activities planned which will certainly incur the sure frowns of heaven above? Sin is still sin whether practiced away from home or in the home environment. Something which is wrong in and of itself cannot be made right by doing it in the home. Concerning all our activities in the home we should ask: Is it right? Would Christ approve of our doing it? Would we want to be engaged in this type of entertainment if Jesus were to come again? What have they seen in the way of recreational and entertaining activities in the home?

What type of spiritual atmosphere have they seen in our homes? Can they leave and say we are a spiritually minded and Bible-centered family? Would they observe us give thanks for every meal? Would it be so common and frequent a habit that our children would automatically wait for an expression of thanks before they passed the first dish of food to the guests? Have they seen the Bible and prayer as occupying places of supreme emphasis in the family framework? How long would a guest have to remain in our home before he saw the family head read the Bible and heard him pray with the family gathered around him? What do guests see the family do if it is Sunday morning, Sunday evening, or Wednesday night? Do they witness every member making preparation to attend the services of the church? Are the guests invited to attend? If they refuse, do the guests see the family set aside their plans to go and remain home to entertain the current visitors? Or do they hear the family say, "If you will not go with us, just make yourselves comfortable. We will be back as soon as worship is concluded." Families teach a very powerful lesson by what they do when it is time for a religious service and guests are present who do not intend to accompany them to worship. Have they seen us rearing our children in the nurture and admonition of the Lord (Eph. 6:4)? Have they seen us giving them the training they need in order that when old they will not depart from the Lord (Prov. 22:6)?

In imitation of the ancient Hebrews have they seen us diligently teaching our children how to make an honorable living? Ancient Hebrews believed if they failed to teach their children a trade, they taught them to steal. Have they seen children who are required to earn their allowance and perform their part of the household and yard duties?

Have they seen courteous treatment in our homes? Is there consideration for each other? Is there a bond of kindness extended toward guests? Do older guests see younger children manifesting real regard and respect for those who are their seniors?

What kind of companions have they seen us bring into our homes? Be it remembered that Paul stated so very tersely, "Be not deceived: evil communications corrupt good manners" (I Cor. 15:33). If those who are living sinful lives are brought into the home in order to teach them the truth, this is noble and commendable. Heaven will smile on such efforts and good people will extend commendation for such earnest endeavors. But if the immoral are brought into the home for the purpose of consorting with them in their grievous sins, then the visit is evil in invitation, intent, action, and conclusion. If people are brought in to drink, gamble, commit immorality, and become more deeply entrenched in drug addiction, then the home has been turned into a den of drinkers, a gathering of gamblers, an inn of immorality, and the arena of addiction to mind-altering drugs. What kind of friends have we chosen for home companionship?

Have they seen our home as a training ground for juvenile delinquency? In *The Commercial Appeal* of July 27, 1971, Ann Landers gave "Helpful Hints On How To Bring Up Delinquents.'" They are reprinted by permission.

1. Begin with infancy to give the child everything he wants. He will then grow up to believe the world owes him a living.

2. When he picks up bad words, laugh at him. He will think he is cute. It will encourage him to think up "cuter" words and phrases that will blow off the top of your head later.

3. Never give him any spiritual training. When he is 21 let him decide for himself what he wants to be. (Don't be surprised if he decides to be "nothing.")

4. Avoid the word "wrong." It might develop a guilt complex. A few years later, when he is arrested for stealing a car, he will feel that society is against him and that he is being persecuted.

5. Pick up after him. This means wet towels, books, shoes, and clothing. Do everything for him. He will then become experienced in evading responsibility and incapable of finishing any task.

6. Let him see everything, hear everything, and read everything smutty he can get his hands on. Make sure the silverware and drinking glasses are sterilized but let his mind feed on garbage.

7. If you have a serious conflict in opinion with your spouse, fight it out in front of the children. It's good for youngsters to view their parents as human beings who express themselves freely and openly. Later, if you get divorced, they'll know what caused it.

8. Give your children all the spending money they want. After all, one of the reasons you have worked so hard all

your life is to make life easier for your children. Why should they have it as rough as you did?

9. Satisfy his every craving for food, drink, and comfort. See that his every desire is satisfied. Denial might lead to harmful frustration.

10. Take your child's part against neighbors, teachers, and friends. This will prepare you to take his part against the police.

11. When he gets into serious trouble, apologize for yourself by saying, "I can't understand why he turned out like this. We gave him EVERYTHING."

12. Prepare for a life of grief. You are apt to have it.

I have included this list because it describes the home in many of its major failings today. It would be well for every parent who reads these lines to look closely and objectively at himself and the child-rearing techniques which he follows. Have the guests in our homes seen future delinquents in the making? What has the Almighty observed along these lines in our homes?

Have they seen the home as a workshop for winning the lost to Christ? Much personal soul-winning is done in the homes of the lost. The passionate soul winner is going with the gospel and he goes to the lost in their own homes if that is where the most good can be accomplished. However, soul winners can often win people to Christ by inviting the lost to their own home. Sometimes this arrangement has many advantages over going to the lost person's home. Sometimes it is difficult in the lost person's home to get everything conducive for Bible study. The lost person may have a close family member strongly opposed to the religious study. This usually necessitates choosing a location for the study other than the prospect's home. Hence, an invitation to a gospel prospect to visit the home of the soul winner for a meal with a stipulated understanding beforehand that the visit will include a serious study of the Bible can be richly rewarding. I have often used my home as a place to talk with people about their need for Christ.

Human guests do not always see everything that goes on in the home. Fallible eyesight and limited opportunities may conceal much of the good and a great deal of the bad characteristics of the home visited. However, God sees all. What God sees in our home is far more important than what human guests witness. The *Christ in the home* concept will help insure that only what should be seen in our homes will be witnessed by God above and man below. Let the home lift up the Christ and His Book, and Christ and His Book will lift up the home.

QUESTIONS FOR DISCUSSION

1. Give the background that produced Isaiah's question, "What have they seen in thine house?"
2. Are sinful pride and heavenly wisdom apt to be found in the same heart? Why, or why not?
3. What evil was once seen in Noah's home? Give reasons why that same evil is common in many homes today.
4. Analyze the statement of the young lady who claimed she and her husband were powerless in keeping drinking friends and strong drink from entering their home.
5. Is any home big enough for the presence of Jesus and liquor at the same time? Why do you answer as you do?
6. Discuss polygamy in Jacob's home.
7. Why will neither polygamy nor polyandry work?
8. Discuss partiality as it existed in Jacob's home.
9. Discuss idolatry as some of Jacob's family practiced it. Tell about Jacob's housecleaning of all strange gods in Genesis 35. Why was a trip to Bethel with the avowed intent of erecting an altar to Jehovah so incompatible with the presence of idols still in the family?
10. What sins were seen in David's household?
11. Why is it so very tragic to commit adultery or fornication in one's own home?
12. Describe some of the things which were seen in the home of Herod Antipas.
13. Describe the home of Luke 15 from the standpoint of the loving father, the restless and returned prodigal, and the elder brother.
14. Take a concordance and make a detailed study of every Mary mentioned in the Bible. Tell the good that is suggested about each one.
15. Discuss Christ living in the home of Mary.
16. In what sense was Jesus Mary's Son and yet her Maker? Can such questions ever be answered separate and apart from His deity? Why, or why not?
17. What would have been seen in the home of Lois and Eunice? Discuss what is meant by an unfeigned faith.
18. What problems must Eunice have faced as Timothy was born and grew toward maturity?
19. At what age did Lois and Eunice begin Timothy's training? What lesson can Christian parents today learn from this procedure?

20. What great tributes did Luke and Paul pay to Timothy in Acts 16:2 and Philippians 2:19-23?
21. What would be the immediate results if all homes today had an unfeigned faith, children trained for God from infancy onward, and a reverent regard for Scripture?
22. Discuss in detail some of the evils found in modern homes.
23. Read and discuss Ann Landers' twelve rules for rearing juvenile delinquents.
24. Discuss some of the spiritual realities that guests should witness in our homes.
25. Discuss how one's home can be turned into a place for winning the lost to Christ.
26. Who sees all that goes on in our homes? What concept will keep the home as it should constantly be?

17

Growing Old Gracefully in the Home

Perhaps this chapter can best be begun by reference to a delightful Scripture passage: "The righteous shall flourish like the palm tree: he shall grow like a cedar in Lebanon. Those that be planted in the house of the Lord shall flourish in the courts of our God. They shall still bring forth fruit in old age; they shall be fat and flourishing; To shew that the Lord is upright: he is my rock, and there is no unrighteousness in him" (Ps. 92:12-15). I am especially impressed with the verbs of this marvelous message "shall flourish," "shall grow," "be planted," and "shall still bring forth." Let us examine how people can and have grown old gracefully.

There is something particularly majestic about the way the Bible unfolds the life of Abraham and Sarah. We do not know their age when they married. But from the time Abraham received the call to forsake Ur of the Chaldees and to head for Canaan down to the times of their decease, we witness the budding and full flowering of their spiritual lives. We can follow Abraham's life for about 105 years. Sarah's life is portrayed for a little less than seventy years. These are the years in which they lived in Haran and Canaan with a brief sojourn in Egypt. During these years we see them growing old. They grew old gracefully. Their love for God and each other deepened. Their faith continued to mature and ripen. The Bible indicates that both expired in the embrace of fervent faith (Heb. 11:13). Their confidence in the Abrahamic promises became brighter as they neared the end of their earthly pilgrimages. Abraham lived to see Isaac married to Rebekah and the birth of Esau and Jacob. Abraham and Sarah lived in pagan times. Much evil surrounded them. However, they made a success of their marriage and their lives.

Some people *get* old. Others *grow* old. They continue to grow in love, kindness, faith, dedication, and hope. Some become sour and senile near the end of their earthly existence. Others become more saintly. Their sunset years are among the most beautiful of their long lives. In this chapter let us note some of the ways in which couples may grow old gracefully in the home, the service of the Lord, and as benefactors to humanity.

GROWING OLD IN FAITH

Paul closes his great chapter of I Corinthians 13 with one of the most beautiful of all tributes to three essential graces of the human soul. Previously he had mentioned the miraculous gifts and above them all he wrote the word *temporary*. Then he eloquently portrays the gifts or graces which abide. They are not supernatural but must be cultivated within the human soul. Paul said, "And now abideth faith, hope, charity [love], these three; but the greatest of these is charity [love]" (I Cor. 13:13). These soul-adorning graces need to abide in the church of our Lord. They also need to abide in the homes of those who wish to please the Lord and live with Him eternally. Every couple must grow in each of these as the marriage days stretch into months, years, and decades.

Through the years of marriage there should be a deepening of faith in all its various facets. John says faith is that which produces a victorious overcoming of the world (I John 5:4-5). Faith can overcome all obstacles that appear in the marital pathway. There should be a deepening of the couple's faith in God, Christ, the Spirit, the Bible, and the church of Jesus Christ. At the time of their marriage there may be a youthful energetic faith in all these eternal verities. As the years come and go there should be a deeper development of faith in these spiritual realities. Marriage should also witness a deepening of faith in each other. True faithfulness toward the marital vows means that the confidence placed in each other becomes an expression of greater and more lasting beauty. There is not the least suspicion that either will ever betray the sacred confidence of the other. It is a richly rewarding thought as a couple grows old that the marriage vows have been kept inviolate. Growing old in faith is an essential part of growing old gracefully.

Christ in the home supplies the spiritual impetus for achieving such upward growth.

GROWING OLD IN HOPE

The second of these abiding graces is hope. Many majestic utterances are given within Holy Writ about this wonderful virtue. Salvation is by hope (Rom. 8:24). It is connected with real love (I Cor. 13:7). Hope constitutes one of the seven unities set forth in Ephesians 4:4-6. Hope is expectation, desire, and anticipation. It looks toward eternal life and will find ultimately its full fruition in the heavenly hereafter (Titus 1:2; Rom. 8:24-25). It reaches into the heavenly world for its power of support (Heb. 6:19-20).

I occasionally tell young people who stand on the threshold of marriage that matrimony is comparable to a building. This building is composed of the foundation of faith, the walls of hope, and the roof of love. Long years of a happy and harmonious marriage should greatly strengthen the foundational element of faith. Just as the walls connect the foundation with the roof, so hope connects faith and love. This connector should become stronger as the years come and go. As their sunset years descend there will come the golden glow of a better world just beyond. The great promises of living in the heavenly hereafter will become grander and more glorious as the end approaches.

Brother Goodpasture relates this story in one of his books: "Mr. Bryan wrote a book, the title of which is *Seven Questions in Dispute,* and one of the questions discussed is the question of the resurrection from the dead. At the top of the chapter under that heading there is a picture more or less illustrative of what the resurrection means. It is the picture of an aged husband and wife. They are sitting beside a table. On the table is the open Bible. The old mother in Israel is reading the Bible. The old father's hands are crossed upon his cane and his chin rests upon his hands, his sightless eyes are directed out into space. The old father said, 'Mother, read. Read it again where it says, 'I am the resurrection and the life. If a man believe in me, though he die, yet shall he live.' The aged couple was finding consolation, as they approached the valley of the shadow of death, in the promise that Jesus is the resurrection and the life and if a man died, he would live again" (B. C. Goodpasture, *Sermons and Lectures,* Nashville: Gospel Advocate Company, 1968, pp. 95-96). How holy must be the growing hope of living again as Christian couples come to the end of their earthly pilgrimages. Growing old in hope is one of the sure ways to grow old gracefully.

GROWING OLD IN LOVE

Love is the greatest, grandest, and most glorious of all emotions. It has no close competitors. Love makes us kin to deity in both attitude and actions, in both motives and mission, for the Bible tells us God is love (I John 4:8, 16). Love is not restricted to any age. The human heart never fully exhausts its ability to increase in love.

The young man and woman who stand at the marriage altar to pledge undying affection and loving loyalty toward each other may feel they care for each other at that happy moment just as deeply as they ever will or ever can. But if they are the right kind of people and walk with God and each other, they will love each other far more deeply when they face the sunset years of life together than during the sunrise of their marriage. By then their love and loyalty will have been tried and tested on a hundred proving grounds. The joys and sorrows of life have been faced together. The joys of the physical union have produced children. These children have brightened their days and gladdened their hearts. Now the children have grown up, married, and have families of their own. They began their life of love together. Gradually there were additions to the family. Now each child has married. They are as they began but now they are much older and much wiser. If the bond of love has been carefully cultivated, the richest part of their marriage can be before them. The last years of their life can see them with a greater love for the Lord, His church, and the Bible. Their senior years should see them with a greater love and regard for each other. The last part of their earthly pilgrimages will witness a growth of their love for people. Love will keep them from becoming soured on the world and toward each other. Love will block the invasion of the frequent intruder, a senile spirit, into advanced age. Love will not close their eyes to the talents of younger successors. Love will not blind them to the fact that worthy young people are arising to take their places in leadership roles. Love will tolerate no envy toward those who are younger in years and more active in work. People can grow old gracefully. It takes a mature and increasing love to allow for such to be a reality. If the Lord allows my wife and me to grow old together, it is our hopeful prayer that we can grow old gracefully in love and the other golden virtues of blissful Christianity.

GROWING OLD IN PATIENCE

Patience is steadfastness. It is endurance. It is the ability to bear up under stress and strain. Patience is keeping on without a cowardly capitulation to weak surrender and impotent defeatism. It is one of the seven Christian virtues and must be supplied or added diligently to the foundation of faith (II Peter 1:5-7). Patience does not produce faith but is a fruit of the faith that has been tried and tested (James 1:2-3). Patience is needed to do God's will and ultimately receive the heavenly reward (Heb. 10:36).

Patience is a vritue frequently unseen in youth. Young people are usually very impatient. Frequently they want something accomplished *yesterday* instead of working for its accomplishment for some tomorrow. Rome was not built in a day. An oak does not grow into a mighty tree overnight. The great evils of our world have not come in one day and they will not be cured in the next five minutes regardless of what idealistic youth may think. The farmer does not plant his grain one morning and reap a harvest the very next morning. James says, "Be patient therefore, brethren, unto the coming of the Lord. Behold, the husbandman waiteth for the precious fruit of the earth, and hath long patience for it, until he receive the early and latter rain. Be ye also patient; stablish your hearts: for the coming of the Lord draweth nigh. . . . Take, my brethren, the prophets, who have spoken in the name of the Lord, for an example of suffering affliction, and of patience. Behold, we count them happy which endure. Ye have heard of the patience of Job, and have seen the end of the Lord; that the Lord is very pitiful, and of tender mercy" (James 5:7-8, 10-11).

Patience is sometimes lacking in advanced age also. In recognition of this Paul wrote in Titus 2:2, "That the aged men be sober, grave, temperate, sound in faith, in charity, *in patience*" (italics added). Growing old gracefully means developing a disposition of patience. As couples grow old there should be a greater exhibition of patience toward each other. It is heartwarming to visit an elderly couple and observe the fine fruits of patience, longsuffering, and sympathetic understanding at work. It adds so much to their last years together.

GROWING OLD IN GRATITUDE

Gratitude seems to be a vanishing art in our thankless generation. Multitudes seemingly have forgotten that such expressions as "thank-you," "I am grateful," and "I appreciate that" still have a welcome ring in the ears of many. Too many people act as though such expressions are now archaic, obsolete, and totally outdated.

Gratitude should be a grace of the soul. Youth should be taught gratitude. Mature people should practice it regularly. The aged should not forget it. A wise elder in the church where I have conducted a number of meetings once said, *"Thanks* and *please* are two of the most powerful words in our language." I heartily concur with this observation.

Gratitude should be one of the most common practices of a household. Couples who form their marriage with an eager determination to be truly grateful for every gift or blessing received from each other have made a wise choice of ingredients for gracious living in a family framework. Throughout their marital lives there should never be a deviation from this godly practice. Their growth in love for each other should have as one of its accompanying fruits similar advancement in appreciation for each other. People who grow old in gratitude in the home will be grateful people in other relationships as well. They will love to do things for people. The joy is doubled when people are truly appreciative. Years ago I helped an unemployed man obtain gainful employment. I had forgotten all about it. Last summer his wife remarked how thankful they still were for that gesture of helpfulness. Her expression of gratitude brightened my day.

Growing old gracefully means growing old in gratitude. Jesus lived in an atmosphere of appreciation during His sojourn on earth. His very spirit was *"I thank thee, O Father,* Lord of heaven and earth, because thou hast hid these things from the wise and prudent, and hast revealed them unto babes" (Matt. 11:25 italics added). Outside the tomb of Lazarus Jesus said, "Father, I thank thee that thou hast heard me" (John 11:41). When people have lived a long time with the *Christ in the home* philosophy predominating they will develop more gratitude and appreciation. This spirit of thankfulness in the home should be both vertical and horizontal. It should be vertical in that it reaches up to Jehovah. It should be horizontal in that it reaches out toward each other and to people beyond the home relationship.

GROWING OLD IN WISDOM

Youth is known for its enthusiasm, energy, idealism, and dreams. But wisdom comes with age. James 1:5 says it is a gift from God and comes in answer to prayer. People of true wisdom have usually lived for quite some years, have profited from life's lessons, have drunk deeply and passionately from the fountain of knowledge, and have spent much time communing with the Father in prayerful requests for wisdom. Knowledge is acquaintance with facts; wisdom is the ability to use well what we know. The Biblical writer said years ago: "With the ancient is wisdom; and in length of days understanding" (Job 12:12).

Couples who have made a success out of their own marriages should be able to give advice to those who are contemplating matrimony. Young couples who are experiencing serious difficulties in the early years of their marriage would do well to seek help from some wise, godly couple in the church. From such people there is much less likelihood of being given false and harmful counsel that might come from some marriage counselor who neither knows nor cares what God's Book teaches about marriage and the home. Couples who are growing old gracefully in the realm of practical wisdom can be of immense aid to those who are young and inexperienced.

GROWING OLD IN SERVICE

The home in which Jesus is the guiding force will be an institution of service from its very beginning. The husband will serve the wife. The wife will serve the husband. Later there will be a mutual exchange of service in the parent-child relationship. This home will experience the ring of friendliness and the echoes of hospitality will sound in the ears of its many grateful guests. It will be a place where people will know the delightful joy of Christian fellowship at its best. The hungry will be fed at its bountiful table. The widow and the orphan will find repose here in its joyful surroundings. The person burdened with sorrow will find an open ear and a sympathetic heart into which he may pour his problems. Later grandchildren and perhaps even great grandchildren will reap the blessed fruits of this good home.

The older should teach the younger to know God's Word, respect His will, and adhere closely to sound doctrine. Those who have been faithful Christians a long time and are growing old gracefully can do much to insure a safe transfer of truth from the generation that is gradually leaving the scenes of earthly activity to the one that is appearing. The aged Paul had taught the youthful Timothy the truths he in turn was to pass on to faithful men possessing the ability to teach others (II Tim. 2:2). In Titus 2:3 Paul says, "The aged women likewise, that they be in behaviour as becometh holiness, not false accusers, not given to much wine, teachers of good things; That they may teach the young women to be sober, to love their husbands, to love their children, To be discreet, chaste, keepers at home, good, obedient to their own husbands, that the word of God be not blasphemed." Older men and women who have been successful as husbands and wives and later as parents can offer much help to those who are just entering these roles. To grow old gracefully is to grow old in service.

GROWING OLD JOYFULLY

Paul wrote the Books of Philemon and Philippians during his first Roman imprisonment. Possibly they were written fairly close together. In Philemon 9 the imprisoned veteran of the cross referred to himself as "Paul the aged." In Philippians 4:4 he wrote, "Rejoice in the Lord alway: and again I say, Rejoice." The advancement of age and the uncertain fate awaiting him at the hands of the infamous Nero did not prevent Paul from having the inward joy of being a Christian and writing an epistle of joyful love and deep appreciation to suffering saints at Philippi.

With all the burdens of coming Calvary weighing so heavily upon Him that Thursday night Jesus still eloquently echoed the message of joy which permeated His heavenly heart (John 15:11). He spoke of hearts free of trouble (John 14:1-3). In John 14:27 He promised the bestowment of peace, a peace that the world was totally unable to give. He desired that His departure from them back to the Father would prompt rejoicing on their part (John 14:28).

We have listed these two great examples of joy to suggest that people can be happy in the advancement of years and that outward circumstances cannot keep holy hearts from rejoicing. It is a joy to see a couple grow old with cheer written on their countenance and the sweet sound of joy in their words. They will be happier individually, together, and before all others if true joy is carefully cultivated all their marital life. There is no reason why joy and age cannot be linked. Paul did it and so have many senior citizens. Certainly elderly Christians can and should for this too is a part of growing old gracefully.

GROWING OLD IN CONTENTMENT

The Bible classifies contentment as a good virtue. The Shunammite woman of Elisha's era is remembered because of her great contentment (II Kings 4:12-13). Paul linked godliness with contentment and said such a holy combination "is great gain. For we brought nothing into this world, and it is certain we can carry nothing out. And having food and raiment let us be therewith content" (I Tim. 6:6-8). Paul was a recipient of many miraculous gifts. However, contentment was not conferred upon him miraculously. He wrote Philippians 4:11-12, "Not that I speak in respect of want: for *I have learned,* in whatsoever state I am, therewith *to be content.* I know both how to be abased, and I know how to abound: every where and in all things I am instructed both to be full and to be hungry, both to abound and to suffer need" (italics added). Paul had learned to be content. He had to work for the spirit of contentment.

Contentment is an imperative for those who wish to grow old gracefully. Aged people who never have mastered this spirit of contentment will make themselves and everyone around them miserable. Those who have grown in this golden virtue will find their sunset years far happier. Years of living together should have mellowed their spirits and sobered their thinking. By the time old age is attained people should have thoroughly curbed their greedy love for things and have recognized that going home to heaven is really the major thing of value. By the time one is old, the restlessness of youth should have long been replaced with a calm contentment to accept things as they are if they cannot be changed and to work patiently to change the things that are changeable and need to be changed. Possession of real contentment is one of the real ways to grow old gracefully.

GROWING OLD IN HELPFULNESS

A marriage cannot survive in a spirit of arrogant independence. Marriage should be entered with the viewpoint of helping the marital partner and being helped in return by one's mate. As the years come and go there should be a beautiful buildup of this spirit of mutual helpfulness. Each should major in the great and lasting work of gentle helpfulness. Happy marriages are begun when each becomes a helper to the other's needs and joys. Each partner should be sustained with an increased dependence upon each other. The sunset years of their marriage can find them happy and contented in helping each other. Now it may take both of them to keep the house clean where once the wife was able to do this alone. It may take both of them to maintain the lawn and flower beds where once the husband did it alone. It may take both of them to move a piece of furniture. During retirement years they may enjoy getting the meals together. With no need to hurry they can take their time for a walk together in the afternoon or call on the sick and afflicted. The going of separate ways each day is a thing of the past. If they both have grown old in the virtues outlined above, some of their happiest days can now be theirs. These can be days of serenity and quietness. They can be days when together they accomplish a desirable work. By growing old gracefully he is not in her way but is her valued helper and companion. She is not in his hair but is a treasured companion. With the deepening furrows in their cheeks, the added bent of their weakening frames toward mother earth, and the settling of many winters upon their silvery heads, they complement each other in the accomplishment of daily tasks. Growing old in gentle helpfulness is also an essential of graceful aging.

GROWING OLD IN THE LORD

Often the Bible speaks of a person dying in a good old age. The penman of the Pentateuch wrote, "Then Abraham gave up the ghost, and died in a good old age, an old man, and full of years; and was gathered to his people" (Gen. 25:8). This tribute is written of Isaac, "And Isaac gave up the ghost, and died, and was gathered unto his people, being old and full of days: and his sons Esau and Jacob buried him" (Gen. 35:29). About David it is said, "And he died in a good old age, full of days, riches, and honour: and Solomon his son reigned in his stead" (I Chron. 29: 28). These three great men of the Old Testament died in a good old age and in fulness of days because they had sought to live for the Lord. They were not perfect men but towered far above the average. When they departed earthly scenes they left "a vast lonesome place across the sky" as Edwin Markham many centuries later would write of Abraham Lincoln. From early life to death they had loved the God of heaven and sought to do His will. These men grew old in the Lord's service. At death they were old in more ways than just in physical age. They were old in service to God and humanity. They were old in knowledge and wisdom. They were old in work and worship. They were old in influencing others for the Lord's cause. They were old in seeking to keep Jehovah's name before their family. They were old in faith and fervency. They were old in hope and holiness. They were old in sincerity and spirituality. They died in a good old age because they had grown old in the heavenly cause. People who wish to die in the Lord must be willing to grow old in the Lord. People who wish to grow old in the Lord must be willing to grow in the Lord from youth and adulthood onward. Couples who grow old in the Lord are the very ones who will grow old gracefully.

Anna is mentioned in only one short passage in God's Word (Luke 2:36-38). She is an excellent example of one who grew old in the Lord. The beloved physician said this of her, "And there was one Anna, a prophetess, the daughter of Phanuel, of the tribe of Aser: she was of a great age, and had lived with an husband seven years from her virginity; And she was a widow of about fourscore and four years, which departed not from the temple, but served God with fastings and prayers night and day. And she coming in that instant gave thanks likewise unto the Lord, and spake of him to all them that looked for redemption in Jerusalem." Anna makes a brief appearance within Holy Writ and then forever fades. But she left her portrait as one loyal to God in old age and as one who was exceedingly grateful for the coming of the Messianic child. Anna truly had grown old in the Lord. He was her joy by day and her peace by night.

The parents-to-be of John are quite old when we first meet them in Luke 1. Together they have grown old in the Lord (Luke 1:6). Luke says, "And they were both righteous before God, walking in all the commandments and ordinances of the Lord blameless." The next verse tells us they were on in years. We do not know how long they lived after John's birth but the final mention of them has them both growing old in the Lord. We cannot believe that the unrecorded part of their final days found them pursuing a different course of behavior. They grew old. They grew old together. They grew old together in the Lord. How fortunate when God-fearing couples can grow old in the Lord. That gives real meaning to their last days on earth.

Christ in the home is the real secret of growing old in the Lord. When older couples lift up Christ and the Bible, Christ and the Bible will greatly help them to grow old gracefully.

QUESTIONS FOR DISCUSSION

1. Discuss Abraham and Sarah as they grew old. In what areas did they grow old?
2. What is the difference between *getting* old and *growing* old?
3. Why do some people become sour in old age while others become more saintly with age?
4. Discuss growing old in faith.
5. How should couples seek to grow old in hope?
6. Discuss growing old in love.
7. Discuss growing old in patience.
8. Why does gratitude seem to be a vanishing virtue in our day?
9. Explain how people can grow old in gratitude.
10. Why will gratitude at home extend to other areas of life as well?

11. Tell of a personal experience where someone expressed gratitude for something you had done.
12. What is meant by vertical and horizontal gratitude?
13. Explain the origin of wisdom. How is it achieved? Distinguish between knowledge and wisdom.
14. Why is wisdom more apt to be found among the aged than among youth?
15. What service can wise couples render to younger couples who are facing serious problems in the early part of their marriage?
16. Discuss the home as an institution of service.
17. How should couples seek to grow old in service?
18. Discuss Paul and Jesus as joyful people while in adverse circumstances.
19. Is real joy dependent upon external circumstances? Give reasons for your answer.
20. List and discuss some texts about contentment.
21. How had Paul obtained his spirit of contentment? Is there any other way for us to obtain it in our time?
22. Why is it important for people to grow old in contentment?
23. Discuss growing old in helpfulness.
24. Discuss growing old in the Lord. Give some examples of Bible people who grew old in the Lord.

18

The Heavenly Home

Heaven and home have much more in common than simply beginning with the same letter. There should be a real touch of heaven in homes on the earth. There will be if the concept discussed in this book, *Christ in the home,* is a living reality in the various facets of the family framework. There surely will be the home atmosphere in all its resplendent beauty and eternal perfection in the heavenly abode. *Home* is a synonym for family togetherness. That is exactly what heaven will be. Ephesians 3:15 says, "Of whom the whole family in heaven and earth is named." Jehovah's family right now is not together. Some are upon the earth. Some are in heaven. Some are in the intermediate state awaiting the resurrection day. In eternity God plans to have His whole family together in heaven. It will be a great day "when all of God's singers get home." Home is a place for the father and his children. Heaven will be just that. God as Father and Jesus as Elder Brother plan to bring all faithful children home in the next world. Home is a place of security. The greatest, grandest, and most glorious security we know upon earth is found in the church of our Lord and in our Christian homes. Heaven will be a place of security. There the tempter will never again seduce us because he will be languishing in the place prepared for his eternal punishment (Matt. 25:41; Rev. 20:10). Suffering saints who lived in the city of brotherly love in the first century were gloriously promised, "Him that overcometh will I make a pillar in the temple of my God, and he shall go no more out: and I will write upon him the name of my God, and the name of the city of my God, which is new Jerusalem, which cometh down out of heaven from my God: and I will write upon him my new name" (Rev. 3:12). A pillar stands for permanence. Pillars in the spiritual Jerusalem are there permanently. Home is a place of love and love will permeate the heavenly abode for righteous souls. The happiest of home life here on the earth is but a faint foreshadowing of the perfect peace, saintly serenity, and holy happiness which will characterize the final abode for God's saved.

Previous chapters have sought to unfold what Christ can mean to our homes on earth. It seems entirely appropriate that the concluding chapter describe what it will be like to live with Jesus in His home on high. Christ desires to live with us in our homes here. He strongly desires that we live with Him in His glorious home when time shall be no more. Those who have desired for the *Christ in the home* concept to pervade the family framework will be the same ones who want to live with Jesus in the Palace of the Universe. What descriptions are given us within Holy Writ concerning this home of all homes — the heavenly home?

THE HEAVENLY HOME IS REAL

Ancient Sadducees and modern atheists have denied the reality of the heavenly home. To these pathetic people who have been duped by the Deceiver, heaven is just a figment of fertile religious imaginations. Their blatant denials do not shake our unfaltering faith in the reality of the heavenly hereafter. Our faith is just as strong in the heavenly home as is our faith in God as Father, Jesus as Saviour, the Spirit as infallible witness to truth, and the Bible as the Word of the living God. Not for a moment could we concede the existence of the Godhead and the divine derivation of the Bible and then erect the sign of imagination over the place of many mansions. In John 14:1-3 Jesus linked faith in the heavenly hereafter with faith in God and faith in Him as Son and Saviour.

The same God who provided Eden as home for the first human couple will surely provide a heavenly Eden for all His faithful children. God knew people needed homes in which to reside on earth. In His great goodness He provided such. Souls of the redeemed will need a home after the resurrection. God has again provided. Let no one misguide you at this point. Heaven is real. It could not be more real if everyone on earth accepted its existence. It could not be less real if everyone on earth denied its existence. The presence of Sadducees in Jesus' day and the appearance of infidels in our day do not affect in the least the reality of heaven. The reality of heaven rests upon God's testimony and not upon how many or how few on earth accept or reject it. The home in which you may read this book is not any more real than is the heavenly home on high.

THE HEAVENLY HOME IS A PLACE OF REST

To the tired traveler there is no sweeter word than *rest*. The anticipation of rest prompts the toiler to keep at the task till the job is done. Knowing there will be rest at the end of the day lightens the burden of the diligent worker. Weary hands stay at the job knowing that soon they can be folded in rest. The Holy Spirit knew of man's great interest in and deep love for rest. Hence He has associated rest with the heavenly home.

In the eloquent extension of the precious invitation Jesus used the word *rest* twice. "Come unto me, all ye that labour and are heavy laden, and I will give you *rest*. Take my yoke upon you, and learn of me; for I am meek and lowly in heart: and ye shall find *rest* unto your souls. For my yoke is easy, and my burden is light" (Matt. 11:28-30, italics added). Employment of the word *rest* twice in this passage prompted the late H. Leo Boles to suggest that the first use of the word may well refer to rest from sins here and the second to that rest which remains in the heavenly realm. I believe Brother Boles was correct. There is no doubt but what other verses make crystal clear that rest now and rest in eternity are two of the grand gifts conferred upon faithful saints by our God on high. The one we have now. The other we have in promise and prospect.

Paul uses the word *rest* in a place that surface readers might easily glide over and totally miss its unique significance. "Seeing it is a righteous thing with God to recompense tribulation to them that trouble you; And to you who are troubled rest with us, when the Lord Jesus shall be revealed from heaven with his mighty angels, In flaming fire taking vengeance on them that know not God, and that obey not the gospel of our Lord Jesus Christ: Who shall be punished with everlasting destruction from the presence of the Lord, and from the glory of his power . . ." (II Thess. 1:6-9). Hasty perusal of this passage might prompt one to conclude automatically that Paul uses the word *rest* as a verb. Able students of the Bible such as David Lipscomb, Foy E. Wallace, Jr., Albert Barnes, Adam Clarke, and others inform us that the word is here used as a noun. It will be noted that Paul talks of two groups:

those who trouble and those who are troubled. God will recompense trouble to the troublers. He will recompense rest to the troubled or those persecuted. Such a blessed hope must have undergirded these bitterly persecuted saints in Thessalonica.

Hebrew saints stood upon the dangerous threshold of apostatizing from Christ and Christianity. The epistle bearing their name was a valiant effort to detour them from their avowed intents. Potent argument after argument is marshaled by the inspired penman to make them reconsider. One of the conclusions reached in Hebrews 4:9 speaks of the heavenly rest. "There remaineth therefore a rest to the people of God." The wavering Hebrews could not claim this prospective reward of rest if they ceased to be God's people. By returning to and remaining with abolished Judaism they would forever forfeit their prospects of one day receiving this heavenly rest. This was a grand and glorious promise to them. It is still a grand and glorious promise to us.

One of the beautiful benedictions gracing the Book of Revelation says, "And I heard a voice from heaven saying unto me, Write, Blessed are the dead which die in the Lord from henceforth: Yea, saith the Spirit, that they may rest from their labours; and their works do follow them" (Rev. 14:13). There is rest from a life of labor on the other side of death. How very sweet and wonderfully comforting is such a precious promise. Here in this vale of tears rest is always temporary. It can be abruptly halted when least expected. There it will be eternal. No intruder will rob us of this heavenly rest.

Years ago Brother Boone Douthitt and I conducted a funeral for a saintly sister in a small middle Tennessee community. Shortly before her death she was heard to say, "I am tired and want to go home." She was quite rational when this utterance was made. She was not speaking of her humble abode where her sunset years had been spent for she was in that house when the statement was made. By the eye of faith and with a heart full of hope she longed for the heavenly rest. Her deep Christian faith and hope connected rest with the heavenly home. How very sweet and comforting it is to be able to lift our eyes from mundane surroundings of an earthly nature and let them rest on the heavenly home where there is permanency of peace and rest awaiting. Infidelity is totally void of conferring such a hallowed hope to one who is about ready to close his eyes in the sleep of death. Thank God for the hope we have in Christ. Heaven is a place of rest. In sharp contrast hell has no rest. "And the smoke of their torment ascendeth up for ever and ever: and they have *no rest* day and night, who worship

the beast and his image, and whosoever receiveth the mark of his
name" (Rev. 14:11, italics added). There is as much difference
between heaven and hell as there is between the opposite terms of
rest and *no rest*. Does not your soul wish fervently to avoid that
awful destiny of "no rest" and to be sweetly at home in that
heavenly abode of "rest"?

THE HEAVENLY HOME IS A BETTER PLACE

The Bible affords us the precious privilege of viewing the great
home of the soul as a better place. The Hebrews had experienced
the spoiling of their goods during past persecutions that came their
way. Yet their hope of the heavenly hereafter should have led them
to look and long for the better and enduring substance reserved in
heaven for all God's redeemed (Heb. 10:34). The Bible's "Hall of
Fame" contains the heroes of the ancient faith (Heb. 11). A
number of them are specifically mentioned as desiring "a better
country, that is, an heavenly: wherefore God is not ashamed to be
called their God: for he hath prepared for them a city" (Heb. 11:
16). *Better,* we recognize, is a relative term. However, it permits
us to compare in a feeble way what shall be with what is, and
allows us to share the expectation that heaven is far more wonderful than the most ideal spot on earth. Men have always evidenced
an eager interest in possessing something better. In the past, hundreds of thousands forsook the Old World and came to the New
World in search of something better. The Holy Spirit knew of
man's unquenchable longing for obtaining the better things and
thus envisioned for us that better country across which the shadows
will never fall. Does not your soul long for that better realm, that
brighter world that lies "beyond the sunset's radiant glow"?

NO TEARS IN THE HEAVENLY HOME

It seems rather fitting that some of the Bible's sweetest and most
beautiful descriptions of the heavenly home are depicted in its
closing chapters. The careful reader of Revelation 21 and 22 is
richly rewarded with a panoramic portrayal of God's new Jerusalem
that is unequaled in any other part of the eternal record. "And
God shall wipe away all tears from their eyes; and there shall be
no more death, neither sorrow, nor crying, neither shall there be
any more pain: for the former things are passed away" (Rev. 21:
4). Jehovah God herein is portrayed as a loving Father who is
deeply interested in removing every cause responsible for a tear
on the cheek and sadness in the heart of His children. Just as a

human father picks up the crying child who has hurt himself and with a loving hand brushes away the tears from the eyes of his child so God's mighty hand is pictured as brushing away the tears from the eyes of His sons and daughters. Is it not a deeply cherishing thought that the same powerful hand that once dipped into limitless space and created a vast universe that functions with marvelous minuteness and perfect precision is just as willing to remove a tear from the eye of a faithful child? Tears are the common lot of humanity as we travel through this land of sin, sickness, and sorrow. Even the strongest are known to weep in the moment of misery and in the day of death. Wonderfully surpassing description is the realization that in heaven no tear will ever dim the eyes or stain the faces of God's redeemed. The things here that have been responsible for causing tears will have long since passed away. In the heavenly home there will be joy, love, contentment, and eternal happiness.

The heavenly home is a realm that the pale horse and his rider death will never invade. How very different from a world that experiences thousands of deaths daily! Here we painfully accept the decease of faithful fathers, marvelous mothers, cherished children, beloved brethren, fine friends, and noble neighbors. There the unwelcomed intruder will never break the circle of heaven's redeemed. Does not your soul desire a holy habitation in that deathless home reserved for the pure and blessed of all ages?

The aged apostle was promised that sorrow will never mar the happiness of those in that "summer land of bliss." From the day that Eve stretched forth her hand of transgression in Eden and plucked the forbidden fruit until now, this world has been writing its constant chapters of sorrow and sighing in the book of human history. Sorrow, like death, knows no respect of persons. Sorrow is the common lot of all classes. No man of wealth can build a wall high enough or thick enough to keep sorrow out. No amount of degrees attached to an educated man's name can make him immune to the certain coming of sorrow sooner or later. One may arise in the morning feeling refreshed and happy. Yet the day may witness a sorrow sweep into his life that a lifetime of grief may fail to erase. Many who read these lines could fill a volume with the sorrows they have faced along life's pathway. As children of sorrow and sighing should we not be eternally grateful that beyond this land of weeping lies a realm protected from sorrow? Are you piloting your soul toward that blissful land?

The heavenly home will be totally void of pain. If an earthly country could truly advertise itself as a refuge completely free of pain, it would soon lack the necessary territory to contain the millions who would quickly congregate there. Pain is universal. It is written on the face of the aged, heard from the lips of the diseased, and witnessed in the mangled forms of the physically injured. I have visited hundreds of hospital rooms and homes where there was intense pain and suffering. On some of these beds were people who had suffered almost beyond human endurance. For them no hour of the day witnessed a moment free of pain. Sobering observations of such pathetic people should prompt the eye of faith to be more strongly centered on that eternal day when all suffering for saints will forever be a thing of the painful past.

THE HEAVENLY HOME IS NEW

The apostle John shared the following glimpse of sublime glory, "And I saw a new heaven and a new earth: for the first heaven and the first earth were passed away; and there was no more sea. And I John saw the holy city, new Jerusalem, coming down from God out of heaven, prepared as a bride adorned for her husband" (Rev. 21:1-2). The heavenly home is new. John witnessed a *new* heaven, a *new* earth, and the *new* Jerusalem. Man has always evidenced an eager interest in the new. Children are thrilled with a new toy, pet, or game. Think how thrilled adults become when they move into a new house or purchase, perhaps for the first time, a new car. Most of us never outgrow this human eagerness to obtain something new though the objects we desire may change as we grow older. God's Spirit knew that humanity is ever characterized with this longing for new things and has vividly stamped "new" on the heavenly home.

THE HEAVENLY HOME IS LIKE A CITY

John saw a city and his description enables us to visualize more accurately what heaven will be like. However, heaven will be far different from any city we have known on earth. Earthly cities have been plagued with crimes, sins, and iniquities of the worst kind. Constant danger and potential violence currently stalk the streets of major cities throughout our nation. In sharp and happy contrast John affirms that holiness will characterize the heavenly city. The enrapturing vision given to John associated Jerusalem with the heavenly home. Due to the events that have transpired in the earthly Jerusalem, that "holy city" has sacred sentiments for both Jew and Christian alike. I am fully persuaded that the Holy Spirit intended to make more graphic His description of the eternal above by referring to Jerusalem. After all, the only earthly city whose name is connected with the heavenly home is Jerusalem.

THE HEAVENLY HOME IS LIKE A BEAUTIFUL BRIDE

The vision given the aged apostle pictures heaven as a bride adorned for her husband. This glimpse of glory is very revealing. How eagerly a bride looks forward to the big day of her wedding. Months of careful and minute planning frequently go into making it a day that will never fade from her mind. How very beautiful she desires to be on this day. It must have been that way also in John's day. Never do young ladies look so strikingly radiant and so beautifully attired as on their wedding day. It is a joyful experience to look into the beaming and happy countenances of a handsome groom and a beautiful bride as they enter the sacred estate of blessed matrimony. The heavenly home is somewhat like the beautiful bride ready to be claimed by her handsome groom. The Spirit knew our finite minds could grasp such a description and that it would become another treasured glimpse of glory. Hope, home, and heaven — what a treasured trio of weighty words these are! Does not your hungry soul long for the heavenly home?

AT HOME WITH GOD

A description of the righteous soul's abode would be very incomplete were we to fail to center attention on the rich fellowship and heavenly association to be eternally enjoyed there. The following verses give us the thrilling promise of one day living with Jehovah God. "Therefore are they before the throne of God, and serve him day and night in his temple: and he that sitteth on the throne shall dwell among them" (Rev. 7:15). "And I heard a great voice out of heaven saying, Behold, the tabernacle of God is with men, and he will dwell with them, and they shall be his people, and God himself shall be with them, and be their God" (Rev. 21:3). "And there shall be no more curse: but the throne of God and of the Lamb shall be in it; and his servants shall serve him: And they shall see his face; and his name shall be in their foreheads" (Rev. 22:3-4).

We can and should be laying plans to be part of heaven's citizenship where God's voice will be heard often and His sacred presence will be enjoyed forever and forever. Earthly contact with the Almighty consisted of short-lived experiences but heaven will provide an eternity filled with uninterrupted associations with the Holy Father. Will it not be worth every feeble effort we have expended to see Him who graciously provided the scheme of human redemption, heard our prayerful petitions, listened to our hymns of homage, and received the reverent adoration paid Him in our sermons and Bible classes? The fulness of how great God is will really dawn upon us when we share an inheritance in His heavenly home. Heaven means being with God. What is home without a father? What would heaven be like without our wonderful Heavenly Father?

AT HOME WITH CHRIST

Heaven will provide eternal fellowship with the Son as the following passages prove. "In my Father's house are many mansions: if it were not so, I would have told you. I go to prepare a place for you. And if I go and prepare a place for you, I will come again, and receive you unto myself; that where I am, there ye may be also" (John 14:2-3). "Then we which are alive and remain shall be caught up together with them in the clouds, to meet the Lord in the air, and so shall we ever be with the Lord" (1 Thess. 4:17). "They shall hunger no more, neither thirst any more; neither shall the sun light on them, nor any heat. For the Lamb which is in the midst of the throne shall feed them, and shall lead them unto living fountains of waters: and God shall wipe away all tears from their eyes" (Rev. 7:16-17).

I am confident that earthly contact with Jesus of Nazareth was filled with a spiritual fellowship and feeling that sinful man had never experienced since Eden was forfeited in Genesis 3. To have beheld Immanuel in human flesh, to have heard the gracious words that always graced His language, to have seen Him in miraculous action and to have witnessed the perfect performance of every task to which He addressed Himself would have been uplifting and rewarding. However, Mary only had Him in her home for a few short years and then His personal ministry claimed His major attention. The teeming multitudes who flocked after Him gazed on the mighty Messiah but for a short time. The disciples were in His presence about three years. Painfully and reluctantly they accepted His declaration of a necessary departure from their midst. A part of Paul's Christian philosophy consisted of the realization that life in the flesh imposed upon him a necessary absence from the Lord he loved and served. In the heavenly home, however, we will be established in a permanent union with Him who lovingly and sacrificially atoned for man's sins. Will it not be wonderful indeed to bask in the light of the "Sun of Righteousness" who showed the way to God's new Jerusalem, provided the truth to free us from our sins, and tendered to His beloved the life that is eternally happy? Heaven means being forever at home with Jesus our blessed Saviour.

AT HOME WITH THE HOLY SPIRIT

In addition to the hallowed fellowship with the Father and the Son, the saved will also possess a fuller and richer knowledge with the third member of the "Sacred Three," the Holy Spirit. I am confident that many of the mysteries which have centered around this eternal personality on earth will then be erased forever from our minds and we shall know Him as we never did before. That will no doubt be true with the other two members of the Godhead also. The Holy Spirit was present at creation and the remainder of the Old Testament contains scattered accounts of various missions He performed. The opening of the New Testament age beholds Him descending in dove-like form on Jesus at the Jordan and He remains with God's anointed throughout His personal ministry. The writer of Hebrews affirms that Jesus made the atoning sacrifice through the "eternal Spirit" (Heb. 9:14). When Jesus ascended to heaven the Holy Spirit came as the promised Comforter, took up His abode with the apostles, imbued the spiritual body of Christ with life, and supervised the composition of the entire Sacred Volume. Since this Divine Agent has filled so signal a role in the scheme that makes possible our redemption, will we not discover pleasant delight in enjoying His fellowship throughout eternity? Heaven means being at home with the Holy Spirit.

AT HOME WITH THE REDEEMED

In Matthew 8:11 Jesus declared, "That many shall come from the east and west, and shall sit down with Abraham, and Isaac, and Jacob, in the kingdom of heaven." Abraham, Isaac, and Jacob are representative of the Patriarchal Age. Those coming from the east and west to join them in the heavenly kingdom of glory were to be from the Christian Age. Second Kings 2:11 tells us that Elijah, a representative of the Mosaic Economy, "went up by a whirlwind into heaven." According to Revelation 15:3 those redeemed in heaven will "sing the song of Moses the servant of God, and the song of the Lamb, saying, Great and marvellous are thy works, Lord God Almighty; just and true are thy ways, thou King of saints." Moses bridges the gap between the Patriarchal and Mosaic Dispensations, having lived in both of them. There seems to be no doubt but what Moses will be in the heavenly home. These passages suggest that the redeemed from all ages will constitute a part of that great heavenly population. God's created beings who have always been in heaven will be there. Hence, angels, faithful patriarchs, loyal prophets, righteous men, godly women, steadfast apostles, devout Christians, and all who have died in infancy or without reaching a responsible mental age will one day surround the rainbow-clad throne and in choral unison will lift their grateful voices in hymning praise to the Godhead. We have all been thrilled by hearing great crowds sing spiritedly and enthusiastically songs such as "How Great Thou Art" or "Amazing Grace." Listening and participating in the song of Moses and the Lamb will be far greater than any song service we have known on earth. Associations with the Godhead and the redeemed of all ages provide glimpses of golden glory which our pen can but faintly depict. Heaven means being with "the spirits of just men made perfect" (Heb. 12:23).

THE HEAVENLY HOME IS ETERNAL IN DURATION

Sometime ago I concluded a meeting in another state. One of the members of the congregation was telling me about the trip home of her daughter and family planned for the very next week. They lived about 2,200 miles away. It had been four years since this mother had seen her daughter and family. I remarked about how happy she must be over this anticipated visit. She was excited but something tempered that happiness in her heart. She remarked that the visit would be so short and then would come that painful good-bye again. That dreaded day of departure kept her from feeling unlimited happiness. From the experiences of the past she knew of what feelings that day would produce.

In sharp contrast to that experience, heaven will be eternal. Jesus said the righteous would go "into eternal life" (Matt. 25:46). According to Paul those raised to the resurrection of life and living saints at the Lord's second advent will "ever be with the Lord" (I Thess. 4:17). For the redeemed there will be no temporary reunions. They will be eternal in their nature. No citizen in the heavenly home will have any need to say a "good-bye" or "so long" ever again. There will be no moist eyes in heaven because someone is about to make a long trip. Separations and departures belong to an earthly existence. We will be together and be there eternally. Have you not asked yourself during a moment of supreme happiness, "How long before a sorrow will replace the happiness I presently feel?" Heaven means joy, happiness, and togetherness for eternity. Jesus said the righteous will go into *eternal* life (Matt. 25:46).

OBEDIENCE: THE KEY

Seventeen chapters in this book have set forth the great need for Jesus Christ in our homes today. This chapter has dealt with living so that we one day can live with Jesus in His home on high. How welcome He has been in our homes and lives will determine how welcome we shall be one day in His heavenly home. Obedience is the key that permits Him a welcome entrance into our home. Obedience is the key that will permit Him to welcome us one day into His heavenly home. "Not every one that saith unto me, Lord, Lord, shall enter into the kingdom of heaven; but he that doeth the will of my Father which is in heaven. Many will say to me in that day, Lord, Lord, have we not prophesied in thy name? and in thy name cast out devils [demons, ASV]? and in thy name done many wonderful works? And then will I profess unto them, I never knew you: depart from me, ye that work iniquity" (Matt. 7:21-23). "And why call ye me, Lord, Lord, and do not the things which I say?" (Luke 6:46). "Jesus answered and said unto him, If a man love me, he will keep my words: and my Father will love him, and we will come unto him, and make our abode with him" (John 14: 23). A family that practices John 14:23 has *Christ in the home.* "Though he were a Son, yet learned he obedience by the things which he suffered; And being made perfect, he became the author of eternal salvation unto all them that obey him . . ." (Heb. 5: 8-9). The last beatitude of the Bible opens heaven's door for doers. "Blessed are they that do his commandments, that they may have right to the tree of life, and may enter in through the gates into the city" (Rev. 22:14).

VITAL QUERIES

How much has Jesus Christ meant to your home in the past? How much does Jesus mean right now? How much are you going to allow Him to mean in the future? In the past how interested have you been in the heavenly home? How interested are you in the heavenly home right now? How interested do you plan to become in the heavenly home in the future? If you have never been interested in heaven, are not now interested in heaven, what makes you think you may become interested at some future day? *Now* is the time to make Christ a part of your home. *Now* is the time to make preparation to go home to heaven. Tomorrow may be too late.

A FINAL PRAYER

Our Father, who art in heaven. Hallowed be Thy name in all the earth. May Thy will be done in homes on earth even as it is done in the heavenly home.

We thank Thee for the righteous homes of the past. For the excellent example and thrilling inspiration they left us we are truly grateful. For every husband, wife, father, mother, and child who has worked toward having a good home we give Thee our unstinted gratitude.

We thank Thee for the righteous homes of today. Wilt Thou bless them that they may become greater citadels for right, truth, purity, and peace. Bless every husband and wife in the marital relationship. May there be a deepening of their love. May their marriage never know the chill of hatred and the freeze of harshness. Bless all fathers and mothers who have brought little children into the world. Impress upon every parent the great responsibility that is daily his to point his children's footsteps toward Thee. Bless our children as they live in a world of woe, an environment of evil, a camp of crime. May they be strong and say decisive NOs to the wickedness that seeks to overwhelm them in the days of their precious youth.

We are so thankful for Jesus and what He has meant and can mean to our homes. Help us to enthrone Him as the ruler and guide of our homes. Help us to build our homes according to the pattern He laid down in Holy Writ.

We thank Thee for our faith and hope in the heavenly home. We thank Thee for the glorious glimpses of its beauty which have been given to us. Help us to be faithful so that one day in the future we may come and live with Thee and Thy Son. Help us to put Christ in our homes in order that one day He may put us into His heavenly home. In Jesus' name. AMEN

QUESTIONS FOR DISCUSSION

1. Discuss the common characteristics of heaven and home.
2. Discuss the reality of the heavenly home.
3. Upon what does the reality of heaven rest?
4. Describe the heavenly home as a place of rest.
5. Discuss the word *rest* as it appears in Matthew 11:28-30, II Thessalonians 1:7-9, Hebrews 4:9, and Revelation 14:13.
6. Does infidelity have anything worthy to offer its passionate patrons at the hour of death and beside the open grave? Discuss in detail.
7. Discuss the heavenly home as a place of no tears. Why will tears forever be absent in this wonderful realm?
8. Discuss the heavenly home as a place of no death.
9. Describe the heavenly home as a place totally free of sorrow.

10. Describe heaven as a place free of pain. How universal is pain here on earth?
11. Discuss heaven as a new place. How does humanity feel about acquiring new things?
12. Contrast the heavenly city on high with cities here on the earth.
13. Why was Jerusalem possibly used as a synonym for the heavenly home?
14. How is the heavenly home somewhat like a beautiful bride?
15. Describe heaven as being at home with God.
16. Discuss the texts which promise the redeemed the privilege of one day living with Jesus.
17. Describe earthly contact with God's Son.
18. Describe heaven as being forever in the presence of Christ.
19. Describe some of the work performed by the Holy Spirit in the Bible.
20. Describe heaven as being forever in the presence of the Holy Spirit.
21. Describe heaven as being forever with the redeemed.
22. What act of worship which we have practiced on earth will be performed in heaven (See Rev. 15:3)? Does the Bible mention anything about preaching and teaching Christ in heaven, partaking of the Lord's Supper there, or giving of our means in the eternal home of the soul?
23. Discuss the eternal duration of the heavenly estate.
24. What is the key which will unlock the heavenly home for humanity? Read and discuss each text listed which speaks of this key.
25. Compose your own prayer for the home of which you are a part.